"*Improvement Science: Promoting Equity in Schools* is a book for all of us who deeply feel the moral imperative to work for equity in our educational system. This book provides concrete steps and a clear methodology to start now and to stop the practice of postponing the work until another school year. This book gives teachers and students hope that change can happen *now*."

Elena García-Velasco, M.A.T.
2012 Oregon Teacher of the Year

"As superintendent, I take seriously the goal of listening to and taking action on our students' and families' perceptions of school culture. I also believe deeply in empowering our teachers and staff to analyze and utilize data to lead and measure improvement in our classrooms and schools so each child achieves their dreams. *Improvement Science: Promoting Equity in Schools* provides numerous examples and ideas for teachers and principals as they collaborate with students, families, and colleagues to implement culturally-responsive, anti-racist practices—with real results."

Dr. Susan Enfield, Superintendent, Highline Public Schools
2020 Women in School Leadership Award by the
American Association of School Administrators

"Collaborating with students, teachers, staff, families, and the broader community to ensure that each student and family has access and opportunity is at the heart of what I do as superintendent. *Improvement Science: Promoting Equity in Schools* is the kind of book that teachers, staff members, principals, community members, and superintendents can use to inspire impactful and lasting change and continuous improvement, building on the expertise of our community to create the high-performing, equity-focused classrooms and schools our children and families deserve. This book shares a multitude of perspectives across a wide-range of topics, all with a singular focus of educational improvement for our students."

Dr. Greg Baker, Superintendent, Bellingham Public Schools
Washington State 2020 Superintendent of the Year

"It is our moral obligation to think about our children and their future with an equity lens, offering all of them the tools they need to succeed in school and beyond. This book, created by educators for educators, is the perfect tool to learn new strategies on how to improve instruction in our classrooms. These are inspirational and motivational examples developed with an equity lens in mind. This book is an essential contribution to all educators who want to reshape our educational system with the hope of closing our academic gaps among the most marginalized students. Thank you, Dr. Peterson and Professor Carlile, for your forward thinking in compiling all this learning in one book."

Dr. Victor Vergara
Executive Director of Equity and Student Success, Edmonds School District
2012 Oregon Middle School Principal of the Year

"In Today's educational landscape we must possess the ability to adapt to change, while holding equity at the forefront of every decision. We make these changes while focusing on the needs of all students. *Improvement Science: Promoting Equity in Schools* provides educators with practical tools they need to make meaningful changes. These changes will positively impact student outcomes by removing barriers, and providing student-focused learning that is culturally relevant and engaging. This book highlights the expertise of teachers, school leaders and practitioners and provides a framework for success. It also includes practices that can be replicated and applied across classrooms, schools and districts."

Dr. Paul E. Coakley, Superintendent
Multnomah Education Service District

"Change does not come easy, but I know it is possible to use a change lens to increase nurturing, culturally responsive and reassuring relationships in schools. The stories in this book recognize the importance of connection, compassion, data and the role of the teacher in improving classroom instruction. This book is a gift to the field!!"

Dr. Karen Fischer Gray
Oregon Superintendent of the Year 2018

"School improvement is a very contextual endeavor. It is about finding what works for which students and under what conditions! Peterson and Carlile have captured the authentic stories of teachers and school leaders engaged in improvement science methods as they seek to advance equitable outcomes for their students within the context of their own schools. A great read for educators looking to get better at getting better!"

Bill Eagle
Associate Director of Student Success
North Central Educational Service District

"*Improvement Science: Promoting Equity in Schools* is a book rooted in timeless theory and grounded in compelling practice. It is highly relevant and useful for teachers and school leaders who seek to urgently advance meaningful improvement in education.

The numerous case studies in this volume weave throughout comprehensive K-12 instruction while reminding the reader that there is no greater theory than good practice. Further, the vignettes provide detailed examples of praxis as the reader's focus is compelled to integrate the essential ethic of equitable education. Educators motivated by improving instruction and its outcomes will find their time is well-spent within these pages."

Rob Larson, Ed.D.
President, RTL Consulting

"Improvement Science: Promoting Equity in Schools demonstrates what collaborative problem solving among practitioners in schools and communities can look like when equity and justice are at the forefront and change is guided by the improvement science process. This important volume offers a firsthand look at improvement in action and shows us how the tools of improvement science are needed for improving and ensuring equitable and just educational systems. Kudos to Peterson & Carlile for putting together this resource!"

Jill Alexa Perry, Ph.D.
Carnegie Project on the Education Doctorate
& University of Pittsburgh

Improvement Science

THE IMPROVEMENT SCIENCE IN EDUCATION SERIES

Improvement Science originated in such fields as engineering and health care, but its principal foundation has been found to be an effective school improvement methodology in education. Although improvement science research is so quickly becoming a signature pedagogy and core subject area of inquiry in the field of educational leadership, the literature is still scant in its coverage of IS models. The Improvement Science in Education series is intended to be the most comprehensive collection of volumes to inform educators and researchers about problem analysis, utilization of research, development of solutions, and other practices that can be employed to enhance and strengthen efforts at organizational improvement. This series concentrates on the elements faculty, students, and administrators need to enhance the reliability and validity of improvement or quality enhancement efforts.

BOOKS IN THE SERIES

The Educational Leader's Guide to Improvement Science:
Data, Design and Cases for Reflection
by Robert Crow, Brandi Nicole Hinnant-Crawford, and Dean T. Spaulding (2019)

The Improvement Science Dissertation in Practice:
A Guide for Faculty, Committee Members, and their Students
by Jill Alexa Perry, Debby Zambo, and Robert Crow (2020)

Improvement Science in Education: A Primer
by Brandi Nicole Hinnant-Crawford (2020)

Teaching Improvement Science in Educational Leadership: A Pedagogical Guide
by Dean T. Spaulding, Robert Crow, and Brandi Nicole Hinnant-Crawford (2021)

Improvement Science: Promoting Equity in Schools
by Deborah S. Peterson and Susan P. Carlile (2021)

Reclaiming the Education Doctorate: The History, Impact, and Implementation of
the Carnegie Project on the Education Doctorate's (CPED) Framework
by Jill Alexa Perry (2022)

Improvement Science as a Tool for School Enhancement:
Solutions for Better Educational Outcomes
by Deborah S. Peterson and Susan P. Carlile (2022)

Improvement Science: Methods for Researchers and Program Evaluators
by Robert Crow, Brandi Nicole Hinnant-Crawford, and Dean T. Spaulding (2022)

Improving Together: Case Studies of Networked Improvement
Science Communities
by Robert Crow, Brandi Nicole Hinnant-Crawford, and Dean T. Spaulding (2023)

Improvement Science Across the Disciplines: Business, Health, and Social Sciences
by Robert Crow, Brandi Nicole Hinnant-Crawford, and Dean T. Spaulding (2025)

Editorial submissions

Authors interested in having their manuscripts considered for publication in the Improvement Science in Education Series are encouraged to send a prospectus, sample chapter, and CV to any one of the series editors:
Robert Crow (rcrow@email.wcu.edu),
Brandi Nicole Hinnant-Crawford (bnhinnantcrawford@email.wcu.edu),
or Dean T. Spaulding (ds6494@yahoo.com).

Improvement Science

Promoting Equity in Schools

EDITED BY Deborah S. Peterson
and Susan P. Carlile

Myers
Education
Press

Gorham, Maine

Myers
Education
Press

Myers Education Press is an academic publisher specializing in books, e-books,
and digital content in the field of education. All of our books are subjected to a
rigorous peer review process and produced in compliance with the standards of
the Council on Library and Information Resources.

Library of Congress Cataloging-in-Publication Data available from Library of
Congress.

13-digit ISBN 978-1-9755-0467-0 (paperback)
13-digit ISBN 978-1-9755-0468-7 (library networkable e-edition)
13-digit ISBN 978-1-9755-0469-4 (consumer e-edition)

Printed in the United States of America.

All first editions printed on acid-free paper that meets the American National Standards Institute Z39-48 standard.

Books published by Myers Education Press may be purchased at special quantity
discount rates for groups, workshops, training organizations, and classroom usage.
Please call our customer service department at 1-800-232-0223 for details.

Cover design by Teresa Legrange.

Visit us on the web at **www.myersedpress.com** to browse our complete list of
titles.

CONTENTS

Part III: Math and Science

Part IV: Health, Wellness, and Physical Education

Conclusion

LIST OF FIGURES AND TABLES

Figures

Tables

ACKNOWLEDGMENTS

Many have inspired us to create this book. Foremost are those who have been historically underserved in our schools: children of color, recent immigrants, those with special learning needs, and those who have been overlooked or ignored in our schools. The teachers and leaders, students, families, and community members who persevere and thrive inspire us.

We would like to acknowledge the leadership of Portland State University's Graduate School of Education Dean Randy Hitz, Educational Leadership and Policy Chair Candyce Reynolds, and School of Public Health Professor Sherril Gelmon, who supported us in our initial exploration of applying improvement science to our focus on equity in our classrooms and schools. We also want to thank the Carnegie Foundation and its support of our iLEAD work; Carnegie Senior Fellows David Imig, Paul LeMahieu, Luis Gomez, Mike Hanson, and Tony Bryk; iLEAD school district partners Tania McKey and Cassandra Thonstad; and our colleagues at Portland State University; Associate Professor Emeritus Pat Burk and Adjunct Professors Larry Becker and Cassandra Thonstad. This book is only possible with their support, along with the encouragement of our families, strong social justice advocates.

Our belief in the power of improvement science to radically enhance the experience of historically underserved students and families is based on the concepts of Paolo Freire and John Dewey, who continue to inspire us.

FOREWORD

MANUELITO BIAG AND PAUL LEMAHIEU
Carnegie Foundation for the Advancement of Teaching

As we continue navigating the epic challenges of the four pandemics (Ladson-Billings, 2021) we have confronted over the past year—the pandemics of long-standing structural racism, the COVID-19 health crisis, growing income and wealth inequality, and climate change—many are asking when will we return to "normal"? This is a question stakeholders in all sectors are wrestling with today, including school administrators, families, policymakers, students, classroom teachers, and caregivers supporting the social, emotional, and cognitive development of children and youth all across America. Yet there are those who argue that a return to "normal," defined as "the way things were," would be to the detriment of many, and particularly those individuals and communities who have been and continue to be excluded from opportunity and learning structures that can help them realize their full potentials. Roy (2020) writes,

> Our minds are still racing back and forth, longing for a return to
> 'normality,' trying to stitch our future to our past and refusing to
> acknowledge the rupture. But the rupture exists. And in the midst
> of this terrible despair, it offers us a chance to rethink the doomsday
> machine we have built for ourselves. Nothing could be worse than a
> return to normality. (p. 10)

Perhaps, and more appropriately, the questions for these unprecedented times are, How might today's challenges precipitate and inform the building of more just educational systems that engage and support a whole range of human experiences and honor our diverse range of knowing, being, and developing? What methods and tools might help us create these inclusive and liberatory systems? And how might we work together to make progress on our shared aims? These questions prompt us, as well as the scholars featured in this volume, to look to the six core and interrelated principles of networked continuous improvement for direction and support (Bryk et al., 2015). Although, individually, each of the principles offers guidance on how to achieve diversity, inclusion, and equity in our efforts to improve, collectively, they do so even more powerfully, as the authors of chapters in this book amply demonstrate. It is worth pausing to consider each of these core principles in terms of the challenge that they pose to us as we confront issues of equity.

Make the work problem-specific and user-centered. This first improvement tenet encourages us to be clear about the question, "What specifically are we trying to solve?" Once we target long-standing problems of inequity, this problem-solving focus sharpens our ability to direct our energy and resources on redressing specific disparities that matter most to those closest to the problem. Moreover, this principle's urging that we focus on "users" in understanding the problem and positing solutions challenges us to elevate those voices (and ensure that they influence our actions) that have historically been undervalued or even silenced.

Variation in performance is the core problem to address. The second principle underscores the notion that understanding what drives variation in our systems, particularly variation in performance by groups of diverse racial, ethnic, or gender identities, is essential in all improvement efforts. If our goal is to achieve quality outcomes and advance effectiveness among diverse educators engaging varied populations of children and families in different organizational contexts, then we must aspire to understand what works, for which populations, and under what circumstances. Seen through such an equity lens, one can argue that variation in performance is, indeed, the core problem to be solved.

See the system that produces the current outcomes. This improvement tenet encourages us to "see the system" so as to ascertain the factors that drive the variability we see and the root causes of our shared problem. We cannot improve what we do not understand. To effectively redesign and reconstruct school systems so that they help all learners thrive, we have to investigate how the interactions among educators, their tools, materials, and processes are joining together to produce (and reproduce) the persistent inequities that have become all too familiar. In doing so, we can also identify the bright spots, important dispositions, and other enabling conditions that afford meaningful learning experiences for all students, especially those placed at risk by the system as currently defined.

We cannot improve at scale what we cannot measure. Sound and appropriate measurement is essential to tracking progress toward shared aims as well as warranting changes as improvements. From an equity perspective, this means ensuring that the measures we use are sensitive to the experience of the diverse populations we serve. This is both a definitional matter (e.g., taking care to measure those conditions and outcomes that have typically varied across diverse groups) and a technical one (e.g., ensuring measures are free from the forms of bias that lead to misrepresentation or misunderstanding of the true conditions and circumstances underlying our efforts). Only with measures that "measure up" in these terms will the understandings that support real improvement appropriately inform our work.

Use disciplined inquiry to drive improvement. The rigorous testing of changes to practice is the engine that drives genuine improvement at scale. Through it, we determine what works, for whom, and under what conditions—improvement knowledge that is essential to ensuring that our ideas are adapted to provide benefit to those traditionally underserved in our systems. The call to disciplined inquiry must not privilege any one method so much as embrace any that is truly rigorous and valid. Plan–do–study–act cycles that examine and adapt changes to best serve equity aims are certainly an example of this, but so, too, are liberatory design experiments or lesson study, when they are executed with discipline and rigor.

Accelerate learning through networked communities. Carefully defined and structured networks provide a unique environment for engaging in rigorous improvement efforts. Such networks embrace and involve all those necessary to realize and spread equitable improvements—notably including the traditionally disengaged or marginalized. The varied contexts of broad networks allow us to explore improvement ideas across multiple settings to accelerate our learning, warrant that changes are indeed improvements, and enable the spread and adaptation to diverse contexts to ensure that these improvements do benefit all.

We see, then, that each of these improvement principles both challenges us to confront equity concerns and guides us in how improvement science can do so. Taken together, they are a blueprint for diversity, equity, and inclusion as they provide us with important grounding, a shared terra firma, to begin tackling the enormity of the complex social challenges we face today, as well as others that await us in the years ahead.

References

Bryk, A. S., Gomez, L. M., Grunow, A., & LeMahieu, P. G. (2015). *Learning to improve: How America's schools can get better at getting better.* Harvard University Press.

Ladson-Billings, G. (2021). I'm here for the hard re-set: Post pandemic pedagogy to preserve our culture. *Equity & Excellence in Education, 54*(1), 68–78.

Roy, A. (2020, April 3). The pandemic is a portal. *The Financial Times.* https://www .ft.com/content/10d8f5e8-74eb-11ea-95fe-fcd274e920ca

CHAPTER ONE

Introduction

DEBORAH S. PETERSON AND SUSAN P. CARLILE

This book was written *by* classroom teachers, principals, and school district leaders *for* teachers, principals, and leaders. We are teachers ourselves. One of our daughters, two sisters, a niece, and a nephew are teachers. We wrote this book with deep respect for our nation's classroom instructors, people who wake up every day committed to improving the life of every child in our care. People who spend their evenings and weekends thinking about how to improve the experience in our classrooms, from the moment the child gets on our school bus or is greeted at the door, even in the environment of COVID-19, or especially in this time when so many children and families are struggling. Continuous improvement, especially for students and communities who have been historically underserved in our schools, is our mission.

When our boss first asked us several years ago if we might consider learning more about improvement science, many of our friends and colleagues in education were aghast that we might take an improvement method from the business community, specifically from the health care and auto industry. However, we were ready to examine something different. Like so many teachers, we were tired of hearing that we just need to "work smarter" in our schools. Or that we just need to implement a change "with fidelity to [the] model." We were tired of top-down mandates with proscribed solutions that might have worked in another county, in another state, in another classroom.

We have taught long enough to know that when even one seemingly small contextual change is made, say, adding one student to the classroom or replacing one classroom assistant with another person or using a new textbook, the instructional strategy for success in the classroom might also have to change—and sometimes change dramatically. So why would any leader mandate the precise change that has to happen in any classroom? *You must post "I can" statements. All PLCs (professional learning communities) must use this template to document your agenda. Principals must use the (name it) framework during walk-throughs.* If these improvement strategies truly were the solution to every instructional problem in every classroom in our nation, we could have reduced our national educational budget tenfold by now because every child would be above benchmark. Instead, we were exhorted to try harder or told we'll be held accountable, or we blame the teachers, their families, our students.

So, why are we so excited about using improvement science to increase equity in schools? What we learned about improvement science from a highly respected professor in the School of Public Health, Professor Sherril Gelmon, was that each unique context requires a potentially different solution based on variables unique to that setting. Through her guidance, we found in improvement science affirmation for Freire (1993) when he declared that freedom is obtained through contextualized, action-oriented, and collaborative actions that enhance the humanity of the individual and the community. We agreed with Dewey (1990) that making meaning by those closest to the learning will best serve our aim. These, we discovered, are the tenets of improvement science.

We have found that people new to improvement science want to know the basic steps before beginning. If you're a beginner, here are some basic steps and a resource (https://www.carnegiefoundation.org/our-ideas/six-core-principles-improvement/) to help you understand the process better:

1. **Form a Team.** Create a team of people in diverse roles and with diverse racial, ethnic, linguistic, and gender backgrounds to form your improvement team: leaders, teachers, community members, and students who will form your improvement team.
2. **Examine Data.** Examine your data to identify an area for improvement in your classroom or school. Collect additional data

through an equity audit to get more information about whom you are not serving. We recommend the equity audit in *Leading for Social Justice: Transforming Schools for All Learners* by Elise Frattura and Colleen Capper (2007), Appendix A.

3. **Ask Why.** Complete a root-cause analysis (fishbone diagram and ask the 5 Whys).
4. **Read Research.** Examine research on this problem.
5. **Get the Perspectives of Those Closest to the Problem.** Conduct empathy interviews and surveys to get more information specific to your context.
6. **Plan the Change.** Design a theory of improvement that includes an aim statement, primary drivers, secondary drivers, and possible change ideas.

After you've done these six steps, then it's time to test one idea, using short **Plan–Do–Study–Act** cycles. These are short improvement cycles. Students are only in our classrooms generally for 1 year, so the cycles should be short, perhaps even as short as one week, to ensure that every instructional move we are making truly does improve the experience of the students!

How did we get started? With so many important and deep problems impacting our lives—systemic racism, the gendered oppression of women, the devastation of our environment, income inequality—it might have seemed reasonable that we might initially have chosen one of these critical projects for our first improvement projects. Professor Gelmon, however, had us learn by doing: She had us engage in our own improvement projects on a topic of our choosing. We identified a problem we wanted to work on—a personal improvement project.

Deborah chose to increase her physical activity after dinner. She thought the reason she wasn't walking after dinner was that she didn't have the right shoes, so she bought new walking shoes. And she still didn't walk after dinner. Then she thought the problem was the socks weren't right. She bought new socks—and still wasn't walking. After several cycles of collecting data on her physical activity after dinner—and spending quite a bit of money on new shoes, socks, rain pants, and a rain jacket, thinking that *those* change ideas would result in increased walking after dinner, she discovered the change idea that really did increase her postdinner walking was having the whole family clear the table and do the dishes so the family could walk together. This is the power of improvement science: She identified a problem she wanted to work on, she thought about what might be the reasons for not walking after dinner, and she tried different change ideas while collecting data on whether the change idea resulted in an improvement.

Susan sought to improve bilateral symmetry and strength in her hips after hip replacement surgery. Through specifically designed change ideas implemented in several Plan–Do–Study–Act cycles, Susan improved strength in each hip and increased her mobility and the muscles in her upper core that had diminished. She learned the power of considering balancing measures—does improving one area negatively influence another area?—when making changes in complex systems like the human body. You have to look at the entire system, not just one part of the system. Similarly, in school improvement efforts, change ideas can focus on social-emotional success and academic success.

Why is the cycle of Plan–Do–Study–Act important to our work in schools? As a classroom teacher or school leader, you might be told by your supervisor that the problem in your school or classroom is attendance or graduation rates or discipline. You're educated, most likely have an MA or higher degree, and you read research. You know research says the problem might be any one of those. But you, the person closest to the problem, have a hunch the problem might be something else. It might be that you have a high homeless population and your students haven't eaten in 18 hours. Or maybe the problem is that the children are experiencing trauma because your area had a wildfire and families are still displaced. Or maybe the local industry shut down and there is a lot of uncertainty in the community.

So how do you respond? What do you do next? How do you "test" whether your hunch is right? How do you collect data that will tell you whether what you're trying is an improvement? How do you adjust what you're doing based on your data? When do you just stop trying one thing and try another? And finally, when do you take the idea that is working in your setting and help others—your grade-level teammates down the hall, the science department, maybe even the whole school, or every school in the district—to adjust the strategy for their context and scale up the change idea so that each child, each teacher in the entire school or district is succeeding? How do you ensure that change in one area is not negatively influencing another? These are the essential questions and strategies of improvement science.

As you read this book, consider the core improvement science questions:

1. What are we trying to accomplish and by when?
2. How will we know the change is an improvement?
3. What changes are within our sphere of influence that will result in improvement?

Think about the following:

1. What personal improvement project could I try to learn how to use the tools and strategies of improvement science?
2. What can I learn about successes in classrooms across the United States and the world that can help me understand the particular and the local within the context of our global community?
3. What are the promising practices that help me recognize and address structural inequities in my school related to race, ethnicity, gender, home language, socioeconomic status, or ability?
4. What is the role of data collection and analysis in my own change ideas?
5. What happens when I (we) make missteps, and how does my organization support risk-taking and trial by error?
6. How can I ensure the voices of families and other community members are included in my improvement project?
7. How can I involve student voices in our classroom or school improvement efforts?

8. How do I ensure that my improvement efforts truly do address issues of equity and truly do result in improvement and not just *change*?

9. What existing resources do we have that could help us take small-scale improvements to scale in our grade levels, department, school, or district?

10. What resources exist to collect, analyze, and discuss data regularly to ensure we use data to adjust our practices? What resources do we have to engage in Plan–Do–Study–Act cycles weekly, monthly, and quarterly?

We've compiled the stories of several teachers, principals, and university professors who are working within their sphere of influence to improve schools, with those being most impacted by any changes informing what the change needs to be, how to measure whether you're improving, and testing the improvement.

We hope the experiences of the teachers and leaders in this book inspire you and motivate you to adapt the strategies to your context. Improvement science empowers each of us to start today, now, in whatever sphere of influence we have, to improve the lives of each student in our care. We encourage you to start today, collaboratively, with your colleagues, students, families, and leaders.

References

Dewey, J. (1990). *The school and society and the child and the curriculum*. Chicago, IL: The University of Chicago Press. (Original work published 1956).

Frattura, E., & Capper, C. A. (2007). *Leading for social justice: Transforming schools for all learners*. Corwin.

Freire, P. (1993). *Pedagogy of the oppressed*. New York, NY: The Continuum International Publishing Group.

Part I:
Reading

Impact by Design: Promoting Equity Through Reading Achievement of Students of Color

NAICHEN ZHAO, ERIN ANDERSON,
SANDY LOCHHEAD, AND LAURA VASTA

Background

This chapter gives an overview of how Academy of Success (AS) Elementary School used an improvement science model to bridge the opportunity gap in literacy for K–2 students of color (SOCs) throughout the 2019–2020 academic year. AS was one of eight schools involved in the third cohort of the design improvement (DI) program, a state-funded program offered by the University of Denver to schools and districts throughout the state. The DI program is a 2-year professional learning model based on liberatory design, design thinking, and the core principles of improvement science (Bryk et al., 2015; Clifford, n.d.; Kelly & Kelly, 2013). The district and university co-constructed the program to reflect the needs and goals of the district. School design teams, made up of the principal and other key school-based teachers and staff, worked closely with an improvement coach to both learn the process and solve a problem of practice selected by the school team. The authors describe the DI process in more detail later in the chapter through a discussion of AS's process.

The program began with a 2-day workshop in August 2019 during which university faculty both facilitated learning the DI process for all eight school design teams and helped them narrow a problem of practice. All teams received a DI handbook provided by the University of Denver to support their learning and utilized a Google site to store and share their learning. The team presented their progress and key learnings to each other in quarterly network convenings held in person in November 2019 and January 2020. From the end of March 2020, after the district decided to turn to remote learning due to the COVID-19 pandemic, the program conducted all coaching and network sessions online. Between network sessions, the schools engaged in action periods during which they moved through five phases of the DI process. The team members at AS met with their improvement coach once a week throughout the action periods to work through the process, discuss issues, and reflect on their practices.

The AS Team

The AS DI team consisted of the assistant principal, Ms. Nora; a reading interventionist and second-grade teacher, Ms. Molly; and a reading interventionist and first-grade teacher, Ms. Claudette. Ms. Nora, an AS alumna, had served as assistant principal for more than a decade. She has a profound knowledge of the AS community and students' needs. She took an active role in leading the DI program by working closely with the improvement coach and supporting the DI team and teachers. Both Ms. Molly and Ms. Claudette had many years of experience working in the D-town Public Schools (DPS) in early literacy. They worked closely with teachers and students, "pushing in" as reading interventionists and providing timely support in the classrooms. They also served an important role in communicating with teachers to help train them in phonics instruction, learn about teachers' vulnerability and professional learning needs in the process, and assist them in improving literacy instruction.

The AS Community

AS serves students from prekindergarten to fifth grade and is one of three public schools in the district to offer International Baccalaureate Primary Years Programs for all students. The majority of AS students are Latinx, 65.37%, out of 76.58% SOC population, and 22.56% are English Language Learners (ELLs). Within the district, Latinx students account for 53.19% out of 74.48% SOCs in the district with a 31.22% ELLs population (Colorado Department of Education [CDE], n.d.-a). AS reflected the demographics of the district.

According to the 2019 School Performance Framework,[1] AS was above average compared with other district schools in academic achievement and academic growth measured by the Colorado Measures of Academic Success (CMAS) tests. AS received the rating of "Meets" for CMAS-English Language Arts in both academic growth and achievement with an "Exceeds" for ELL academic growth and "Meets" for SOCs in both (CDE, n.d.-a). Despite these promising data, the school recognized the need to improve on their literacy instruction. Specifically, the team explored variation in disaggregated data, a core principle of improvement science, and found they were underserving their SOCs in reading (39.5% of first- to third-grade SOCs met the grade-level expectation compared with 60.8% of non-SOCs). The design team knew they needed a new approach to better prepare SOCs to become skilled readers.

The teachers at AS were largely well prepared and effective. AS's teachers had, on average, more than 11 years of classroom experience and a majority of teachers held master's degrees. The Educator Effectiveness Metrics *EducatorView*[2] (CDE, n.d.-b) reposted that 72% of AS's teachers were rated as "Highly Effective" and "Effective" while 56.74% of all teachers in the district received the same rating in 2018–2019. For the four quality standards, (1) Know Content, (2) Establish Environment, (3) Facilitate Learning, and (4) Professionalism, about 66% of AS teachers received "Exemplary" and "Accomplished" rating while approximately 55% of all teachers in the district reached the same levels. Sixty-two percent of teachers met or exceeded expectations based on the same measures of student learning in 2018–2019, which was 12% more than the district.

---

1 See https://www.cde.state.co.us/accountability/performanceframeworks for more information about School Performance Framework (SPF).
2 See https://www.cde.state.co.us/educatoreffectiveness/eemetrics#:~:text=Educator %20Effectiveness%20Metrics%20Overview,as%20the%20Educator%20 Effectiveness%20Metrics for more information about Educator Effective Metrics.

Equity Focus

AS used the DI process to focus its improvement work on structural and systematic changes in literacy instruction for SOCs. Aligned with district goals, the AS team researched and reflected on closing the opportunity gap. The district focus resonated with AS's early literacy team as they focused on grade-level phonics as a lever for change, especially for SOCs. Phonics and phonemic awareness were a new focus for the school.

Previously, the approach to supporting struggling readers was to reteach and provide extra support. Literacy teachers pulled out the struggling readers from the general classroom and provided guided reading. The early literacy team designed instructional support with the expectation that struggling readers needed more remedial instruction. As a result, it was perceived as normal and acceptable that some students were not receiving grade-level phonics. With this approach to guided reading, teachers unintentionally perpetuated the reading literacy gap and contributed to underserved students, most of whom were SOCs, struggling with grade-level reading skills. The principal shared:

> But then I think we also started to see other things, like we were doing intervention over multiple years, but we were pulling them out, so that was actually also increasing the gap for those kids, who a lot of times were our students of color, so we were actually withholding core in the name of support. And so then again, I think, just the problem, we started to understand more the complexity of it. It wasn't just, "We're not teaching phonics." It got more into like, "Oh, the structure is a problem."

Through the DI process, AS focused on bridging the early literacy equity gap by focusing on three areas: changing teachers' mindsets, redesigning grade-level phonics instruction, and providing strategic support.

Through root-cause analysis, including a fishbone diagram, the team identified two primary drivers: SOCs' access to grade-level phonics and teachers' professional development (PD). From there, the team embarked on Plan–Do–Study–Act (PDSA) cycles to test change ideas aligned with the two drivers. After abandoning their first instructional model, through iteration, they moved from a pull-out model to a differentiated push-in model focused on grade-level phonics instruction. To develop teacher content knowledge in phonemic awareness, they responded to teacher feedback and modeled practices to apply in the classroom immediately.

Understanding the Problem

Root-Cause Analysis

A key principle of improvement science is to understand deeply the problem by being user-centered and problem-focused (Bryk et al., 2015). This principle aligns with the *discovery* phase of DI and requires schools to spend a significant amount of time developing a more in-depth understanding of their problem and identifying the root causes of the problem. During the initial training, the DI coaches introduced ways to gather a variety of data sources, including exploring local data, systems, and process mapping; consulting research; consulting successful practicing professionals through visiting analogous settings; and, most important, conducting empathy interviews with those closest to the problem—the users.

Two other core principles of improvement science are to see the system in which the problem is embedded and to analyze variation in data within that system (Bryk et al., 2015). The AS DI team gained a better understanding of the problem by conducting root-cause analysis. The team utilized "Istation" data, an online learning program that provides a regular assessment of student learning, and empathy interview data, which involves asking questions to understand experiences to inform analysis throughout the process. From there, the improvement aim was created: Kindergartners through second graders would improve reading achievement in phonemic awareness and phonics by 10% as measured on a monthly basis by Istation by the end of the 2019–2020 academic year. To track this aim, they created a color-coded data wall that elevated inequity and intentionally tracked student success.

Empathy Interviews

The leadership teams and teachers had focused on early literacy for several years before the DI program. The team had done research and prepared to introduce phonics instruction during the Fall 2019 term. The DI process helped the team to explore the problem deeper and successfully implement changes to literacy instruction with a focus on equitable opportunities and outcomes for all students. The team wanted to understand the opportunity gap and did research about the impact of poverty on learning and the critical role of phonemic awareness in developing beginning readers. In the *discovery* phase, as early as August and September 2019, the team started their first round of empathy interviews with teachers and students, which they completed by October (see Table 2.1 for empathy interview questions).

Using local data, the team put AS students into three categories according to the Istation[3] data: Tier 1—on grade level, Tier 2—between grade levels, and Tier 3—below grade level. The team used "at-promise readers" instead of "struggling readers" or "below grade-level students." After identifying these categories, the team conducted empathy interviews with students who were Tier 3 at-promise readers in kindergarten to third grade. They found an interesting and concerning trend. Students in kindergarten and first grade had confidence in their reading, but in second and third grade, the confidence had dropped, and all students used the word *hard* to describe their reading skills. They shared that they were unsure how to attack a word they did not know. The DI team knew that they needed to improve their approach to early literacy to help students maintain their enthusiasm and comfort with reading.

The team also did empathy interviews with literacy teachers. Teachers were in favor of the changes and understood the importance

---

3 See https://www.istation.com/About/StateApprovals for Istation state specific Colorado.

of a new approach to the literacy block; however, they expressed a lack of awareness about how to deliver quality phonemic instruction and a lack of training around phonics instruction. The team followed up with teachers for more information after the empathy interviews, and teachers confirmed that they needed consistent support in their classroom to support at-promise readers. Teachers needed PD to increase teachers' understanding of effective phonics instructions and phonemic awareness.

The DI team discovered from the interview results that teachers did not have a solid foundation in how to teach phonics but were committed to learning through PD that met their needs. The DI design team had developed a deeper understanding of the significance of fundamental skills and the role of phonics instruction in students' early grades. Based on the empathy interview data, there was a need for systematic phonics instruction through different grades, phonemic awareness, and structural support for teachers' learning needs. The DI team was poised to provide that support but hoped to learn more about how to deliver that support. The team also conducted classroom observations, held informal conversations with teachers, and administered Google surveys to determine teachers' content needs (see Table 2.1).

Table 2.1. Academy of Science Design Improvement Program—Empathy Interview Questions 2019 September

Empathy Questions	Students	Teachers
Question 1	What kind of reader are you? Do you like to read? What do you like to read?	Describe your thinking, preparation, and implementation of literacy instruction
Question 2	What do you do when you get to a word you do not know?	Tell me about a time a lesson went well for all students
Question 3	What have you learned about letters and sounds?	Tell me about a time you felt unsure about how to help a student
Question 4		What was your best coaching/professional development experience, and why? What has been your worst experience, and why?

Variation in Local Data

The AS team took a different approach to analyzing data using the DI process. Prior to the DI, teachers and leaders at AS primarily paid attention to the high-level student data. Although they pinpointed at-promise students and looked into students' percentile ranks, they focused on large gains with groups of students (e.g., how should we support 40th-percentile students' move to the 68th percentile?). Through the DI, they shifted their data analysis strategy by analyzing Istation subcategory data, including letter knowledge, alphabetical decoding, phonemic awareness, and spelling and fluency, which allowed them to have a deeper understanding of the root causes of where students started to have misconceptions. The AS team analyzed students' subcategory data and collectively summarized what they learned. The analysis enabled the leadership team and teachers to use the students' data trends as a reference to inform their next steps in instruction.

Theory of Improvement

After this *discovery* phase, schools narrowed the problem statement and created an aim statement, or SMART (i.e., specific, measurable, achievable, relevant, time-bound) goal, to guide the theory of improvement. Through *interpretation* and *ideation*, the design teams also identified several drivers that surfaced as the levers for change based on research, empathy data, and local data. These drivers identify the systems, structures, and processes related to solving the problem and meeting the stated aim. From there, the team brainstormed change ideas that aligned with one or more drivers. These ideas come from research, creativity, and existing practices. The aim statement, drivers, and change ideas make up a theory of improvement depicted in the driver diagram. This theory suggests that implementing a certain change idea will improve the driver and, in turn, lead to progress on the aim. The team then tested and iterated the change ideas in *experimentation* through a PDSA cycle.

Problem Statement

AS's early literacy initiative aligned with district learning on closing the opportunity gap and also their school's vision and mission. After the team collected and analyzed data from the empathy interviews, they revised the problem statement. AS's problem statement was to address the long-term issue of underserving SOCs in early literacy. They found out that 39.5% of first- to third-grade SOCs were on track as compared to 60.8% of non-SOCs according to end-of-year Istation data. They realized that they had unintentionally withheld grade-level phonics instruction from their SOCs in early literacy instruction. The leadership team made assumptions, instead of using data, to determine student needs. They also realized they had made assumptions of literacy teachers' PD needs and preferences.

Aim Statement

AS aimed at improving its SOCs' reading achievement in kindergarten to second grade measured by monthly Istation data by 10% by the end of 2019–2020 academic year. Reading achievement refers to phonemic awareness and phonics. The team analyzed and looked at the trends of data in disaggregated data for different grades: phonemic awareness and letter knowledge in kindergarten; phonemic awareness, letter knowledge, and alphabetical decoding in first grade; and spelling and fluency in second grade. The AS DI team tracked progress toward solving these issues by analyzing monthly Istation data and narrowing the Istation data from "reading" to "phonics instruction" subcategories. They built a data wall where they color-coded the at-promise students based on their ethnicities. SOCs received yellow dots and non-SOCs red dots. The data wall elevated the inequities between AS's SOCs and non-SOCs and helped the team track progress toward improvement.

Drivers and Change Ideas

The team identified two drivers that targeted teachers' and students' needs, respectively. One driver was PD for teachers and the other focused on access to grade-level phonics and providing strategic support. The team constantly revised the change ideas throughout the DI process (see Figures 2.1 and 2.2 for two versions of drivers' diagrams).

The change idea in response to the driver of addressing students' needs in improving reading skills was to change their model of support. Throughout the DI process, the team iterated a model for intervention and ended up with a push-in model with the interventionists in the classroom instead of pulling students out. All students would receive 20 minutes of grade-level instruction differentiated within the classroom. The team intended a gradual release of core phonics instruction to classroom teachers by removing interventionists' support during core instruction. They revised the classroom structure to capitalize on the 40-minute blocks to allow classroom teachers to deliver core instruction to small groups and interventionists to serve more students. Tier 1 students had opportunities for independent application and practice of newly learned skills. The at-promise students not only had access to grade-level phonics in the classroom but also had a second chance to learn the phonics with the intervention teachers. Teachers and interventionists also allowed at-promise students to practice phonics principles to confirm understanding and ensure mastery.

To better support teachers, the teachers changed their PD model. The reading interventionists in the DI team supported teachers' capacity with phonics instruction and changed teachers' mindsets by emphasizing phonemic awareness. The three interventionists also supported planning time for teachers. Teachers analyzed Tier 3 students' data with the support of the leadership team to set goals, identify next steps, and continue their practices of building a tracker for teachers to monitor student learning. The interventionists supported teachers in getting a deeper knowledge of their work: identify celebrations and notices, set goals, and clarify the next steps. The DI team designed and implemented the PD primarily based on teachers' recommendations.

PDSA Cycles

The AS team completed PDSA cycles to test and refine their change ideas. To determine their teaching model, they tested several configurations to move from a pullout to a push-in model. The DI team tested a model of co-teaching for 6 weeks in September and October and then turned to the teaching in differentiated blocks for the remainder of the year. First, they tried to have interventionists co-teach with teachers, but through PDSA cycles, the team learned they were not able to target sufficient numbers of at-promise students when co-teaching, so they abandoned this approach. They needed a different way to support teachers in delivering strong phonics instruction. For the next PDSA cycles, they tested different models of differentiated blocks of instruction.

The DI team tested the pullout model in kindergarten. Teachers used the first 20 minutes of the literacy block to teach core phonics to the whole classroom at once, while the interventionists supported the teacher. During the second 20 minutes, the interventionist would pull a small group of students (Tier 3, at-promise students) to further support the skills taught in the first 20-minute block. In this pullout model, some students stayed with the teacher for supporting practices while some did not. The DI team adopted a push-in model to strategically support more students after the first round of the PDSA cycle. The students were divided into two different groups. The first group was either getting a core phonics lesson with a teacher or independent work based on past days' lessons, while the second group was with the interventionist for the first 20-minute block. The two groups of students would switch during the second 20-minute block. The new push-in model doubled the amounts of students seen by the interventionist, and all the students were able to receive core-phonics instruction from their teacher and practice independently. Any student below the 50th percentile in the Istation was taught by interventionists while still getting grade-level core phonics instruction in AS's second round of PDSA cycles.

The team then tested the push-in model in kindergarten and first grade and the pullout model for the second grade. The push-in model mixed students in different tiers together instead of putting students into homogenous groups (at-promise students and non-at-promise students). The DI team found that the heterogeneous grouping was the most effective. By having heterogeneous groups, teachers were able to help more students in the classroom and knew every student's progress. All the students in the classroom received grade-level phonics instruction, and at-promise students got support from interventionists immediately on the spot. Throughout the PDSA cycles, the DI team took teachers' recommendations and teachers felt more valued in the DI process.

For the driver of PD, the DI team continued to support teachers in understanding phonemic awareness. In the second set of PDSA cycles, the interventionists modeled how to deliver a 10-minute strategic phonemic awareness lesson and how to develop a scope and sequence for teaching phonics. The teachers were also given resources, such as Haggerty Resources and phonic awareness curriculum to support their learning in PD (see Figure 2.1).

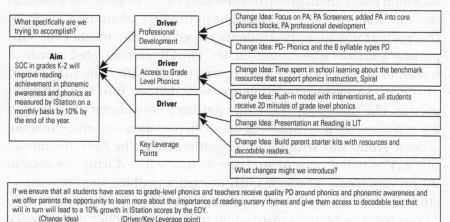

Impact by Design: Promoting Equity Through Reading Achievement of Students of Color

What specifically are we trying to accomplish?

Aim
SOC in grades K-2 will improve reading achievement in phonemic awareness and phonics as measured by IStation on a monthly basis by 10% by the end of the year.

Driver Professional Development

Driver Access to Grade Level Phonics

Driver

Key Leverage Points

Change Idea: Focus on PA; PA Screeners; added PA into core phonics blocks, PA professional development

Change Idea: PD- Phonics and the 6 syllable types PD

Change Idea: Time spent in school learning about the benchmark resources that support phonics instruction, Spiral

Change Idea: Push-in model with interventionist, all students receive 20 minutes of grade level phonics

Change Idea: Presentation at Reading is LIT

Change Idea: Build parent starter kits with resources and decodable readers.

What changes might we introduce?

If we ensure that all students have access to grade-level phonics and teachers receive quality PD around phonics and phonemic awareness and we offer parents the opportunity to learn more about the importance of reading nursery rhymes and give them access to decodable text that will in turn will lead to a 10% growth in IStation scores by the EOY.
      (Change Idea)   (Driver/Key Leverage point)

Figure 2.1. AS's First Driver Diagram for 2019-2020 Program in Nov. 2019

The final version of the driver diagram is displayed in Figure 2.2.

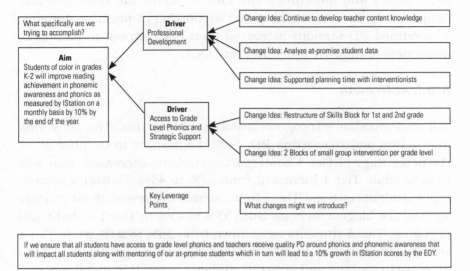

Figure 2.2. AS's Final Driver Diagram for 2019-2020 DI Program

DI Outcomes and Lessons Learned

Through this process, AS began to see "impact not by accident" but by design and found more students moved to grade level than in previous years. The DI team also recognized they had operated with deficit thinking. They had pulled struggling readers (renamed as "at-promise" students) out of grade-level instruction for different support, assuming they were not capable of grade-level phonics instruction without interventions. They recognized the supports the school provided were actually an impediment to the goal of having all students reading on grade level or above. The team learned that students, including SOCs they thought were struggling readers, actually needed to be exposed to phonemic awareness, which is a building block to reading. Also, they realized previous PD had been built around assumptions about what teachers needed and not what teachers identified they needed. By changing their PD model, the literacy teachers became more transparent and honest about their experiences and difficulties and clearer about the resources and support they need in teaching and supporting at-promise students. The refined PD sessions increased their engagement in phonemic awareness to improve outcomes for SOCs.

Student Growth

The students showed progress based on this new model for delivering instruction and supporting PD. From September to October 2019, the percentage of Tier 3 kindergarten students decreased from 56% to 36% while Tier 1 increased from 27% to 43%. Fourteen percent more students entered Tier 1 in phonemic awareness. First graders showed the biggest increase from 33% to 43% in Tier 1 alphabetical decoding. Tier 3 students went down from 36% to 24% while Tier 1 students increased from 32% to 40%. The second graders had a 9% increase in spelling and 20% (20 students in total) in text fluency.

By January 2020, the Istation data has shown great improvements in the students' outcomes in kindergarten and first grade and promising results in all grades. The kindergarten students showed a 14% increase and a 20% decrease in Tiers 1 and 3. There was a significant decrease (33%) and increase (35%) in Tiers 1 and 3 letter knowledge. About 10% of students moved from Tiers 3 to 1 in phonemic knowledge. The team aimed at increasing Tier 1 students to 60% for the next phase. The first graders showed the same trend. Their change ideas would be refined around the first graders who were still receiving instruction in phonemic awareness, 49 in total. The second-grade students didn't show a great increase (8%) in Tier 1 or decrease in Tier 3 (6%) after passing the 60% mark. The second-grade data are a result of a culmination of years of early literacy work. AS's initial data revealed that they had begun closing the opportunity gap (meeting expectations/Tier 1), with a reduction from 22% to 11% between SOCs and non-SOCs by January 2020.

Figure 2.3 is a comparison of students' Istation data before and after the implementation of DI program that shows SOCs' improvement in keeping grade-level literacy. After 7 months (September

2019–March 2020) of the DI program, more than 25% of kindergarten students, 17% of first-grade students, and 10% of second-grade students had reached grade level. The students also moved from Tier 2 and Tier 3 faster than they had in previous years.

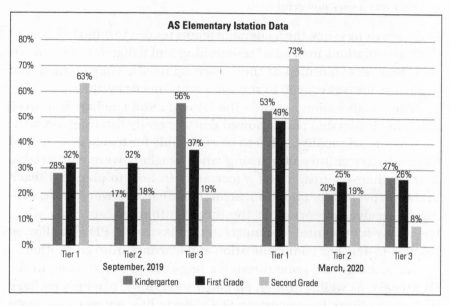

Figure 2.3. AS Istation Data 2019-2020 Yearly Comparison

Change of Mindsets

AS's leadership team and teachers also recognized a shift in mindsets throughout the DI process. The leadership team valued the importance and the power of data and had deep reflections on their assumptions. One area in which they shifted their understanding was in how they organized and delivered PD. Ms. Nora shared:

> We've always delivered, I would say, quality PD around the assumption that this is what teachers needed, versus this is really what teachers needed. And so the way that they showed up for this year, they were all in, and as the process continued, they even were very

vulnerable and being like, "So, now how do we teach those high-frequency words? I'm unsure." So, because we had given them a space for their voice, and then given them something they can apply literally the second they leave PD, their voices just became stronger, and what they needed was what we delivered. And I just think that that was a very powerful tool.

In the previous years, the leadership teams tended to build PD around their assumptions instead of researching and using data to find out what teachers identified as their learning needs. They learned that teacher voice was crucial to serve students' needs better.

The collaboration between the DI team and teachers improved when the leadership team showed trust by really listening to teachers' voices and modifying PD to be applicable for teachers. It helped form a better culture of learning when teachers were comfortable sharing their confusion and uncertainty in how to plan and teach literacy, specifically phonics instruction. Teachers were more willing to receive support from the interventionists, especially while teaching with the interventionists in the classroom. PD also allowed teacher-to-teacher communication and learning from each other.

AS teachers had gone through a huge change of mindset in the DI process, as well. Through empathy interviews, teachers realized that their efforts in supporting SOCs' early literacy were the right thing, and they allowed themselves to be vulnerable in the process. Veteran teachers and novice teachers alike were willing to reveal their vulnerability and change in instruction to serve their at-promise students. An acceptance of vulnerability gradually became an essential part of AS's school culture. Teachers were much more open to learning and growing when the PD met their own learning needs.

Systematic PD

The DI processes used to understand the problem such as empathy activities and analyzing data more deeply helped systematize PD and narrow the focus. The AS team reflected that the DI process helped them not only pinpoint students in need of urgent help but also narrow and keep their focus on PD in a systematic way. AS's

PD was based on teachers' voices and recommendations along the journey.

In the past, the team designed high-quality professional learning opportunities but found out that the teachers felt it was vague and unfocused. DI aligned with AS's leadership team's focus on closing the opportunity gap for students of color. The AS's DI process also benefited from district resources and learning. Collectively, the school's alignment and culture improved, leading to increasingly equitable results for students. During a research interview for the design improvement program, one member of the leadership team found that they had

> the best results on school ratings because we are so focused on what we are doing in PD. There has been structure built in classrooms, empathy data recognizes what we have done, there is more clarity in what we are doing, and alignment exists for all systems. There has been change in [the] second-grade data, second grade has not complained about the new structure and instructional time has increased.

The culture of professional learning and relationships among teachers, leaders, and support staff improved through the DI process.

Remote Learning

There was a pause and change of the DI process and schedule because of the COVID-19 situation. The structured differentiation model in the classroom helped a smooth transfer to the challenging remote learning situation. It is expected that the current DI outcome will prevent an increasing opportunity gap between SOCs and non-SOCs in the remote learning setting in AS's community. A school leader shared:

> I do think that because we were able to change this model, it really helped going into remote learning, because our interventionist understood not only what they were doing with the curriculum, but then like how to implement benchmarks, and then giving all kids opportunities. So, like that is one thing we can celebrate.

The work they had done to improve literacy instruction helped them to face inequities in remote learning as well.

Conclusion

The DI process gave the teachers in AS the opportunity to understand the experience of the students and the teachers to design improvements to the structures to support literacy. With the DI process, the implementation of phonics instruction was successful because the leadership team and literacy teachers in AS were aware of how important the instructional model and PD were in advancing equitable access and outcomes for SOCs. They were able to solve the actual problems and not just base solutions on assumptions about the students' and the teachers' learning needs. This approach led to better designed instruction, which resulted in greater student outcomes, particularly for students historically underserved, our SOCs, as well as an increase in teachers' voices in leadership decisions.

Discussion Questions

1. What do your data, disaggregated by race and ethnicity, indicate might be a potential area for improvement in literacy in your classroom or school?
2. What is your or your team's current thinking on best practices in literacy instruction, and what recent research supports your practices?
3. How does the cycle of inquiry discussed in this chapter inform your approach to literacy instruction?
4. How did the use of the PDSA data and empathy interview data create the conditions for continuous growth in reading? How did this impact the final problem of practice and theory of improvement?
5. What sociopolitical considerations must be addressed in your grade level or school to begin an improvement process focused on equity in literacy outcomes?

References

Bryk, A., Gomez, L., Grunow, A., & LeMahieu, P. (2015). *Learning to improve: How America's schools can get better at getting better*. Harvard Education Press.

Clifford, D. (n.d.). *Equity-centered design deck*. Stanford d.school & design school X. https://dschool.stanford.edu/resources/equity-centered-design-framework

Colorado Department of Education. (n.d.-a). *SchoolView Data Center* [Infographic]. https://edx.cde.state.co.us/SchoolView/DataCenter/reports.jspx?_adf_ctrl-state=pac20phbp_4&_afrLoop=3523805992817892&_afrWindowMode=0&_adf.ctrl-state=oo75sd6hq_4

Colorado Department of Education. (n.d.-b). *EducatorView* [Infographic]. https://www.cde.state.co.us/ee-metrics

Kelley, D., & Kelley, T. (2013). *Creative confidence: Unleashing the creative potential within us all*. Crown Business.

CHAPTER THREE

University Academy Lab Schools: Closing the Gaps in Literacy

JENNIFER RASBERRY, MICHAEL ODELL,
TERESA KENNEDY, KELLY DYER,
JACLYN PEDERSEN, AND JO ANN SIMMONS

According to the 2020 *What's Hot in Literacy* report, citing findings from a survey conducted in 64 countries and territories, "increasing equity and opportunity for all learners" was found to be the third-most critical focus for improving literacy outcomes in the next decade after "determining effective instructional strategies for struggling readers" (most important focus) and "building early literacy skills through a balanced approach" (second-most critical focus; International Literacy Association, 2020, p. 6). The report also found that "equity and professional development are among the top five most important topics to improve literacy outcomes, and they are both deserving of more focus and attention among education policymakers" (International Literacy Association, 2020, p. 7). Addressing inequity in literacy is a nationwide issue and warrants attention to help close gaps for not only underserved students but all students as well.

Quality and equitable literacy instruction is the basis on which students gain literacy knowledge that not only helps them achieve success during their school-age years but also can increase their confidence as productive citizens as they grow and work in society. Oftentimes, educators face barriers that impede their abilities to close the achievement gaps and increase equality of literacy instruction for all students. Obstacles include a lack of teacher knowledge and teaching effectiveness and teacher preparation programs that inadequately prepare preservice teachers for meeting the needs of historically underserved students. Another barrier worth noting is the lack of professional development and opportunities to participate in professional learning communities (PLCs) where equity in education and serving the needs of all students are a focus of discussion. In the *What's Hot in Literacy* report, 71% of teachers "believe that variability of teacher knowledge and effectiveness is one of the greatest barriers to equity in literacy" (International Literacy Association, 2020, p. 21).

According to Haycock (2001), "to increase the achievement levels of minority and low-income students, we need to focus on what really matters: high standards, a challenging curriculum, and good teachers" (para. 1). Too often in education, our model is to serve through the lens of one size fits all. Serving students under those types of constraints can be detrimental to students' academic growth. Emerging research demonstrates that differentiated instruction, when fully implemented, can significantly improve student achievement (Goddard et al., 2007) and close educational gaps, whereas other traditional-style instructional methods do not. With a demanding need for teachers to focus on the vast variety of students that come to their classrooms each year, providing literacy education that is individualized and meets the needs of students will equip them with the tools they need to become strong literate individuals. Differentiated instruction through a blended learning model, a research-based practice that helps serve the individual needs of students, continues to surface as one of the many practices for ensuring that equity is met in education. In short, improving academic success for all students.

Many teachers struggle to meet the needs of the diverse learner populations in their classrooms, and unfortunately, some teachers are not strategic enough to design modifications necessary to serve the heterogeneity in their classrooms. Ultimately, our goal as educators should be to close achievement gaps for all learners, increase equity in education, provide multiple different opportunities for students to acquire content, grow to their highest potential, as well as achieve individual student success. One way the University of Texas at Tyler Academy Lab School has achieved this is by focusing our improvement aim on student progress for all, commonly referred to as "closing the gaps."

Background

The University of Texas at Tyler School of Education has a long history of school improvement work in Texas schools. In 2012, the university invested in the development of the University Academy Laboratory School District and opened three laboratory schools, or "academies." Each academy is located on the university proper or at one of the satellite campuses. The schools serve K–12 students and focus on achievement in science, technology, engineering, and mathematics (STEM) through project-based learning (PBL) strategies closely aligned with the school design model and the deeper learning outcomes associated with the approach (Odell et al., 2019; Odell & Pedersen, 2020).

The schools also provide authentic environments for faculty to prepare new educators in the educator preparation programs at the bachelor's, master's, and doctoral levels and with research opportunities that facilitate longitudinal studies that are difficult to implement and maintain through traditional school partnerships. The laboratory school platform has also increased the credibility of the School of Education and its faculty by keeping faculty current in their practice. Innovation and improvement are most effective when grounded in practice (Duggan, 2013; Fullan, 2011). Too often, university faculty can become dated in their experience. Involvement in the laboratory schools allows faculty to ground their research in the practical applications of school improvement using improvement science principles and tools and, specifically, through the utilization of Plan–Do–Study–Act (PDSA) cycles in the process of school improvement.

University students enrolled in the educator preparation programs participate in unique clinical experiences that utilize innovative instructional approaches including project-based learning (PrBL) and PBL, effective strategies to closely engage students with their learning content (Bender, 2012), as well as participate in alternative classroom management strategies and PLCs that include both K–12 and university faculty, and engage in graduate-level education research.

The academies also serve as demonstration sites for other school districts throughout the state. Schools thinking about adopting certain methodologies can send personnel to the laboratory schools for visits or short immersion periods to experience a potential intervention that may be of interest for implementation locally. More recently, the university was approved to offer a doctorate in school improvement, and the laboratory schools are taking on a new role as demonstration sites for active Network Improvement Communities (NICs). The laboratory schools and the School of Education are both units within the College of Education and Psychology. As a result, the NIC is sustainable and is capable of achieving its annually defined aims.

As an ongoing NIC, personnel from all units in the college and the laboratory schools work together on one or two goals annually. According to Bryk et al. (2015), an NIC is marked by four characteristics. It is

1. focused on a well specified common aim.
2. guided by a deep understanding of the problem and the system that produces it, and a shred working theory to improve it.
3. disciplined by the methods of improvement research to develop, test, and refine interventions.
4. organized to accelerate the diffusion of these interventions out into the field and support their integration into varied educational contexts. (p. 144)

Each year, a new iteration of improvement is designed and implemented to build on the work of the previous year. Using this approach, the laboratory schools have shown continuous growth over the last 7 years in academic achievement and accountability ratings. NIC personnel meet as needed to

- develop a theory of practice for improvement.
- utilize improvement science tools.
- identify sources of evidence to be collected and analyzed.
- refine the logistics and operations of the network.
- refine culture and norms for the network.
- create the next iteration of the PDSA cycle.

Each iteration of the PDSA cycle is characterized by leaders and stakeholders from units within the college, meeting to continue refinements to the school model with an emphasis on student outcomes, evidence from previous cycles, and identification of root causes and potential primary and secondary drivers. Each PDSA cycle coincides with each semester. Normally there are two iterations during the academic year. There have been cases of shorter term PDSA cycles when looking at specific instructional interventions. These are typically 9 weeks in length, coinciding with a grading period. Summer is used for additional analysis, reflection, and preparation for the next year's iteration. The PDSA model currently in use at the laboratory school is illustrated in Figure 3.1.

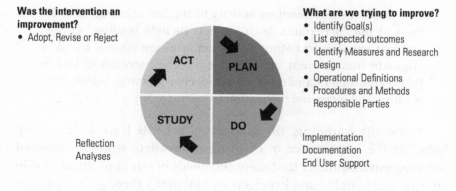

Figure 3.1. UT Tyler PDSA Model

One early goal of the NIC was that the district be rated in the top 10% of school districts in the state while demonstrating fidelity to the PBL/PrBL instructional model unique to the school as compared to more traditional instructional strategies being used in traditional partner districts. Through an iterative approach, the University Academy Laboratory School District has received an accountability rating of A by the Texas Education Agency. However, in the early days of the laboratory school, the implementation of the PBL instructional model and the anticipated teacher and student outcomes were not realized. Improvements were required to the instructional model and how that model was supported at the teacher and student levels. As new iterations of the PDSA cycle have concluded and met the operationally defined aim, the focus has shifted away from achievement and is now focused on equity in achievement and in nonacademic areas such as social-emotional learning (SEL).

Closing the Gaps in Reading

The University Academy Laboratory School District's goal since opening in 2012 is to provide a PBL approach for K–12 students to increase both academic and 21st-century skills. According to Bell (2010),

> PBL is not a supplementary activity to support learning. It is the basis of the curriculum. Most projects include reading, writing, and mathematics by nature. Many inquiries are science-based or originate from current social problems. The outcome of PBL is [a] greater understanding of a topic, deeper learning, higher-level reading, and increased motivation to learn. (p. 39)

Since our founding, the laboratory schools have held a deep belief in the importance of creating innovative, student-centered learning environments that meet the needs of our community while sharing our insights and experiences nationally through our unique university partnership. The mission of the University of Texas Tyler

University Academy is to develop students who leave school STEM college- and career-ready. STEM college-ready indicates students are prepared to enroll in a STEM major at a university. Typically, this means they are calculus-ready upon graduation or have completed calculus in high school. In pursuit of this mission, we have found that as the needs of our students grow in complexity, it has become vitally important that our approach to pedagogy and providing social/emotional support is increasingly tailored for their individual growth and development.

Each year, Texas provides an accountability rating to its public school districts, public charters, and schools. The ratings are based on student performance on state standardized tests, graduation rates, and postgraduate outcomes. The ratings examine student achievement, school progress, and whether districts and campuses are closing achievement gaps among various student groups. Table 3.1 shows the 2019 district accountability report. There are also campus-level reports as well.

Table 3.1. District Accountability Summary Report

	Component Score	Scaled Score	Rating
Overall Score		92	A
Student Achievement		91	A
STAAR Performance	63	91	
College, Career, Military Readiness	100		
School Progress		82	B
Academic Growth	71	82	B
Relative Performance EDS 20.9%	63	79	C
Closing the Gaps	92	93	A

Source: Texas Education Agency (2019).
Note: EDS = Economically Disadvantaged Students

The District Accountability report can be used to identify broad areas for improvement. This is one of the tools utilized by the NIC to identify problems of practice. It should be noted that there were no ratings in 2020 due to the COVID-19 pandemic. In this case, going forward, there is a need to examine school progress in the areas of academic growth and relative performance of students who are economically disadvantaged (ECD). This is an equity issue as the district could improve meeting the needs of ECD students.

The information in Table 3.2 enables the team to drill down into the English language arts (ELA) data. A review of the data shows that ECD students and English Language Learners (ELLs) are struggling to "meet" grade-level standards. An examination of the data reveals that only 62% of ECD students are meeting grade-level expectations and only in ELA compared to all students as measured by the state accountability exam, and only 26% are "mastering" the content. The ELA data show other areas of concern, such as scores among students who are African American and/or Hispanic, who receive ELL services, and who are also lower than scores of all students and White students. In a review of the data, ECD students include the majority of students from these other subgroups. Although the district is rated A, there is still much work to be done to bring all students to higher levels of achievement. The NIC also looks at other data, such as nonacademic data, including discipline, attendance, and other factors, that may have an impact on student achievement (see Table 3.2).

Tables 3.1 and 3.2 are current snapshots driving the most recent iterative PDSA cycle for our school improvement journey to date. However, it is important to provide a historical perspective. When the laboratory schools opened, the district and the schools struggled to meet the expectations. The district received its first accountability ratings in 2013. The format of the accountability charts has evolved over time, but the outcome is quite clear. The school did not initially meet accountability standards. Table 3.3 illustrates the initial accountability outcomes for the district. Schools in 2013 did not receive a letter grade, but the system utilized the same accountability domains currently used to hold schools accountable. Although there has been obvious improvement based on 2019 scores, the district is still focused on student growth and closing the gaps (see Table 3.3).

Table 3.2. 2019 English Language Arts/Reading Achievement Scores by Demographic

Percentage of Tests	All Students	African American	Hispanic	White	Asian	Two or more Races	ECD	EL Current	EL Current and Monitored	SPED
Approaches Standard	92%	87%	84%	93%	94%	100%	90%	73%	84%	83%
Meets Standard	71%	58%	55%	74%	89%	86%	62%	18%	42%	48%
Masters Standard	35%	23%	22%	37%	61%	43%	26%	9%	32%	10%
Number of Tests										
Approaches Standard	463	27	64	329	17	21	129	8	16	33
Meets Standard	358	18	42	261	16	18	89	2	8	19
Masters Standard	174	7	17	129	11	9	38	1	6	4
Total Tests	504	31	76	353	18	21	144	11	19	40

Source: Texas Education Agency (2019).
Note: ECD = economically disadvantaged; EL = English learner; SPED = special education.

Table 3.3. 2013 Accountability Rating: Pre-A–F Ratings

Performance Index	State Target	District Score	A–F Rating Equivalent Under Current System
Student Achievement	50	59	C
Student Growth	21	14	F
Closing the Gaps	55	45	F
Career, College, and Military Readiness	N/A	N/A	N/A

Source: Texas Education Agency (2013).
https://rptsvr1.tea.texas.gov/perfreport/account/2013/index.html

The ELA Improvement Journey

At the end of the 2012–2013 school year, district leaders gathered to reflect and make decisions regarding school improvement to increase academic success and close gaps for our students. The 2013 statewide assessment scores resulted in the district performing at the bottom 5% of schools in the state on standardized tests in ELA. Before we started the implementation of formal improvement cycles, the director of professional development, in consultation with district and School of Education personnel, started traveling to all campuses and implemented content rubrics for PBL as an initial intervention. In addition, the district provided professional development on PBL, with observational feedback based on teacher needs as voiced by teachers struggling to implement PBL. To accommodate teacher learning, time was created in the master schedule for teachers to plan and learn together and resulted in the implementation and institutionalization of embedded PLC as part of the improvement approach.

As part of the PLC, the leadership team examined statewide assessment data from years 1 and 2 of the organization to understand how students were performing in each of the domains within the accountability system and identify actionable areas for improvement. The "aim" that was identified was to improve Domain I scores, which focuses not only on overall student achievement but also on knowing that improvement was needed in Domain II, school progress, and Domain III, closing the gaps. The problem of practice (POP) at that time was to improve Domain I, overall student achievement, of our Texas accountability results. This work occurred in the summer as accountability results are typically released after the school year ends.

Our primary drivers identified in Table 3.3 led the conversations within the NIC leadership team to help determine how each would be implemented and carried out in the coming year. At the time of these conversations, there was a recognition of the need for instructional coaching throughout the year. Because content coaches had not yet been hired, the team recognized that would be one of the first major steps in driving the intended change within the laboratory school. Coaches were identified from existing teachers that had shown results and fidelity to the PBL approach. The NIC and district administration developed a theory that the implementation of content-specific coaches to target areas of concern would be a high-impact driver to facilitate improvement and expand the voices of teachers in the "plan" and "do" components of the PDSA cycle. It was believed at this point in the development and growth of the organization that systems were not in place to drive educational change forward and this implementation would be largely impactful in ensuring progress for all students. This was a recognition of the school improvement concept "seeing the system as it is." It was hypothesized that if we intentionally examined student achievement in ELA through the implementation of our primary drivers, as shown in Table 3.3, that we would begin to see an increase in our Domain I score.

Once the content coaches were implemented as an intervention, the NIC team decided during the early iterations of the PDSA cycle that the coaches would travel to each of the district's three campuses to provide PBL instructional support through a content lens. Strengthening PLCs that had been implemented was a complementary intended goal for the district as an improvement support structure.

PLCs would be not only a time that content coaches could meet with teams but also a structured, consistent scheduled time for teachers to plan, meet, and intentionally discuss student data, instructional approaches, and nonacademic factors such as discipline and school culture. During this initial PDSA cycle, teachers would be provided support with looking at data through the lens of each student and tracking overall class and individual student data. This would help us ascertain whether our students were showing progress and facilitate making plans centered around data (see Figure 3.2).

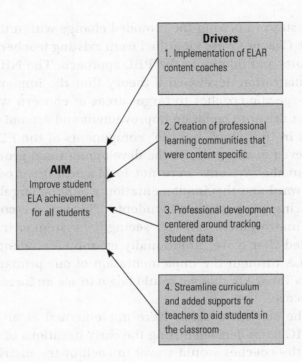

Figure 3.2. Initial Driver Diagram for English Language Arts

When looking at our ELA/reading and writing district data from 2013 and 2014, it can be noted that our averages when compared to the state averages were well below expected levels. The NIC determined that not only our team but also the teachers needed to be intentionally and consistently looking at data much closer than in the pre-intervention cycles of the schools in the district. Teachers became an important essential voice in the NIC as part of the improvement team. The English Language Arts and Reading content coach–led professional development on each campus through PLCs centered on best practices in tracking student data to closely monitor scores for each student. The ELA coach also helped the teachers plan and, when necessary, co-teach PBL lessons to build instructional capacity within ELA. In the 2014–2015 school year, a more systematic data collection plan was implemented to include fall and spring benchmark assessments that would help the district and teachers track student data on assessments that would mirror the manner in which they would be assessed by the state. Teachers were also provided training in a data-analysis software that can be used by teachers and students to track progress. The district utilizes DMAC, a software platform that allows teachers to do the following:

- Data disaggregation
- Generate, administer, and report on state standards-based local assessments
- Student achievement/progress monitoring
- Create curriculum maps
- Develop campus/district plans
- Facilitate student self-monitoring plans

Our final primary driver that helped our team make some initial changes in our POP was using the ELA coach to help implement and streamline curriculum for teachers to better assist them in the classroom with their students. Some of the changes included vertical alignment of scope and sequences as well as literacy-specific curricula to support the standards.

Earlier in the chapter, Tables 3.1 and 3.3 highlighted the current accountability status (rated A) and the initial accountability status (rated Improvement Required). Over the last 7 years, the PDSA iterations have resulted in significant improvements. Table 3.4 provides a longitudinal view of ELA scores since the lab schools opened during the 2012–2013 academic year.

In examining Table 3.4, after implementing our first PDSA methodology in the 2014–2015 school year, there was a 13-point gain in reading scores and an 8-point gain in writing. In 2014, we learned that the primary drivers contributed to growth in our overall Domain I scores, but we still needed to target our Domain II and Domain III scores to help each student show growth and close the literacy gaps we were seeing as an academy.

Between 2015 and 2017, the NIC for the district became more of an oversight NIC. Mini-NICs were developed within each area

Table 3.4. Annual Outcomes Data for English Language Arts

Year	2013	2014	2015	2016	2017	2018	2019
Subject	Pre-Intervention		Post-Intervention				
ELA/Reading							
District Average	75	74	90	87	86	87	92
State Average	80	76	77	73	72	74	75
Difference	−5	−2	+13	+14	+14	+13	+17
Writing							
District Average	48	53	80	79	78	79	75
State Average	63	72	72	69	67	66	68
Difference	−15	−19	+8	+10	+11	+13	+7

Source: Texas Education Agency. (2021)

targeted for improvement, bringing the expertise of the college and the academies on each discipline area to better refine the improvement interventions. These mini-NICs were led by the instructional coaches in collaboration with teachers and curriculum experts from the School of Education when appropriate. In the case of ELA, the literacy coach helped teachers plan instruction through the intentional use of modified ELA scope and sequences designed to align the approved state curriculum (state standards), the assessed curriculum (state assessments), and the taught curriculum (teacher lessons). The ELA coach worked with teachers to create cross-curricular PBL lesson plans aligned with district and statewide assessments and to track data on each individual student with an increasing level of fidelity to the PBL instructional model.

The POP at the start of the 2014-2015 school year was to improve student achievement for all students, and although the academy had seen gains in overall student achievement and the district had climbed out of the bottom 5% of the state regarding test scores, the data still showed the schools needed to grow in the areas of equity among all students by ensuring all students were meeting or exceeding their progress measure targets. Willie (2006) found that quality and equity can occur together and can and must be interlinked:

Education should focus neither on cultivating excellence at the expense of equity nor on cultivating equity at the expense of excellence. In a well-ordered society, the goal of education is to seek both excellence and equity because they are complementary. One without the other is incomplete. (p. 16)

During the 2016–2017 academic year, teachers used district-created spreadsheets to track individual student data at the classroom level. The addition of a uniform data-tracking system allowed the district to be more intentional with student data tracking. The primary focus in these data tools was to track past state assessment scores and district assessments through the lens of each student, focusing on Domain III, referred to as "closing the gaps" or subpopulation data. Within the spreadsheets, teachers highlighted subpopulations (Hispanics, Asians, and African Americans) to ensure an intentional emphasis on these students and their progress could occur. Teachers used these data to provide targeted instruction in ELA for students who were underserved and struggling to meet growth and achievement measures. Perhaps most important, they must be able to connect data analysis with effective interventions, monitoring processes, and instruction (Jimerson & Wayman, 2015; Mandinach et al., 2015; Mandinach & Friedman, 2015a).

Our state testing system, the State of Texas Assessments of Academic Readiness, defines progress measure classifications by comparing a student's gain score and the difference between the student's 2020–2021 scale score and 2018–2019 scale score to a progress target. The amount of improvement a student makes from year to year is classified in one of the following ways:

- Limited Progress
- Expected Progress
- Accelerated Progress

"Limited Progress" means that the student has shown little to no academic improvement. If a student's progress measure is "Expected," they have shown expected academic improvement from the previous year to the current year based on Texas Education Agency's formulas. If a student's progress measure is "Accelerated," a student has shown a significant amount of academic improvement from the previous year to the current year, much larger than expected.

Progress measures are reported within a content area (mathematics, reading, and high school English). As previously noted in Table 3.4, after implementing our improvement strategies, students made considerably more growth over pre-intervention growth. As shown in Table 3.5, all students, Hispanic students, and African American students showed particular growth. It is important to note that the district has a low number of Asian students, ranging from 8 to 15 students over the course of 7 years. Also, the number of students who had Expected or Accelerated Progress grew, which helped our district conclude that what we were modifying and changing within our organization was working.

Table 3.5. Domain III Academic Improvement based on State of Texas Assessments of Academic Readiness

Population	Limited 2013	Limited 2019	Expected 2013	Expected 2019	Accelerated 2013	Accelerated 2019
All Students	41%	30%	22%	37%	5%	18%
Hispanic	67%	32%	11%	34%	11%	21%
Asian	20%	50%	0%	0%	20%	25%
African American	61%	25%	17%	64%	6%	18%

Source: Texas Education Agency. (2021)

It should be noted that from 2016 to 2017, overall reading and writing scores dropped slightly (see Table 3.5). Our hypothesis for this drop was not having a focus on progress measures for all students, Domain II, but instead having a focus on closing the gaps for our subpopulations. Despite low numbers of students of color, we had to focus on their progress more intently. Although this was a primary aim during this PDSA cycle, the district's goal was to shift from a laser focus of Domains I and III to start providing equity and growth for all students. In the coming years, our anticipated goals are centered on Domain II, which is student progress for all students.

Between 2017 and 2019, our coaches changed their schedules from traveling to each campus to being stationed at one campus. If content expertise was needed, the implementation of the Zoom platform became robust enough to address communications. Evidence supports that this change has helped provide continuous daily support through coaching cycles, feedback, and professional development around areas of growth for each campus. The elimination of travel time has allowed more time for coaches and teachers to interact. For example, coaches and teachers spend more time together to continue to adjust resources and streamline ELA curricula to PBL best practices.

Also, during this time, the coaches on each campus were able to prioritize teachers on a differentiated need basis and determine how often the coach spent with each teacher. This was determined by walk-throughs, years of experience as a teacher, years of experience within our district, and past state data summaries. As a result, the coach was able to provide tiered levels of support through the instructional coaching model. The instructional coaches used a three-tiered approach to determine the levels of support each teacher would need. Tier 1 included experienced teachers who demonstrated excellence in teaching and data-driven decisions. These teachers only needed monthly observations and coaching. Those in Tier 2 were teachers who could be experienced or new but still needed modeling or co-teaching instruction with the instructional coach and assistance with planning and looking at data. Tier 2 teachers participated in biweekly meetings and had two coaching cycles per month. The tier with the most teacher support is Tier 3. This could be for new teachers or even experienced teachers who were struggling with the laboratory's model of instruction. These teachers received weekly support with the instructional coach on an as-needed basis. By doing this, the coach and teacher were able to build a strong relationship and work together in specific individual data meetings, make plans, and target students not making progress. Based on these meetings with teachers, lesson plans were revised, classroom assessments were modified in some cases, and tutorial and intervention group-ings were designed to target instruction for all students. The teacher tier system was fluid, and teachers could move in and out of those levels of support based on data through observations and meetings.

During the 2019–2020 school year, the NIC and the district started the year off with the same plans for continuing closing gaps for all student by tracking student data in the district created spread-sheets, as well as continuing the tiered level of support within the coaching cycles conducted by the instructional coaches.

One change made during the 2020–2021 school year was to add the layer of tiered support for our students within the district-cre-ated student progress monitoring spreadsheets. The district wanted to add in and strengthen the response-to-intervention process for our schools. The tier system for the students is similar to the teach-er-tiered level of support. Tier 1 students included all students in the general education classrooms, all receiving the same amount and types of instruction. Tier 2 and 3 supports for students allowed for those students to be served in a smaller group capacity through intensive targeted instruction, with Tier 3 being the highest level of support for a specific student. This helped the teachers see which students specifically needed extra support and targeted literacy instruction, which they were already doing to some degree but were not documenting and tracking intervention progress for each of their Tier 2 and 3 students.

This adjustment enabled teachers to closely examine the inter-ventions in place and determine if they were helping students make progress academically. Intervention meetings occurred every 9 weeks. If the students were not showing progress, the intervention was changed and new goals for that student were set. This process allowed teachers and district personnel to follow each student's progress intentionally by tracking their tiers and the level of aca-demic support they were receiving. Unfortunately, due to COVID-19, our school instructional model changed to remote learning in March 2020. The district was unable to document end-of-year data per the state assessment. At the start of the 2020–2021 academic year, the Texas Education Agency released beginning of the year assessments for schools to utilize to see academic gaps from the closure of COVID-19. These data were imperative to the teachers and helped them know where their students were academically at the start of the year due to the lack of end-of-year state assessment data at the close of the 2019–2020 school year. This was extremely valuable data and helped start the year off with data to drive instruction. These data were placed in the student progress monitoring system that we continued from the year prior.

In the eight years our district has been open, it has implemented multiple iterations of PDSA improvement cycles, each building on the last. As a new organization in the 2012–2013 academic year, tightly aligned systems were not in place to support equity within our academic systems. While the first 2 years of operation did not result in expected outcomes, the PDSA cycles helped the district stay true to its PBL instructional model. It would not be uncommon for a district to abandon a model that was not initially working, but the research literature indicated that PBL was the best instructional paradigm for our school model.

PDSA cycles helped the district to investigate the undesirable outcomes that were occurring and shift the focus toward adopting practices and systems that would help drive student achievement and close the educational gaps for our underserved students. The district's primary intervention in ELA from pre- to post-intervention was the implementation of instructional coaches and teacher input that helped shift classroom curriculum, assessment, and instruction. Tracking student data with fidelity to ensure that progress for *all* students was occurring has been institutionalized and is a common discussion reference at all levels of the organization and within the NIC structure itself.

All academic subjects are essential, of course, but it's literacy that unravels them all. There is significant evidence in the research literature that the ability to read affects achievement during a student's academic career and beyond. It is ultimately our charge as educators to ensure that all students have the tools at hand to become well-rounded literate students.

Datnow et al. (2014) report that "thoughtful data-informed decision making and, more specifically, data-informed leadership involves more than collecting and looking at student data. A deep process of inquiry using multiple assessments and types of data is essential" (p. 97). By implementing evidence-based methods in schools that help teachers track individual student progress and adjust instruction based on data, teachers can help all students show progress by differentiating instruction based on need. For any academic organization to increase access and equity in schools there has to be a focus on data to identify areas of weakness and improvement. The University of Texas Tyler University Academy Laboratory Schools have developed a learning culture designed to identify and close gaps to develop more equitable schools. Knowing where students are on a deeper level academically, we begin to view our students in a new way. According to Powell and Rightmyer (2011), "honoring students' knowledge changes us as teachers. We see students differently" (p. 9).

The work around the PDSA cycles points in a promising direction for future studies that look to illustrate instructional improvement in literacy. Based on the iterations of cycles of study at the lab school, the work is still ongoing and will continue to improve the ELAR outcomes for students. A central lesson is that all stakeholders must work collectively to ensure students are provided the appropriate educational opportunities and individual support to grow. These laboratory schools reflect a vision for what is possible in schools when everyone is focused on growth for all students, of all backgrounds.

Discussion Questions

1. While this chapter focused on a districtwide strategy with a university partner, in what ways could you, as a classroom teacher or building principal, adapt the concepts presented here to start small in your classroom or your school?
2. What are the dispositions that enable equity-centered collaboration among students' teachers?
3. How could you, as a classroom teacher, promote these dispositions in your classroom, grade-level teams, or school?

4. What data do you collect, or could you collect, and analyze at the classroom level to start small and test improvement strategies in your classroom or school?

References

Bell, S. (2010). Project-based learning for the 21st century: Skills for the future. *The Clearing House, 83*(2), 39–43. https://www.jstor.org/stable/20697896?seq=1 #metadata_info_tab_contents

Bender, W. N. (2021). *Project-based learning: Differentiating instruction for the 21st Century*. Corwin.

Bryk, A. S., Gomez, L. M., Grunow, A., & LeMahieu, P. G. (2015). *Learning to improve: How America's schools can get better at getting better*. Harvard Education Press.

Datnow, A., & Park, P. (2014). *Data-driven leadership* (Jossey-Bass Leadership Library in Education). John Wiley & Sons, Inc.

Duggan, W. (2013). *Strategic intuition: The creative spark in human achievement*. Columbia University Press.

Fullan, M. (2011). *Change leader: Learning to do what matters most*. Jossey-Bass.

Goddard, Y. L., Goddard, R. D., & Tschannen-Moran, M. (2007). A theoretical and empirical investigation of teacher collaboration for school improvement and student achievement in public elementary schools. *Teachers College Record, 109*(4), 877–896. http://www.tcrecord.org/Content.asp?ContentId=12871

Haycock, K. (2001, March). Closing the achievement gap. *Educational Leadership, 58*(6), 6–11. http://www.ascd.org/publications/educational-leadership/mar01/ vol58/num06/Closing-the-Achievement-Gap.aspx

International Literacy Association. (2020). *What's hot in literacy report*. https:// www.literacyworldwide.org/docs/default-source/resource-documents/whats hotreport_2020_final.pdf

Jimerson, J. B., & Wayman, J. C. (2015). Professional learning for using data: Examining teacher needs and supports. *Teachers College Record, 117*(4), 1–36. https://www.tcrecord.org/Content.asp?ContentId=17855

Mandinach, E. B., & Friedman, J. M. (2015, April 15–21). *Case studies of schools of education: What we can learn about improving data literacy among educators* [Paper presentation]. Annual meeting of the American Educational Research Association, Chicago, IL, United States.

Mandinach, E. B., Parton, B. M., Gummer, E. S., & Anderson, R. (2015, February). Ethical and appropriate data use requires data literacy. *Phi Delta Kappan, 96*(5), 25–28. http://www.thecircleofdata.com/uploads/7/8/8/2/78829528/ethical_and_ appropriate_data_use_requires_data_literacy_.pdf

Odell, M. R. L., Kennedy, T. J., & Stocks, E. (2019). The impact of PBL as a STEM
    school reform model. *Interdisciplinary Journal of Problem-Based Learning,
    13*(2): Article 4. https://docs.lib.purdue.edu/ijpbl/vol13/iss2/4/

Odell, M. R. L., & Pedersen, J. L. (2020). Project and problem-based teaching and
    learning. In B. Akpan & T. J. Kennedy (Eds.), *Science education in theory and
    practice* (pp. 343–357). Springer International Publishing. https://link.springer.
    com/chapter/10.1007/978-3-030-43620-9_23

Powell, P., & Rightmyer, E. C. (2011). *Literacy for all students: An instructional
    framework for closing the gap*. Routledge.

Texas Education Agency. (2019). *A parent's guide to STAAR progress measure*. State
    of Texas Assessment of Academic Readiness. https://tea.texas.gov/sites/default/
    files/2019_STAAR_Progress_Measures_Parents_Guide_English_final_tagged.pdf

Tomlinson, C. A., & Allan, S. (2000). *Leadership for differentiating schools and class-
    rooms*. ASCD.

Willie, C. V. (2006, Winter). The real crisis in education: Failing to link excellence and
    equity. *Voices in Urban Education, 10*, 11–19.

CHAPTER FOUR

Equity Matters: Witnessing the Stories of Students and Families

LYNDA TREDWAY, MATTHEW MILITELLO,
MORAIMA MACHADO, AND JOLIA BOSSETTE

Context and Background

As we know from Cornell West (2017) on matters of equity and race, what we do matters a great deal. In this chapter, we first frame the East Carolina University (ECU) Education Doctorate (EdD) program and then share first-person stories of Principal Moriama Machado and fifth-grade student Jolia Bossette. In analyzing their stories as examples of equity and antiracism actions, we show how the participatory action research (PAR) project and study embody what we value about PAR and activist research. Furthermore, in this chapter, we marry the asset-rich approach to the equity of the PAR process with the improvement science methodology.

In our reimagined equity-focused EdD program, we redesigned a complementary set of courses and experiences that reflect equity as a moral imperative (Harris & Jones, 2018; Rivera-McCutchen, 2014; Theoharis, 2010). By design and in practice, equity matters in the EdD as a *noun* and a *verb*. As a *noun*, equity matters are a through line in course work and a required element for PAR dissertations. And we espouse equity matters as a *verb*—signifying the importance of explicit and consistent equity actions. Being an antiracist school leader of equity is what matters most in the EdD program (Kendi,

2019; Khalifa, 2019; Leverett, 2002); that means that instructors and students embrace an equity principle that includes antiracism. The equity frame from Rigby and Tredway (2015) is a guide: Equity leaders enact an equity perspective by explicitly naming the structural elements of inequities and working tirelessly to diminish those inequities. An antiracist school leader is always in the process of being and becoming aware of how policies and practices solidify racial inequities and work to change them (Kendi, 2019). And, in the EdD, what matters even more than a moral imperative to address equity is enacting equity as an antiracist, equitable leader. In our course design and sequence, interactions with and in support of students, and in the dissertation methodology, we have a set of frameworks and practices that support how leaders address equity matters and how leadership actions for equity matter.

The ECU EdD framework is an amalgamation of the Carnegie Project for the Education Doctorate (CPED; J. Perry, 2013), the improvement science (IS) core principles (Bryk, 2015; Bryk et al., 2015), axioms from the community learning exchange (CLE) (Guajardo et al., 2016), and PAR and activist research (Hale, 2008, 2017; Herr & Anderson, 2015; hunter et al., 2013). Together, CPED, CLE, and IS anchor our EdD as a "principled and practical degree that is tough-minded and tender-hearted; rigorous and relevant; and, most importantly, designed to help students reach their full potential as educational leaders of equity" (Militello et al., 2019, p. 217).

More important than equity as a principle, however, is the critical matter of equity in action—explicitly naming inequities and working to correct them. In this chapter, we discuss our methodological approach, CLE axioms, and the IS principles as they play out in one PAR inquiry, which, at ECU, qualifies as a dissertation. Moraima Machado is an elementary principal in an East Bay school district in California. She collaborated with teachers, counselors, parents, and students to co-design, analyze data, and make decisions about how to proceed in three PDS+A (Plan–Do–Study + Act) cycles of inquiry (Bryk et al., 2015). In her activist researcher role, she structured a project and study in which critical pedagogy and dialogic practice were at the forefront (Freire, 1970; Hale, 2008; Hale, 2011; hunter et al., 2013). Her PAR question was, "How can elementary school teachers incorporate family and student stories as the text for redesigning the fifth-grade curriculum?" As a part the inquiry, Jolia Bossette, a student participant in Machado's PAR project, wrote a response in her fifth-grade class to the George Floyd murder; later, the principal and the teacher chose her response for the graduation speech. Subsequently, Vox's (2020) *Today, Explained* podcast invited Jolia to co-host an entire episode about systemic racism (Hassenfeld & Pinkerton, 2020) and supported the animation of Jolia's story, "My Skin Is Not a Threat," which has had nearly 400,000 views. In September 2021, Jolia, now in middle school, presented at the school district board meeting, and Principal Machado and her team presented to district teachers and administrators.

Equity Imperative in the Educational Leadership Doctorate

As we designed a reimagined EdD, explicitly enacting our values about equity matters was of prime importance (Khalifa, 2019: Rigby & Tredway, 2015). How could we ensure that the processes and the outcomes reflected our values and incorporated key frameworks in ways that made sense to graduate students who were school or district leaders? *One goal became clear to us: School and district leaders should become different kinds of leaders for the long term, not only for the duration of the doctoral work.* We wanted to build school and district leaders' capacity to use different processes as school leaders, not only as an episodic skill for the dissertation and degree completion. In particular, we wanted students to effectively collect and analyze evidence to diagnose, design, and make better informed decisions as a collaborative endeavor with other constituents in their contexts. And students could more fully enact their roles as curricular, instructional, and socially just leaders (Spillane, 2013; Theoharis, 2010).

In enunciating the importance of a curricular stance that mirrors our equity values, several preconditions are necessary for graduate student success: student readiness as researchers and writers, relational trust, and differentiation (Allen, 2019). Each course builds on these critical preconditions while addressing issues of equity and social justice because, simultaneous to course work, students steadily produce dissertation chapters throughout the program of study using participatory action research methodology.

The students admitted to the EdD are successful school leaders; however, they have not been in an academic environment for quite some time, and perhaps at no time did they have substantial preparation for the academic writing required for a strong dissertation. To achieve success as researchers (and writers) of a high-quality dissertation in 3 years is no small feat; thus, we practice the warm demander approach to adult learning that they, in turn, must model as leaders: Strong relationships coupled with high expectations and supports are vital to program success (Bondy & Ross, 2008; Delpit, 2012; Drago-Severson, 2012; Safir, 2019; Ware, 2006). Additionally, two preprogram sessions support graduate students: reading and writing for graduate school. To further augment their learning support, we hired dissertation coaches to work with students. Students can hire editors who know the program and our expectations and become fully acquainted with the methodology.

The importance of networks and cohort structures is well established; these structures bolster participants to disrupt inequitable systems and address injustice (Theoharis, 2009, 2010). Therefore, we invest time and attention in building a strong cohort in which relational trust undergirds horizontal and dialogical learning (Bryk & Schneider, 2002; Bryk et al., 2010; Grubb, 2009). In the first course, Leader as Self, students produce autobiographies and digital stories in which they examine themselves through political, biological, historical, and cultural lenses. They continue exploring self as leader through writing and analyzing reflective memos to document and understand the ways they change as leaders. These processes fortify a collective focus on course work, candidacy, and completing the dissertation in 3 years.

Finally, we differentiate assignments and schedules for students, some of whom are students with learning disabilities, using the universal design for learning principles (Hall et al., 2003). Knowing that the universal design for learning requires multiple modalities of learning, we use design thinking (Nash, 2019) and arts-integrated learning (Marshall, 2014). Three processes support student learning: reading guides, encouraging students to crowdsource annotations, and making accommodations for oral responses by using Flipgrid (a video discussion board) as a frequent platform for assignments. The coaching structure is a differentiation consideration: All graduate students are in research groups with a dissertation coach who can enhance support from program coordinators and course instructors.

Our international EdD program track record is strong: Fourteen students in Cohort 1 completed in 3 years, with four needing an additional semester. In the second cohort, 12 of the 14 are on track to finish in 3 years, and two need an additional semester. Sixteen students are currently in Cohort 3. The five dissertation coaches who support the students' PAR meet with the program coordinator each month, and coaches meet with students individually and in teams. By fusing the content and design course work, the EdD program "walks its equity talk" and supports all students differentially. Another proof of program success is represented in the case study we share in this chapter, but first, we discuss how the content course work and research methodology in the design courses align in key equity matters.

Course Work

The EdD curriculum includes content courses for the fundamental learning necessary in a doctoral program, design courses for research methodology, and internships that support students to integrate their experiences by engaging in *praxis*—reflection and action (Freire, 1970). While the official syllabi and coursework communicate one story of the EdD, ever present is another curriculum—a high degree of relational trust that includes accessibility of coordinators and instructors leads to forming strong networks of support and equitable support systems for differentiating and supporting student learning, particularly in areas of academic writing. Second, we are engaged in a meta-PDS+A cycle of inquiry tied to improving the program content and processes.

Content Courses

We begin with two core content courses: Leader as Self, and Equity for Educational Leaders. In the course Leader as Self, students and instructors engage in self-analysis by writing and sharing autobiographies, drawing a mandala to investigate moral imperatives, and creating a digital story of self (Militello & Guajardo, 2013). Using the resilience manifesto as a way of reminding ourselves why and how we do the work for equity, we engage in call-and-response with an emphasis on one part of the manifesto: "We cultivate our resilience and become stronger so that we can help others become stronger; we cultivate our resilience so that we have energy to heal and transform the world" (Aguilar, 2018, p. 19; see the Appendix). Finally, the students read *Pedagogy of the Oppressed*, Freire's (1970) seminal text to investigate and interrogate current situations and actively and humanely address oppressive and racist systems and structures.

In the Equity for Educational Leaders course, theory to practice and practice to a new theory of leadership action is emphasized. Students document equity examples in their contexts and, in tandem with PAR methodology, code the equity examples (Eubanks et al., 1997; Khalifa, 2019; Leverett, 2002; McKenzie & Scheurich, 2004; Rigby & Tredway, 2015; Saldaña, 2016). Several theoretical frames are used to investigate equity: philosophy (Mills, 1997), psychology (Steele, 2010), political and economic (Anderson et al., 2013; Kantor & Lowe, 2016), and sociocultural (Gutiérrez, 2016; Wilkerson, 2020). Students apply the theoretical readings to their experiences as school leaders. The culminating course activity has students write the equity section of Chapter 1 of the dissertation and a legacy letter in which each student commits to the ongoing journey of being and becoming an antiracist leader of change.

In the readings and pedagogical activities (synchronous and asynchronous, in-person and virtually), students learn about race and racism as a contract, albeit unwritten, of those in power and those not in power (Mills, 1997, 2017; Pateman & Mills, 2007). As such, attention to equity and antiracism anchors all content courses, including teaching and learning, the history of education, change theory, organizational theory, and policy.

Intersection of Content With Design Courses

As students proceed in the content courses, the students prepare to be practitioner-researchers. Each semester, they take design courses and practice coding as a critical practice for qualitative research methodology. Students code and generate categories and emerging themes from a variety of data prior to engaging in their PAR projects (Saldaña, 2016). Coding as a heuristic is a cyclical act of analysis, akin to the Bryk et al. (2015) cycle of inquiry model in which school-based practitioner-researchers should plan, do, and study before they decide on actions. By introducing qualitative research to students who are in dynamic school environments, students become more aware that action research is a "messy, iterative and generative approach that is constantly being remade within diverse place-based contexts" (hunter et al., 2013, p. 26). Because they and their environments are ever-changing, we subscribe to Hale's (2008) admonition:

> Activist scholarship is a matter of critique, not just advocacy. It is a part of a project of producing new knowledge, of integrating more abstract and universal sorts of knowledge with more concrete and particular sorts of knowledge, and of keeping action and its possibilities at the center of attention. (p. xxv)

To emphasize coherency across course work, participant-observer evidence, reflective memos, and coding evidence are part of the content courses and then the dissertation chapters.

To help students complete the program in 3 years, we rely on a single methodology—PAR as activist research. The process offers an equitable approach to how schools can take up reform work (Hale, 2008; hunter et al., 2013). In the PAR projects and studies, EdD students initiate or improve on a focus of practice in their schools or districts. In this chapter's PAR case study, for example, Principal Machado wanted to understand how family stories could become an intrinsic part of the fifth-grade curriculum. The PAR participants manifested what can happen when a collaborative team has equity as a North star and uses iterative evidence from inquiry cycles for decision-making. The PAR findings highlight how we can and should work more systematically from the inside out to address issues of equity in schools (Grubb & Tredway, 2010), but her PAR work and that of all students rely on two foundational frameworks: CLEs and IS.

Foundational Frameworks

The CLE axioms and the IS principles guide our program design. In adapting the axioms and protocols, the CLE approaches to data collection and revised the IS tools and processes fit with equity, asset-based values, and iterative qualitative data analysis. In adapting the improvement science to the EdD, we added an equity dimension to the tools and processes. Critical to our work is relying on adaptive and innovative forms of scaling up tools and processes for use in the doctoral program (Morel et al., 2019; Riddell & Moore, 2015). As a result, school and district leaders who become practitioner researchers in the EdD see themselves as being and becoming equity warriors for the long term (Leverett, 2002).

Community Learning Exchange: Axioms and Methodology

The CLE philosophy and practices comport with an emphasis on generative knowledge and the need to deeply reflect in order to act—*praxis* (Freire, 1970). The CLE approach axioms appear obvious on the surface but are more complex to enact (see Table 4.1).

Table 4.1. Community Learning Exchange Axioms

1. Learning and leadership are dynamic social processes.
2. Conversations are critical and central pedagogical processes.
3. The people closest to the issues are best situated to discover answers to local concerns.
4. Crossing boundaries enriches development and the educational processes.
5. Hope and change are built on assets and dreams of locals and their communities.

Source: Guajardo et al. (2016).

The CLE tools and process provide a methodology—a way to collect and organize evidence in more organic and humanistic ways. The entire research process is about a renegotiation of power relationships. As hunter et al. (2013) note,

> by learning how to listen and take care of each other, the focus is on personally and collectively enacting the changes we want to see in the world on a day-to-day basis—even if such efforts and messy and imperfect. (p. 2)

In Moraima's case, the primary methodology is storytelling and analysis of the stories to construct the curriculum, but the primary finding is that by listening differently, we become witnesses for each other's stories in ways that are transformative, not simply transformational (Shields, 2010). Because the stories sustain a focus on social justice, the leaders build a capacity for moving beyond allyship to stronger co-conspirators who can interrupt injustice (Love, 2019).

IS Adaptations

The improvement science guidelines and tools underpin the PAR methodology (Bryk et al., 2015). However, in iterative use and analysis of PDS+A cycles, we found the tools at times are too technical and interrupted meaningful dialogue. As a result, in scaling up use of the IS and tools, we changed the term *problem of practice* to *focus of practice*, revised the fishbone design to include assets, attended to relational trust as a necessary precondition, and focused more systematically on equity. Other IS processes remain critical—understanding the drivers of improvement, Networked Improvement Communities, and an emphasis on useful metrics to make iterative change at the classroom level, where it matters most (Safir, 2017; Popham, 2003):

- Using the term *focus* of practice (FoP) instead of *problem* of practice supports students in diagnosing assets as well as challenges for the dissertation topic and research questions (Spillane & Coldren, 2011). Each EdD student identifies an FoP that attends to the student's equity moral imperative and passion and action space (do-ability) for iterative inquiry (PDS+A) cycles.

- The original fishbone is a graphic organizer designed as a needs analysis with attention only to the challenges or issues in a given context. Instead, we have found that when practitioner-researchers effectively identify and build on current assets, they can more effectively address challenges or needs. Second, students analyze the FoP to understand how different levels of the organization may impact the research: micro, meso, and macro (Rosenthal, 2019). With these shifts, students can better examine root causes and grapple with the complexities of the change project; they use the fishbone diagram as an analytical tool to assess their action space and sphere of influence for their PAR.

- In Bryk et al.'s (2010) work in Chicago, the findings indicated an emphasis on relational trust as a key factor in school improvement. To us, that emphasis seemed diminished in the IS framing as we know that relational trust is a necessary precondition and abstract resource for school improvement (Bryk et al., 2010; Bryk & Schneider, 2002; Grubb, 2009; Tschannen-Moran, 2004).

- The PDS+A syncs with PAR inquiry cycles. The students conduct three PDS+A cycles of inquiry: a pre-cycle, or what is called a probe in the complex systems literature (Riddell & Moore, 2015; Snowden & Boone, 2007) and two cycles of inquiry. The iterative cycles emphasize planning, doing, and studying before deciding how to act with larger numbers of students or teachers.

We adapted other improvement science processes in less dramatic ways. We call the Networked Improvement Communities (NICs) in the PAR process a co-practitioner research (CPR) group. Students select a small group of local educators who become a CPR group that works closely with the EdD student throughout the program. The CPR groups function as networks or communities of practice (Bryk et al., 2015; Lave & Wenger, 1991; Theoharis, 2009; Wenger, 1998). In the PDS+A cycle, iterative evidence is critical, and the CPR group collects and analyzes evidence to understand (study) what happens after initial attempts or probes (plan–do). In reframing the importance of evidence, Safir (2017) makes a distinction among the grain sizes of data; what she terms "street data" comports with the fine-grained and ubiquitous data available on a regular basis to analyze for decision-making. Cobb et al. (2011) call these types of data pragmatic evidence that is timely and useful for making decisions. The pre-cycle is a place where probing and studying this level of evidence happens so that the actions in Cycles 1 and 2 are consistently moving toward the aim and using key drivers to do so (Bryk et al., 2015).

Combining the community learning exchange and improvement science frameworks supports the overarching principles to which the program is committed. The principles of disciplined inquiry that afford students the necessary metrics for making iterative evidence-based changes are essential. In the same vein, we are committed to scaling up in ways that use dialogical processes for uncovering the assets of local communities and schools to address their challenges in adaptive and innovative ways meaningful to them (Guajardo et al., 2016; Morel et al., 2019).

Counternarratives of Students and Families: Principal and Student Stories

In Moraima's project and study, she married community learning exchange protocols with IS practices to address an equity concern in her school: fully engaging students of color in their learning. Her experience from the principal and principal-researcher points of view is complemented by Jolia Bossette's experience as a storyteller and video author; Jolia finished fifth grade at the school in June 2020. They each relate their stories in first person; then, we discuss how their stories reveal how CLEs and IS frameworks combined with school-based inquiry focused on equity and antiracist practices.

The Story of Moraima Machado, Principal

As the school principal and principal researcher in a PAR project and study, I investigated how the curriculum could be more culturally responsive to the lived experiences of students and families in the school community. As we relied on CLE protocols, we began to understand how the stories of the families could become an integral part of the curriculum and a learning experience for the students. Like the Foxfire stories on using the experiences of students and families in Appalachian region of Georgia (Wigginton, 1972), the oral histories of families are a part of critical literacy that we often ignore in school curricula. Because our purpose was to counteract the dominant narrative of students as deficient, low-income, and unable to succeed, I shared my story of growing up in a poor section of Caracas, Venezuela, and immigrating to the United States. From my experiences, I knew that communities of color can engage in counter-storytelling to create narratives that include their hopes, dreams, and aspirations for their children. I wanted to support teachers to co-design a strength-based critical pedagogy of storytelling that honored the voices and histories of students of color and their families. If we could use successive cycles of inquiry, PDS+A cycles, we would learn together how to fully act to incorporate the stories in the fifth-grade curriculum.

We used the fishbone process to analyze our assets and challenges and focused on using the assets we might uncover to address the challenges (see Figure 4.1). How could our stories and our processes be powerful enough to overcome students' feelings of inadequacy? How could we ensure that families thought their stories were worth telling? How could the storytelling undo the feelings of negativity about the life challenges our students and families faced "on the daily"?

I enlisted a CPR group that included three fifth-grade classroom teachers, a counselor, a parent, and a community based-organization leader who acted as a CPR group for the duration of the PAR inquiry cycles (September 2019–Fall 2020). We engaged in three short PDS+A cycles of inquiry. In the first cycle of inquiry at a CLE, we concentrated on bringing together families to understand the power of their stories and then meeting to tell our stories. As a result, we co-designed and implemented a fifth-grade curriculum based on student and family storytelling that we fully implemented

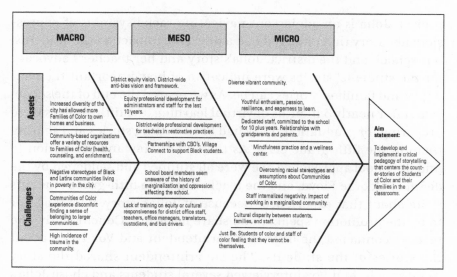

MACRO	MESO	MICRO

Assets

District equity vision. District-wide anti-bias vision and framework.

Diverse vibrant community.

Increased diversity of the city has allowed more Families of Color to own homes and business.

Equity professional development for administrators and staff for the last 10 years.

Youthful enthusiam, passion, resilience, and eagerness to learn.

Community-based organizations offer a variety of resources to Families of Color (health, counseling, and enrichment).

District-wide professional development for teachers in restorative practices.

Dedicated staff, committed to the school for 10 plus years. Relationships with grandparents and parents.

Partnerships with CBO's. Village Connect to support Black students.

Mindfulness practice and a wellness center.

Aim statement:

To develop and implement a critical pedagogy of storytelling that centers the counter-stories of Students of Color and their families in the classrooms.

Challenges

Negative stereotypes of Black and Latinx communities living in poverty in the city.

School board members seem unaware of the history of marginalization and oppression affecting the school.

Overcoming racial stereotypes and assumptions about Communities of Color.

Communities of Color experience discomfort finding a sense of belonging to larger communities.

Lack of training on equity or cultural responsiveness for district office staff, teachers, office managers, translators, custodians, and bus drivers.

Staff internalized negativity. Impact of working in a marginalized community.

Cultural disparity between students, families, and staff.

High incidence of trauma in the community.

Just Be. Students of color and staff of color feeling that they cannot be themselves.

Note: An adaptation of the Bryk et al. (2015) fishbone.

Figure 4.1. Fishbone Analysis of Assets and Challenges

in the third PAR Cycle. However, I knew that if the adults, especially the teachers, did not have experiences in storytelling, I was not sure they would know how to engage the students. While the teachers had relationships with their students, the notion of interrupting the curriculum and revising the typical fifth-grade curriculum with stories would be new for them. We recognized from the outset that the adult and student experiences needed to be symmetrical and that we needed to anchor those experiences at the intersection of creativity and identity (Mehta & Fine, 2015). In other words, if the teachers do not have sufficient experience, they could not confidently facilitate the dialogue and storytelling they wanted from student–student interactions and we could not engage in the necessary praxis—reflection to action—that Freire (1970) says is necessary for deciding on subsequent actions.

By empowering students and families to tell their stories of immigration and cultural and historical experiences, we authorized compelling stories to emerge. One student's story coincided with the murder of George Floyd and became a powerful example in the PAR project. Jolia is an adolescent navigating racial systems of oppression; her story that emerged had a dramatic impact on the students, our school, and the district. Jolia's story and her teacher's advocacy for the students' stories were indicative of how important the children's and families' stories can be. As we neared the end of the school year, after nearly 3 months of virtual learning, the fifth graders were preparing for graduation. They had been writing stories and sharing them in the fifth-grade class. As the end of May and promotion to middle school approached, we were all stunned and saddened by the death of George Floyd, and the teacher had the fifth-grade students write about that experience. Because of Jolia's story, we asked her to be the promotion speaker and share her story. Concurrently, the teacher contacted the district superintendent and Vox News about the stories of the students. The superintendent shared the story more widely, and Vox interviewed several students and chose Jolia's to animate. The experience was a powerful one for Jolia, her classmates, and the teacher; the entire process verified what I had hoped for in the inquiry project—to lift up the voices of students and families to share their experiences as a central part of how we teach and learn in our school. The teachers and I have since shared our process with our district colleagues.

In the third cycle of inquiry, the fifth-grade teachers, with a new class of students, utilized "I am coming from poems" to share memories of family hopes, aspirations, and resilience. The teachers had used these poems before, but this time they invited students to ask family members about where they were coming from. Students researched their histories and wrote poems to share with the class. Parents joined their children when students shared their stories, and we, as staff members, could see the sense of pride in the parents as the children honored their ancestral knowledge. I recall Ah'mani's mother whispered words of encouragement to her son as he was nervously presenting to his class his poem "Get to know me and you'll find out who I am." Sharing stories has now become a way of being in our community and in classrooms. Teachers observed that their students connected to each other in a deeper way through the telling. Cerise, a fifth-grade teacher and CPR group member, shared, "The most exciting part about the project was definitely the community that was built, and the questions they were asking each other and how excited they were getting about their connections." Through careful use of the community learning-exchange (CLE) protocols and the cycles of inquiry that built on each other with evidence, we were able to collaboratively build a revised curriculum that centered the experiences of families and youth in the curricular experiences of the students.

In examining the CPR work in terms of participatory action + activist research, we maintained a clear focus on equity, antiracism, and the importance of counternarratives. In each PAR cycle of inquiry, we collected and analyzed evidence to ensure that we were clear about next steps and the pace of implementation and logistics but, more important, about linking our collective interpretation of results to future work. As we moved to the last activity of PAR Cycle 3 in the fall of 2020, we designed the fifth-grade curricular content and processes on the basis of evidence from two prior PDS+A cycles or of inquiry.

Two findings are significant. The research process is a one of "witnessing." By redefining relationships as horizontal and reciprocal, we became researchers of our experiences and moved toward *witnessing the stories, instead of only listening*. These are more than stories; they are *testimonios*, which has a stronger quality of a public spoken statement that is proof of the existence of something—centering the experiences of the students and families is a public statement of how we value them and the students. As a result, we developed more authenticity in the curriculum and deeper relationships as a part of student learning. The research itself is not a process of extracting but a process of listening more deeply for the epiphany moments that we can tether to a larger focus on storytelling as an act of critical literacy (Freire, 1970; McDonald, 1996; Velasco, 2009). We are using the stories to engage students in their schooling and as a curricular experience for reading and writing. By drawing on the assets at the micro level—the people closest to the issue who have hopes and dreams for their children—we redesigned a curriculum, but in the process, we built a stronger community that is now sharing our learning with the others who want to adapt this process to their contexts. Jolia's story, of course, is but one example of why this work is important to the students and how the process changes the students' experiences. By offering a safe space for students to speak their truths, we are modeling for them what school could look like if we engaged their stories and their family's stories.

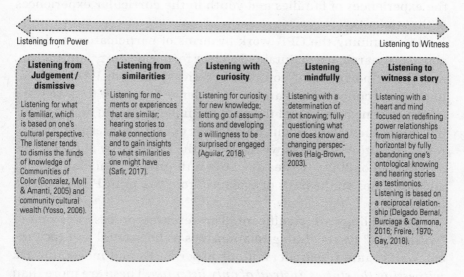

Figure 4.2. Storytelling through Testimonios: The Path to Witnessing

The Story of Jolia Bossette, Fifth-Grade Student

As a fifth-grade student, writing stories about our lives was really hard at first because there are a lot of things that students don't want to share. For some students, there are parts of their lives that they feel they don't need to share because they are painful stories. Sometimes, they want to share because they want another adult to help them. Unfortunately, when a student is trying to share something confidentially to either a counselor or teacher, then, often, the teacher or counselor does speak to the parents about it. This is why my classmates don't feel comfortable sharing things. So digging deep to figure out what I wanted to share was really hard.

As for me, my main goal was to share the facts of my experience. I think you can see that in the statements I use in "My Skin Is Not a Threat." Making sure that what I said made sense was the most important thing for me because my goal wasn't to offend anybody; it was to get my message out. They asked us to write stories about our reaction to George Floyd murder, but Miss Rachel, my fifth-grade teacher, didn't actually know what I was writing about, and neither did Miss Machado, but they helped a lot as during the school year. They showed us a lot of support through our writing and that is how I was able to write "My Skin Is Not a Threat." When I showed the writing to Miss Rachel, she sent it to Miss Machado.

I learned a lot about myself in writing the story and making the video. First, I have a lot of patience and, once my patience builds up, I can make a great story. I was done after the death of George Floyd, and I needed to express myself. Our teacher knew that and gave us the opportunity to write about it. That's how I made "My Skin Is Not a Threat" because I was patient with myself to write a story that seemed to be a factual story of how I felt. Through all the rewrites, editing, and video production, I had to be patient to make it the best. Making the video and reading my story over and over again helped me, and it helped others. Doing it this way makes the message even more permanent for me and more important.

Storytelling: An Equity Emphasis for PAR

A key factor in Moraima's PAR project was the emphasis on combining the EdD foundational frameworks of CLE and IS with a strong and consistent equity focus. To solidify program methodology as PAR, Principal Machado included all inquiry cycles as separate chapters in her dissertation. As she engaged other constituents in the research context to analyze and proceed with subsequent cycles, telling the story of how the families and teachers told their stories before they incorporated student stories in the curriculum was a critical component of the PAR study. In her internship classes, she concentrated on reflective memos and coding as integral to keeping a focus on the research question related to her leadership: *How does my leadership change and improve as a result of the PAR process?* As she knew in theory and now in practice, the PAR process is not solely for the dissertation; rather, it is a process of using qualitative evidence that she can transfer into her leadership repertoire as she relies on foundational frameworks from the EdD to guide future school change and decision-making.

She developed a conceptual and action-oriented understanding of the critical consciousness—*conscientização*—that she needed to enact her values (Freire, 1970). She had a deeply rooted awareness of what is going on and attended to generative themes that emerged from the context of the work; she looked for sightings as a process of change in analyzing the qualitative evidence and tethered the iterative learning and actions to the evidence and subsequent actions (McDonald, 1996; Velasco, 2009). Moraima invoked and practiced the axioms in interlocking ways as she convened families and students and teachers in CLEs and used the processes to collect and then analyze evidence in three iterative PAR cycles of inquiry. She was acutely aware of building on the assets and dreams of the families and students. One of the key findings involves her definition of witnessing; this discussion from the last chapter of Moraima's (Machado, 2021) dissertation describes the difference between listening and witnessing.

Centering the voices of students of color in schools and in classrooms necessitates engaging in dialogue that moves away from listening or hearing from judgment toward listening to witness stories. Listening from judgment dismisses the funds of knowledge and community cultural wealth of people of color (Yosso, 2006). Listening to witness stories or testimonio requires redefining power relationships from hierarchical to horizontal, whereby students, teachers, and administrators are both simultaneously teachers and learners of each other stories. (Freire, 1970; Gay, 2018; Howard, 2019). Witnessing requires "breaking down the walls" that separate schools from communities of color and being willing to be vulnerable in the moment to share your story (Guajardo et al., 2016; this entails being open to new knowledge and stories beyond our experiences (Delgado-Bernal et al., 2016).

Witnessing requires the listeners of the testimonio or story to self-reflect and open their hearts and minds to understand the storyteller's point of view. If listeners and speakers are open to bearing witness of each other testimonios, then the testimonio is a gift to the listener. As a result of listening without judgment, participants experienced vulnerability and connectedness, and a different sense of community emerged.

Student and family stories are the backbone of the PAR project. While Jolia "was done," meaning frustrated and ready to give up after the death of George Floyd, she did not. Jolia's experience in storytelling an authentic story—the factual story of how she felt— became a window to other experiences but, more important, to her sense of self and the importance of her truth telling. By incorporating the stories in the fifth-grade curriculum, teachers saw student stories as integral to learning, and students began to see themselves as authors of their learning. We believe that the horizontal experiences of witnessing Principal Machado's and Jolia's stories and inviting them as coauthors provide a counternarrative in and of itself that is vital to graduate students' seeing themselves being and becoming practitioner-researchers and antiracist equity leaders. Jolia's story of personal growth offers a wisdom we seek. As the reader witnesses her story, we invite you to imagine how we can see a way forward in schools and districts.

Conclusion: Lessons Learned

Increasing equity in schools requires boldness and risk-taking. Like Jolia, it is a courageous act—an act requiring structural supports and individual champions. The ECU design and the specific action space for equity in student PAR projects creates the necessary synergy for students like Moraima and Jolia to acknowledge and engage in the power of place and wisdom of people. We offer three lessons for those looking to support the next generation of equity leaders in our schools.

In the PAR project and study, critical literacy means

> finding ways to make literacy instruction meaningful and relevant
> by recognizing and incorporating students' out-of-school ways of
> practicing literacy, and [incorporating how] families and commu-
> nities practice literacy in ways that may differ from those in the
> mainstream or in positions of power. (K. Perry, 2012, p. 50)

Because Freire (1970) said that critical literacy is both reading the
word and *world*, teacher, student, and parent stories are crucial
components of understanding inequities and reframing. The stories
of families and students as counternarratives are vital, and the stories of teachers who have different experiences in the social dynamic
are just as vital to come to the knowing and doing—the new epis-
temological and ontological understandings of how to engage in
authentic equitable practices. Moraima's PAR project provides a
response to Gutiérrez's (2016) question about what a third space for
literacy can look like: "What role can education play in advancing
a more expansive social and pedagogical imagination for all youth
across all schools and communities?" (p. 195).

Second, participatory action research as a methodology requires
that EdD programs and instructors authorize an equity action space
in the research design and projects that advances our understanding of what schools could look like if they were more equitable and
antiracist. This is not a tinkering project of fixing this or that in
the technical rational change ways we have been so schooled to do
(Grubb & Tredway, 2010; Tyack & Cuban, 1998). This is using what
we know about IS principles and iterative evidence to become exper-
imenters on the equity front and build the capacity of all members
of a school to use pragmatic, street data to make decisions that put
equity at the center of our praxis (Cobb et al., 2011; Safir, 2017; Safir
& Dugan, 2021).

Finally, our work is made possible by the courage to reimagine, "mash-up" constructs and have trust, hope, and confidence in
our students. We found possibilities in multiple frameworks (CPED
principles, CLE axioms, IS processes, and PAR methodologies). Only
when we let go of any one framework, were we able to reimagine a

new, combined power of frames that we wove together. Blending the technical with the context of place and stories of people created the right space for our students to excel.

In the end, the reimagined EdD creates opportunity for a new kind of dissertation, one focused on the relentless pursuit of equity and justice. While one goal for Moraima is a doctorate degree partially fulfilled with a dissertation document, the power of her work is that she will continue the process. And, as guides, we have a front-row seat to witness the stories of our students and their families.

Discussion Questions

1. In what ways could the key concepts of this chapter support you and colleagues to reimagine and redesign an existing program in your organization to increase equity?
2. How could the core activities of the course Leader as Self be adapted to your organization, district, school, or classroom and your equity goals?
3. The authors of this chapter substitute asset-rich language to increase their focus on equity; what terms or language that are a regular part of your organization's lexicon could be revised to enhance the dignity of those in your organization or those you serve?
4. How could you use student and family stories in your classroom or organization to increase resiliency and affirm the lived experiences of people in your classroom or organization?

References

Aguilar, E. (2018). *Onward: Cultivating emotional resilience in educators.* Jossey-Bass.

Allen, J. (2019). *The productive graduate student writer.* Stylus Publishing.

Anderson, G. L., Mungal, A., Pinit, M., Scott, J., & Thomson, P. (2013). Politics, equity, and diversity in global context: Educational leadership after the welfare state. In L. Tillman & J. J. Scheurich, (Eds.), *Handbook of research on educational leadership and equity and diversity* (pp. 43–61). Routledge.

Bondy, E., & Ross, D. E. (2008). The teacher as warm demander. *Educational Leadership, 66*(1), 54–58.

Bryk, A. (2015). Accelerating how we learn to improve. *Educational Researcher, 44*(9), 467–477.

Bryk, A., & Schneider, B. (2002). *Relational trust: A core resource in schools.* Russell Sage.

Bryk, A. S., Gomez, L. M., Grunow, A., LeMahieu, P. G. (2015). *Learning to improve: How America's schools get better at getting better.* Harvard Education Press.

Bryk, A. S., Sebring, P. B., Allensworth, E., Luppescu, S., & Easton, J. (2010). *Organizing schools for improvement: Lessons from Chicago.* The University of Chicago Press.

Center for Applied Special Technology. (2019). *Universal design for learning guidelines.* CAST Publishing. https://www.cast.org/impact/universal-design-for-learning-udl

Cobb, P., Jackson, K., Smith, T., Sorum, M., & Henrick, E. (2011) Designing research with educational systems: Investigating and supporting improvements in the quality of mathematics teaching at scale. *National Society for the Study of Education 112*(2), 320–349.

Delgado-Bernal, D., Burciaga, R., & Carmona, J. F. (Eds.). (2016). *Chicana/Latina testimonios as pedagogical, methodological, and activist approaches to social justice.* Routledge.

Delpit. L. (2012). *"Multiplication is for White people": Raising expectations of other people's children.* The New Press.

Drago-Severson, E. (2012). *Helping educators grow: Strategies and practices for leadership development.* Harvard Education Press.

Eubanks, E., Parish, R., & Smith, C. (1997). Changing the discourse in schools. In P. Hall (Ed.), *Race, ethnicity and multiculturism: Policy and practice* (pp. 51–80). Garland Publishing Inc.

Freire, P. (1970). *Pedagogy of the oppressed.* Continuum.

Gay, G. (2000). *Culturally responsive teaching: Theory, research, and practice.* Teachers College Press.

Grubb, W. N. (2009). *The money myth: School resources, outcomes, and equity.* Russell Sage.

Grubb, W. N., & Tredway L. (2010). *Leading from the inside out: Expanded roles of teachers in equitable schools.* Paradigm Press.

Guajardo, M., Guajardo, F., Janson, C., & Militello, M. (2016). *Reframing community partnerships in education: Uniting the power of place and wisdom of people.* Routledge.

Gutiérrez, C. (2016). Designing resilient ecologies: Designing social experiments and a new social imagination. *Educational Researcher, 45*(3), 187–196.

Hale, C. R. (2008). *Engaging contradictions: Theory, politics, and methods of activist scholarship.* University of California Press.

Hale, C. R. (2017). What is activist research? *Items and Issues, 2*(1), 13–15.

Hall, T., Vue, G., Strangman, N., & Meyer, A. (2003). *Differentiated instruction and implications for UDL implementation*. National Center on Accessing the General Curriculum. http://www.cast.org/products-services/resources/2003/ncac-differentiated-instruction-udl

Harris, A. & Jones, M. (2018). Leading for equity: a moral imperative. *School Leadership & Management, 38*(3) 239–241. https://doi-org.proxy.lib.pdx.edu/10.1080/13632434.2018.1432094

Hassenfeld, N., & Pinkerton, B. (Host). (2020, August 29). *Today, explained to kids* [Audio podcast]. https://www.vox.com/today-explained-to-kids

Herr, K., & Anderson, G. (2015). *The action research dissertation: A guide for students and faculty* (2nd ed.). Sage Publications.

Howard, T. (2019). *Why race and culture matter in schools: Closing the achievement gap in America's classrooms* (2nd ed.). Teachers College Press.

hunter, l., emerald, e., & Martin, G. (2013). *Participatory activist research in the globalised world: Social change through the cultural professions*. Springer.

Kantor, H., & Lowe, R, (2016). Educationalizing the welfare state and privatizing education: The evolution of social policy since the New Deal. In W. J. Mathis & T. Trujillo (Eds.), *Learning from market-based reforms: Lessons for ESSA* (pp. 37–59). Information Age Press.

Kendi, I. X. (2019). *How to be an anti-racist*. One World.

Khalifa, M. (2019). *Culturally responsive school leadership*. Harvard Education Press.

Lave, J., & Wenger, E. (1991). *Situated learning: Legitimate peripheral participation*. Cambridge University Press.

Leverett, L. (2002). *Warriors to advance equity: A case for distributing leadership*. The Mid-Atlantic Educational Laboratory.

Love, B. L. (2019). *We want to do more than survive: Abolitionist teaching and the pursuit of educational freedom*. Beacon Press.

MacDonald, J. P. (1996). *Redesigning school: Lessons for the 21st century*. Jossey-Bass.

Machado, M. (2021). *Family stories matter: Critical pedagogy of storytelling in fifth-grade classrooms* [Unpublished doctoral dissertation]. East Carolina University.

Marshall, J. (2014). Curriculum and arts integration as an agency for change: Transforming education through arts-centred education. *Visual Inquiry: Learning & Teaching Art, 3*(3), 361–373. doi:10.1386/vi.3.3.361_1

McKenzie, K. B., & Scheurich, J. J. (2004). Equity traps: A useful construct for preparing principals to lead schools that are successful with racially diverse students. *Education Administration Quarterly, 40*(5), 601–632.

Mehta, J., & Fine, S. (2015). *The why, what, where, and how of deeper learning in American secondary schools*. Jobs for the Future.

Militello, M., & Guajardo, F. (2013). Virtually speaking: How digital storytelling can facilitate organizational learning. *Journal of Community Positive Practices, 13*(2), 80–91.

Militello, M., Tredway, L., & Jones, K. (2019). A Reimagined Ed.D.: Participatory, progressive on-line pedagogy. In J. Keengwe (Ed.), *Handbook of research on blended learning pedagogies and professional development in higher education* (pp. 214–242). IGI Global.

Mills, C. W. (1997). *The racial contract.* Cornell University Press.

Mills, C. W. (2017). *Black rights/White wrongs: The critique of racial liberalism.* Oxford University Press.

Morel, R. P., Coburn, C., Catterson, A. K., & Higgs, J. (2019). The multiple meanings of scale: Implications for researcher and practitioners. *Educational Researcher, 48*(6), 369–377.

Nash, J. (2019). *Design thinking in schools: A leader's guide to collaborating for improvement.* Harvard Education Press.

Pateman, C., & Mills, C. (2007). *Contract & domination.* Polity Press.

Perry, K. (2012). What is literacy? A critical overview of sociocultural perspectives. *Journal of Language and Literacy Education, 8*(1), 50–71. http://jolle.coe.uga.edu/wp-content/uploads/2012/06/What-is-Literacy_KPerry.pdf

Perry, J. A. (2013). Introduction Carnegie Project on the Education Doctorate: The education doctorate—A degree for our time. *Planning and Changing Journal, 44*(3/4), 113–126.

Popham, W. J. (2003). The seductive allure of data. *Educational Leadership, 60*(5), 48–51.

Riddell, D., & Moore, M. L. (2015). *Scaling up, scaling deep: Advancing systemic social innovation and the learning processes to support it.* J. W. McConnell Family Foundation.

Rigby, J., & Tredway, L. (2015). Actions matter: How school leaders enact equity principles. In M. Kahlifa, N. A. Witherspoon, A. F. Osanloo, & C. M. Grant (Eds.), *Handbook of urban educational leadership* (pp. 426–440). Rowman & Littlefield.

Rivera-McCutchen, R.L. (2014). The moral imperative of social justice leadership: A critical component of effective practice. *Urban Review, 46*(4), 747–763. doi:10.1007/s11256-014-0297-2

Rosenthal, L. (2019). *Fits and starts: One elementary school's journey toward trauma-informed leadership* (Order No. 27629324). East Carolina University. Available from ProQuest Dissertations & Theses A&I; ProQuest Dissertations & Theses Global.

Safir, S. (2017). *The listening leader: Creating the conditions for equitable school transformation.* Jossey-Bass.

Safir, S. (2019). Becoming a warm demander: Adopting an equity-centered coaching model for school leaders. *Educational Leadership, 76*(6), 64–69.

Safir, S., & Dugan, J. (2021). *Street data: A next-generation model for equity, pedagogy, and school transformation.* Jossey-Bass.

Saldaña, J. (2016). *The coding manual for qualitative researchers.* Sage Publications.

Shields, C. (2010). Transformative leadership: Working for equity in diverse contexts. *Educational Administrative Quarterly, 46*(4), 558–559.

Snowden, D. J., & Boone, M.E. (2007, November). A leader's framework for decision making. *Harvard Business Review*, 1–15. https://hbr.org/2007/11/ a-leaders-framework-for-decision-making

Spillane, J. (2013). Diagnosing and designing for schoolhouse practice: Educational administration and instructional improvement. In H. J. Malone (Ed.), *Leading educational change: Global issues, challenges, and lessons on whole-system reform*, (pp. 37–41). Teachers College Press.

Spillane, J., & Coldren, A. F. (2011). *Diagnosis and design for school improvement*. Teachers College Press.

Steele, C. (2010). *Whistling Vivaldi: And other clues to how stereotypes affect us*. W. W. Norton.

Theoharis, G. (2009). *The school leaders our children deserve: Seven keys to equity, social justice and school reform*. Teachers College Press.

Theoharis, G. (2010). Disrupting injustice: Principals narrate the strategies they use to improve their schools and advance social justice. *Teachers College Record, 112*(1), 331–373.

Tschannen-Moran, M. (2004). *Trust matters: Leadership for successful schools*. Jossey-Bass.

Tyack, D., & Cuban, L. (1998). *Tinkering toward utopia*. Harvard University Press.

Velasco, C. (2009). *Tracking, tethering and transfer: The expedition of a second grade team* [Unpublished master's thesis]. University of California, Berkeley.

Vox. (2020, August 21). *What Black Lives Matter means to an 11-year-old* [Video]. YouTube. https://www.youtube.com/watch?v=muy5zpqslRc

Ware, F. (2006). Warm demander pedagogy: Culturally responsive teaching that supports a culture of achievement for African American students. *Urban Education, 41*(4), 427–445.

Wenger, E. (1998). *Communities of practice: Learning, meaning and identity*. Cambridge University Press.

West, C. (2017). *Race matters* (25th anniversary ed.). Beacon Press.

Wigginton, E. (1972). *Foxfire stories*. The Foxfire Fund.

Wilkerson, I. (2020). *Caste: The origins of our discontents*. Random House.

Yosso, T. J. (2006). *Critical race counterstories along the Chicana/Chicano educational pipeline*. Routledge.

Appendix

The Resilience Manifesto
Elena Aguilar (2018, p. 19)

1. A wellspring of resilience is inside us. We are stronger than we think.
2. We were born with individual and collective resilience. Our quest is to find our way to these internal springs and nourish them.

3. We cultivate resilience so that we can thrive, not simply to survive.

4. Resilience is cultivated through daily habits and thoughts that strengthen dispositions.

5. It is a human right to explore and express emotions.

6. To help students build their emotional intelligence and resilience, we must simultaneously tend to our own emotional intelligence and resilience.

7. Powerful and effective educators talk about emotions at work.

8. How we interpret events and tell our story matters. In our interpretation, we exercise the freedom to choose our attitude.

9. We are all connected and responsible for each other: Caring for the other is caring for the self.

10. We cultivate our resilience and become stronger so that we can help others become stronger; we cultivate our resilience so that we have energy to heal and transform the world.

CHAPTER FIVE

Increasing Reading Engagement in Middle Level Learners: How to Reverse the Decline

RHIANNON YOUNG

The Setting/Background

Gorge Middle School is located in the Columbia River Gorge in a rural area. There are two campuses; Gorge Middle School resides on the main K–12 campus. Some of the core values of the district, which has 1,100 students, include looping K–9 students for 2 years with one teacher to establish stronger relationships and deepen understanding through project-based learning, as well as place-based learning, to build connections to the surrounding environment.

Gorge Middle School houses six heterogeneously mixed classrooms of 157 sixth- and seventh-grade students with multiple subject-area teachers. Subjects are integrated, with the exception of math and enrichment classes (music, art, Spanish, culinary arts). English Language Developing (ELD) students are placed in one core class that receives push-in support each day from our ELD specialist. Placements in math are by ability and in enrichment classes by choice. Students with a learning disability are placed throughout the core classes and receive both push-in support by a learning specialist as well as small-group, specially designed instruction; they also receive small-group math instruction if designated in their

77

individualized education plan (IEP). Intervention support consists of small-group work with a core classroom teacher for additional instruction and work time. Students receiving services for Talented and Gifted (TAG) programs are given multiple opportunities throughout the curriculum to challenge their thinking at their rate and level of learning. The school strives to have a completely inclusive environment for activities and instruction.

In the last 5 years, multiple teachers and administrators have been attending the Teachers College Reading and Writing Project (TCRWP) at Columbia University. This work has supported and furthered a focus on the workshop format for both reading and writing instruction. Recently, there has been a renewed focus on support for culturally and linguistically diverse learners within the literacy program, as well as student engagement in reading. A focus on student engagement, equity, and literacy is supported by Calkins and Ehrenworth (2017), who state, "It is critically important for schools to create communities of practice where teachers work together to learn from each other's best practices to position students to develop into skilled, proficient, expert readers and writers" (p. 19), thus corroborating the school's belief that relationships are essential in all areas of growth and reinforcing the mission to increase engagement in readers.

The staff at Gorge Middle School believes that middle school is a critical time in a student's life to foster resilience, critical thinking, and creativity. All students are met where they are, and we establish goals of high expectations for each individual in all areas of learning. The improvement team consists of classroom teachers, specialists, and administrative support. The Improvement Science Team consists of the following members:

- Lead teacher and administrative intern
- Sixth- and seventh-grade teachers: Both of these teachers have attended the TCRWP reading institute, are trusted colleagues, and have worked extensively with middle schoolers.
- Learning specialist: This specialist understands the specific needs of various students across the middle school.

- Paraeducator: This colleague implements reading inventories and provides important interventions for struggling readers.
- Curriculum director: An essential resource for data information, standards, and resources, this colleague also offers a K–12 perspective with significant experience in the district.
- Superintendent: This colleague is a support person for policy changes, data analysis, and a K–12 perspective.

This team composition provides a full understanding of the literacy needs in the building for all learners and how strategies can be built to address any inequities.

Need for Improvement

Gorge Middle School values relationships, hands-on learning experiences, student choice, and an integrated, authentic curriculum. Students from Gorge Middle School generally do well on high school standardized tests in comparison to students across the state and nation. However, the achievement rate for English language arts (ELA) in Gorge Middle School is below the state average and has room for improvement. One of the main issues for all middle-level readers is the decline in reading engagement. Interventions need to be put into place to reverse this trend.

Data Collection and Analysis

Equity Audit Information

Two equity audits were completed for this analysis, focusing on student engagement. Results on the first audit, modified from Frattura and Capper's (2007) audit, generated a general overview of the student population, as well as the status of labeling at the school. Data from this audit suggested comparing the passing rates to identify any disparities (see Table 5.1).

The team also wanted to examine passing rates by gender as shown in Table 5.2.

These data indicated that boys were underperforming in ELA. Members of the IS team identified this as an area of future examination. Although not the focus of this project, the data indicate an additional area for improvement.

Student Survey

Results of a survey from *Building Equity: Policies and Practice to Empower All Learners* (Smith et al., 2017) provided data that indicated our need was to focus on increasing intrinsic motivation. The results of this survey are presented in Table 5.3.

Table 5.1. Equity Data Sixth/Seventh Grade

Label	Number of Students	Percentage of Student Population	Passed 18/19 ELA Exam	Percentage Passing*	Percentage Passing**
Gifted	7	4.3%	7	100%	4.3%
Disability – IEP	18	11.2%	1	5.5%	.6%
Disability – 504	2	1.2%	1	50%	.6%
ESL	4	2.5%	0	0%	0%
Intervention Support	9	5.6%	5	55%	2.5%
No Label	117	72.7%	63	54%	39.1%
No Score (new)	4	2.5%			
Total Number	161		77		47.2%

Note: IEP = individualized education plan.
*Passing rate is based on that label.
**Passing rate compared to overall population.

Table 5.2. Passing Rates by Gender

Gender	Number of Students	Percentage of Student Population	Passed 18/19 ELA Exam	% of Gender That Passed in 2018/2019 Year	% of Population by Gender
Female	67	41.6%	36	53.7%	22.4%
Male	94	58.3%	41	43.6%	25.5%
Total Number	161	47.8%	77		

Table 5.3. Equity Survey Results

Descriptor of Survey Question	Family Strongly Agree	Student Strongly Agree	Family Agree	Student Agree	Family Neutral	Student Neutral	Family Dis-agree	Student Dis-agree	Family Strongly Dis-agree	Student Strongly Dis-agree
Students learn about things they are interested in	20.3%	27.5%	35.6%	46.4%	23.7%	24.6%	13.6%	1.4%	6.8%	0%
A trusted adult at school	52.5%	36.2%	39%	34.8%	3.4%	17.4%	3.4%	7.2%	1.7%	4.3%
Encouraged to have commitment, perseverance, and flexibility	15.3%	24.6%	54.2%	47.8%	18.6%	23.2%	10.2%	2.9%	1.7%	1.4%
Receiving excellent instruction	22%	20.3%	69.5%	56.5%	6.8%	21.7%	1.7%	1.4%	0%	0%
Know how to be successful in class	37.3%	40.6%	55.9%	50.7%	6.8%	7.2%	0%	1.4%	0%	0%

Data from the survey of 23 students of all genders indicated that for both enjoyment and a student seeing themselves as a reader, 43.5% strongly saw themselves as a reader and 47.8% only sometimes did. Of the male respondents, only 41.3% saw themselves as readers, 50% sometimes saw themselves as readers and 8.7% did not feel like a reader. In general, there is no meaningful difference between how the males and females perceive themselves as readers.

Empathy Interviews

We sought additional insight by conducting empathy interviews. The author completed multiple empathy interviews as well as an additional survey to identify students' attitudes toward reading and themselves as readers. During these interviews, book choice was a primary factor in increasing reading engagement in the eyes of the students. This is supported by research and the team's observations. Also, students indicated they desire a quiet, distraction-free time each day to read in class.

After completing the survey and analyzing the empathy interview data, the team also wanted to examine academic articles that support our focus on culturally responsive literacy and student engagement in reading. One compelling and pertinent article describes how focusing on equity in reading can address the inequities inherent in society (Wigfield et al., 2016). Wigfield et al. identify factors that contribute to motivation to read, which include social motivation, ethnic and gender differences, perceived autonomy, competence, and self-efficacy. Self-efficacy is an important link between reading engagement and our other goal of increasing achievement on the Smarter Balanced Assessment Consortium (SBAC) tests. To improve self-efficacy, we realized we needed to increase time for reading and accessing fascinating books and expert instruction—information that helped the team prioritize the primary drivers.

Wigfield et al. (2016) indicated that motivation and engagement in reading typically decline in the middle-grade years. Because Gorge Middle School already places a high value on providing time to read each day in the classrooms, the team decided to focus on the primary drivers of instructional and assessment strategies, increasing book selection, and increasing social aspects around literacy. The literature review is further discussed within the theory of improvement and testing the change.

Theory of Improvement

Student reading engagement declines from fourth to eighth grade (National Assessment of Educational Progress, 2019). Upon a close look at the district's SBAC scores, in surveys, classroom observations, and in empathy interviews, this trend is also apparent. The goal of this project, to increase reading engagement in sixth- and seventh-grade students by May 2020, addressed this trend, aiming to increase the ELA passing rate by 20%. After reviewing the data collected, the team identified the wide range of factors that influence reading engagement represented in the fishbone diagram shown in Figure 5.1.

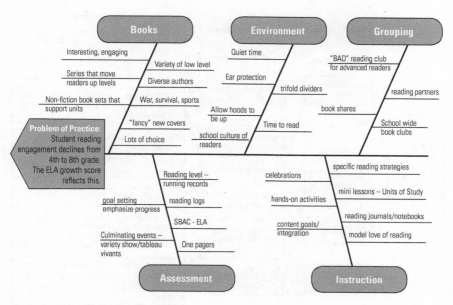

Figure 5.1. Fishbone Diagram

After completion of the fishbone diagram, the team prioritized which change ideas to focus on to disrupt the current educational norm of lower SBAC scores at the middle level by increasing reading engagement for all student groups. The team discussed which components held the most potential to increase reading engagement, including a further review of the information found from the author's literature review. The team identified the primary drivers that needed to be prioritized to create the most immediate change within our school environment and that could be implemented within our time, personnel, and fiscal constraints. The driver diagram in Figure 5.2 shows primary, secondary, and change ideas generated from this review.

Before looking at the data, most of the team members predicted that the engagement of reading for male students was lower than for female students and that this disparity needed to be addressed. This correlates with the data analyzed from ELA scores. Gender played a more significant role than any other demographic indicator. We decided to place priority on increasing the number and types of novels

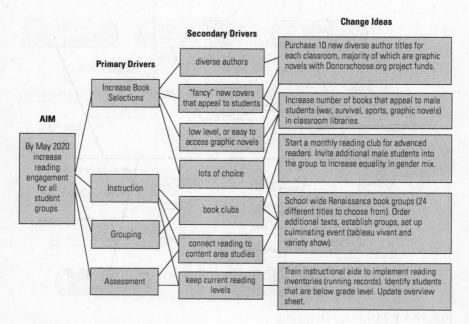

Figure 5.2. Driver Diagram

students could choose from, with titles that might appeal to male students; we also aimed to increase the number of male students in a higher level extracurricular reading club. The team also agreed to test the change idea of increasing the number of student-led, in-class book shares of the new novels to generate more interest. There were numerous different change ideas that could be implemented, but it was essential to prioritize the changes that would be most effective in the given scope and timeline of the project.

Testing the Change

Plan–Do–Study–Act (PDSA) Cycle 1

Plan

After identifying which drivers were the priority, the team implemented the project with the PDSA process for each cycle. We decided to administer running records and reading inventories to determine both the fluency and comprehension levels of our students. This helped us identify if interventions were needed and the comprehension levels of books for our classrooms and library (Calkins & Ehrenworth, 2017). This process helped students feel efficacy in their continuous learning.

Do

The administrative intern hired, trained, and organized a schedule for a paraeducator to complete reading inventories for 20 minutes each day. This educator was given access to the reading levels of all 157 middle school students. After completing the inventories, the paraeducator shared the written documentation with the student's core teacher and then updated the reading-level data collection chart. The goal was to have an updated reading inventory for all students not already reading at Level Z each trimester. The team chose to use guided reading levels because it easily translated to IEP and intervention goals, as well as aligned with our reading curriculum, *Units of Study for Teaching Reading* by Lucy Calkins.

Study

The team quickly realized that we would not be able to get our targeted number of reading inventories completed. Priorities for assessments were shifted to new students, those students well below their grade reading level, and any other students who teachers felt needed intervention support. Then the team circled back to completing reading inventories on all students not currently at Level Z.

Act

The paraeducator figured out how to complete the reading inventory with two students at a time rather than one. It was decided this would really increase the number of inventories that could be completed. We made a note that the following year, additional personnel would be extremely helpful at the beginning of the year for the initial round of inventories. From the information gathered, students were identified for intervention support, which book levels needed to be additionally ordered, and which students would need to be closely tracked for reading progress later in the year.

PDSA Cycle 2

Plan

The change idea behind PDSA Cycle 2 was increasing our book selection by adding titles from authors of diverse backgrounds. The choice of novels is imperative to increasing skillful, versatile, engaged readers (Calkins & Ehrenworth, 2017). The new novels included not only fascinating reads but also books at a low enough reading level so that readers can move through them easily. The data from the first cycle helped the team determine at which reading levels books needed to be purchased. In addition, we recognized the need to further increase the diversity of the authors. These books would address the important points outlined in Bishop's (1990) work on windows, mirrors, and sliding glass doors that has been foundational in multicultural literacy. Books can serve as a window or even a sliding glass door through which students can see into other people's worlds and deepen their understanding of the "multicultural nature of the world they live in" (Bishop, 1990, p. 1), whereas with a mirror lens, readers can identify themselves in the text and feel a sense of belonging. Ivey and Johnston (2013) also support the concept that books are of high interest, are compelling, and will engage students. This led us to our next change idea: Bring in the social connections by conducting student-led "book shares" of these novels.

Do

Twelve book titles were purchased for each classroom library, at comprehension Levels N–Z, including various genres and a wide variety of social issues. Funds for the books were donated through donorschoose.org and supplemented by a matching anonymous grant. The act of asking for outside funding engaged families. In doing so, it also generated excitement for the novels among students and families.

Study

How we introduced texts became the focus of its own PDSA cycle. The introductions generated an overall buzz in the classroom and the titles were passed around quickly to be read and discussed. Half of the students responded that reading the new books increased their enjoyment of reading.

Act

This step inspired the team to increase the amount of time we spent instructing and leading book groups around important social issues. The students found them to be engaging. One student with whom we had conducted an empathy interview had responded that he never enjoyed reading; he wanted to do the interview again so he could change his answer.

PDSA Cycle 3

As middle-level educators, the team believed that the social aspects of school, activities that connect, build relationships, and authenticate learning, are important. Grouping that supports positive partnerships so that social interactions can happen often (Au, 1997; Daniels et al., 2011; Ivey & Johnston, 2013). This helped us determine that the next change should be built on book shares. Relationships were a central part of the process, both because students wanted friends with whom to share the experience and conversation and because students built new relationships because of books (Ivey & Johnston, 2013). In addition, book shares allow readers to talk and write about what they are reading, which helps make their thinking concrete and supports a deeper level of engagement.

Do

After reading the books over their winter break, students shared the titles with the class via a book presentation. These book presentations were multimedia and allowed for dialogue around the shared titles. The books were then added to the classroom libraries.

Study

To determine if the strategy of student book presentations increased student interest in reading, 13 of the 19 students surveyed who had not yet read one of the titles in one classroom were now motivated to do so. When we asked all students in the grade the same question, 59% of students answered affirmatively.

Act

Beyond the book shares in this cycle, the team decided to also implement two different book group sessions: historical fiction book groups (Cycle 4) and social issues book groups (Cycle 5). This would allow us to leverage the social forces around reading engagement and support content studies, as well as foster important social justice conversations. Both of these cycles were temporarily halted due to the COVID-19 transition to distance learning. However, after the initial transition time, the team found ways to implement similar book groups in distance learning.

Implementation and Challenges

In the six classrooms that are in the middle school, three were committed to following through with the parts of each PDSA cycle. The other three did not commit to the surveys and plans at the same level, increasing the challenge of a schoolwide collective teacher effort in each cycle. However, the diversity of commitment among the classrooms provided an opportunity to compare the effectiveness that IS brought to each cycle. Given that, according to Carlile and Peterson (2019), the primary goal is to "understand variations in the context, facilitate effective collective action, employ rapid learning cycles, fast feedback, continual reflection and ongoing coaching; experience firsthand ecological, context-based and community data-driven solutions guided by the foundational concepts of improvement science" (p. 197). Analyzing the different levels of implementations for each cycle would increase the knowledge about which modifications increase collective efficacy. Table 5.4 synthesizes the focus of each cycle, including full and partial implementation of IS strategies.

Table 5.4. Plan–Do–Study–Act Cycles

Cycle 1 Guided Reading Levels Obtained Full Implementation: - Guidance given by teachers to para-aeducator on who to prioritize for testing (communication of concerns) - Reflected on reading levels obtained and intervened in a timely fashion - Used the data to help students select appropriate books for their level	Partial Implementation: - Reading levels completed on new students and those with levels below grade level - Interventions implemented in a separate setting
Modifications: - Establish biweekly meetings with all teachers to review results and establish interventions necessary. - Encourage/model reflective practice to help determine additional students that need to be targeted especially early in the school year to leverage the most strategies possible. - Review SBAC scores from previous year more closely to determine additional students that need supports.	

Cycle 2 Additional Titles by Diverse Authors Full Implementation: - Books introduced by teacher - Books placed in special spots within classroom libraries to showcase - Students have access to all titles - Survey given–measure engagement (remind students of new titles)	Partial Implementation: - Books placed in classroom libraries - Students have access to all titles
Modifications: - Introduce books at morning meeting (daily schoolwide assembly). - Emphasize how this activity aligns with our school's core values (Deal & Peterson, 2016, p.13). - Increase teacher buy-in by having them choose next titles.	

Cycle 3 Book Shares of Diverse Book Titles Full Implementation: - Encourage individual students to read specific titles over winter break - Winter Break Book Share Assignment - Increase dialogue after shares - Survey students to identify if engagement was increased	Partial Implementation: - Winter Break Book Share Assignment
Modifications: - Celebrate reading accomplishments and share schoolwide. - Bulletin board with student work pulled from book share assignment.	

The team of three teachers implemented the PDSA cycles completely, which allowed for enough data to be obtained from a wide variety of students and to test the change ideas. The data indicated significant increased engagement. The team implemented PDSA Cycles 4 and 5 in the late winter and spring to build on what they had learned in the previous PDSA cycles. PDSA Cycle 4 consisted of historical fiction book groups to support the students' Renaissance studies. Students were able to participate in schoolwide book groups that culminated with a variety show skit and a tableau vivant of an important scene from the book that advertised their skit. The final event and the follow-up survey were scheduled the day school was shut down due to COVID-19. However, the success of the book groups in Cycle 4 and the introduction of the diverse authors' texts that addressed various social issues in PDSA Cycle 2 made the team decide that they wanted to implement schoolwide books in the spring. PDSA Cycle 5 would include current titles, with some favorite middle-level "classics," that addressed important social issues. The modifications mentioned in PDSA Cycle 3 were implemented in the planning and design of the book groups. Unfortunately, the books were not ordered prior to the pandemic shut down. However, the team was able to place the order that summer and begin the next school year, entirely in a distance-learning model, with engaging social issue books written by a very diverse group of authors.

Finally, the last measure to determine the effectiveness of our improvement project, spring SBAC scores, was canceled due to

COVID-19. Although the team was not able to identify if the goal of increasing the ELA passage rate on the SBAC by 10% was achieved, the *aim* of increasing reading engagement by 20% was accomplished. Another measure that was going to be used was the completion of reading inventories at the end of the school year to determine reading-level growth. Due to the constraints of the pandemic environment, the administration decided to allocate support services in engaging students in distance learning with their core curriculum rather than targeting resources for one-on-one tests. Additional ways of assessing fluency and comprehension in future years using online technology have been considered and may be given priority given the uncertainty regarding in-person or online instruction. No matter the mode of instruction, reading engagement remains a priority in Gorge Middle School's curriculum.

Lessons Learned for Increasing Reading Engagement

Every day at Gorge Middle School, students have time to read a book of their choice during quiet time and are read aloud to by their teacher. This is a foundational pillar for building literacy. The classroom libraries are filled with a wide variety of genres and levels of books. Students get to choose their book, take the time to improve their literacy, and dive into another world. Even though the school has some of the lowest levels of racial diversity in the county, that fact only increases the need for additional books representing the diversity of our nation. Historically underserved students in the classrooms need to see themselves in their books and our White students need to experience the rich world of those whose background is different from their own. The classroom libraries are the windows and sliding glass doors into other people's lives for our students. Reading helps deepen all students' understanding of the world and strengthens their empathy when they can identify with characters in more diverse books. The team quickly realized that this was an area of equity that needed to be addressed during this improvement science project. By increasing the diversity of the authors represented in the classroom libraries, we did increase engagement for independent reading, dialogue around important issues, and, most important, we increased the social justice orientation of our classroom and school library collection.

One of the areas that the team wanted to place special attention to was increasing the engagement of Gorge Middle School's male readers. The survey was written so that students did not have to give their gender or name, but with the 26 self-identified boys surveyed, 54% of them said that having access to titles of high interest to them increased their reading engagement. Additionally, 52% of the male students surveyed said that listening to presentations increased their desire to read them.

Change Is Intentional

An important takeaway from improvement science is to not just identify a problem but to also engage in PDSA cycles to ensure any change results in an improvement. We found support in the statement: "Systems don't change just because we identify them; they change because we disrupt them" (Minor, 2018, p. 31). One cycle within the project can have significant results, and each of those changes can be enacted quickly. It does not take the agreement of everybody within the large system or a full and expensive curricular overhaul or an elaborate protocol to increase reading engagement. It does take reflective practice, identifying what is missing, and setting in place the actions necessary to disrupt the norm. For Gorge Middle School, that meant engaging in several PDSA cycles that resulted in building equity while increasing motivation to read.

Emphasize the Culture of the School

To increase teacher collective efficacy, it's important to share leadership for the improvement project and to integrate improvement cycles into the school's way of doing its work. Improvement projects are an opportunity to strengthen the school culture. When there are high expectations for students and a focused mission by the staff, there will be an increase in engagement (Deal & Peterson, 2016). PDSA cycles also ensure that the staff are key players in identifying the data, making sense of the data, and identifying whether to abandon, adopt, or adapt the change idea. Although reading has long been a pillar in the Gorge Middle School community and all teachers are committed to uninterrupted choice reading and read aloud every day, using improvement science tools and engaging in several PDSA cycles caused us to increase the engagement of the most reluctant readers.

Discussion Questions

1. How could your school leaders promote collective teacher efficacy to ensure a schoolwide culture of reading?
2. More research needs to be examined around gender differences and literacy. How could improvement science teams address this further in their districts?
3. How could your school increase culturally responsive teaching in the area of reading?
4. How could your school adapt the reading curriculum to best meet the needs of our students and sustain reading engagement during distance, hybrid, or in-person learning?

References

Au, K. (1997). Literacy for all students: Ten steps toward making a difference. *Reading Teacher, 51*(3), 186–194.

Bishop, R. S. (1990). Mirrors, windows, and sliding glass doors. *Perspectives: Choosing and Using Books for the Classroom, 6*(3). https://scenicregional.org/wp-content/uploads/2017/08/Mirrors-Windows-and-Sliding-Glass-Doors.pdf

Calkins, L., & Ehrenworth, M. (2017). *A guide to the reading workshop middle school grades*. Heinemann.

Carlile, S. P., & Peterson, D. S. (2019). Improvement science in equity-based administrative practicum redesign. In R. Crowe, B. N. Hinnant-Crawford, & D. Spaulding

(Eds.), *The educational leader's guide to improvement science: Data, design and cases for reflection* (pp. 197–216). Myers Education Press.

Daniels, E., Marcos, S., & Steres, M. (2011). Examining the effects of a school-wide reading culture on the engagement of middle school students. *Research in Middle Level Education Online, 35*(2), 1–13.

Deal, T. E., & Peterson, K. D. (2016). *Shaping school culture* (3rd ed.). Jossey-Bass.

Frattura, E. M., & Capper, C. A. (2007). *Leading for social justice: Transforming schools for all learners*. Corwin.

Ivey, G., & Johnston, P., (2013). Engagement with young adult literature: Outcomes and processes. *Reading Research Quarterly, 48*(3), 255–275.

Minor, C. (2018). *We got this: Equity, access, and the quest to be who our students need us to be*. Heinemann.

National Assessment of Educational Progress. (2019). *2019 reading findings*. https://nces.ed.gov/nationsreportcard/reading/

Smith, D., Frey, N., Pumpian, I., & Fisher, D. (2017). *Building equity: Policies and practices to empower all learners*. ASCD.

Wigfield, A., Gladstone, J., & Turci, L. (2016). Beyond cognition: Reading motivation and reading comprehension. *Child Development Perspectives, 10*(3), 190–195.

Part II:
Writing

CHAPTER SIX

Small-Group Instruction in Writer's Workshop: A Surprising Obstacle

DANIEL F. BARNARD

Background

This improvement science project took place in a K–5 school in rural Oregon in a community located within an hour of a suburban area. The school in the case, Cambridge Grade School, has a unique population of students that live in Cambridge proper and those who live in nearby suburban communities. Students who lived in neighboring towns were also allowed to attend Cambridge Grade School due to a statewide law. This law allowed students to attend neighboring school districts if they were accepted into the desired district. As a small rural school district, Cambridge has grown its student population by 40% to 45% during the past decade by admitting students from neighboring towns.

According to the most recent statewide district report card, Cambridge School District was home to 1,200 students in kindergarten to Grade 12. At the time of reporting, 85% of the student population was White, 95% of the teachers in the district were White, 20% of students were on the free and reduced-price lunch program, and 40% of third graders met grade-level expectations for English language arts.

The five teachers in the second and third grades are all White. The principal and student teacher, who both also participated as part of the improvement science team, are White as well. The intervention specialist, who led the improvement science project during

97

his principal licensure program, is White. Four of the second- and third-grade teachers are female, and one is male. Overall, the team members' average years of teaching in their own classroom was about 5 years, with one female teacher in her 1st year of teaching, two female teachers in their 2nd year of teaching in their own classroom (one had previously worked as the intervention specialist), one female teacher in her 7th year, and one male teacher in his 11th year of teaching.

Of the 70 K–5 students who received intervention services, 15 students were kindergarteners and first graders, 30 were second and third graders, and 26 were fourth and fifth graders. Thus, 42% of students receiving intervention support were from a second- and third-grade classroom. The demographics of each of the second- and third-grade classrooms are shown in Table 6.1.

Table 6.1. Demographics of Second- and Third-Grade Classrooms

	Jon	Maren	Leona	Amanda	Jordyn
Number of Students	27	27	28	26	26
Boys/Girls/Nonbinary	12/15/0	15/12/0	11/17/0	10/16/0	12/14/0
Second/Third Graders	13/14	14/13	12/16	13/13	12/14
English Learners	4	0	0	0	0
IEPs	2	6	7	4	3
504 Plans	0	0	0	0	0

Note: IEPs = individualized education plans.

Problem of Practice

The improvement science project started with a focus on small-group instruction within a Writers' Workshop. The initial working theory of improvement started with a focus on classroom management. Upon creating the fishbone diagram, it became clear that student behavior was a major obstacle to administering small-group instruction successfully. In November, teachers all agreed that the biggest challenge they faced when trying to lead a small group was the behavior of the rest of the class.

Tools Used in the Improvement Science Process

The improvement science process included planning for the Plan–Do–Study–Act (PDSA) cycles by engaging in a fishbone analysis; conducting empathy interviews; completing equity surveys; examining data from a student engagement survey; analyzing data received from a survey administered to staff, students, and community members in alignment with our school's Student Success Act proposal; examining literature on the use of small groups and on classroom management; and engaging in PDSA cycles.

Empathy Interviews and Survey Data

Six empathy interviews were held for this improvement science project; one for each teacher and one for a student teacher who played an active role in the first two cycles of the improvement project. Her interview was performed alongside her mentor teacher's interview. These interviews were held during the month of September as the team began its work. Empathy interview data revealed that teachers being asked to lead a class of 26 diverse learners was not a problem. But hosting a small group of three to five students within a Writers' Workshop was panic-inducing. During the empathy interviews, each teacher was asked about small groups with the open-ended question: "Please share your thoughts or fears regarding leading small groups" (see Table 6.2).

The range of survey responses showed a disconnect between teachers' understanding of the value of small-group work and teachers' abilities to host small groups, which are an integral part of the Writers' Workshop model. Throughout this process, it became clear that teachers' relationships with their own abilities to utilize small groups as an effective teaching tool varied greatly.

Literature Review

Each teacher read an article regarding small groups, classroom management, and student behavior related to the improvement

Table 6.2. Teacher Responses Thoughts or Fears

Teacher Name	Response
Jordyn	*I've really enjoyed many of the small groups I've done. My trouble is putting them together and knowing I'm placing them in a group that will serve them best in the moment. I'm using the on-demand scores and goal sheets to place them, and I struggle with prioritizing which areas for which kids.*
Jon	*So one of my fears is based on running small groups this year. If we're worried about a group of kids having the same goal, getting to the advice that would help that individual kid. That advice might not help the other kids in the group. I worry about wasting the time of the other kids in the group if what we're talking about doesn't advance their own writing. I don't have a good way to recognize when it's time to conference versus have a small group. I'm obsessed with efficiency. When it's not efficient, it doesn't feel right.*
Leona	*I feel good about running them. My biggest fear is that I'm not going to get around to enough students and teach them all the skills I need to teach them. Maybe I won't be able to reach all of their needs. Because of time and maybe because I'm too slow at doing small groups. I honestly don't know how anybody is able to do it faster. Lucy [Calkins of Teachers College] says this, and the conferencing, and I spent all this time with one student. I guess a part of it is me. I'm not going to be the one to make the growth. Maybe it's me being self-centered.*
Amanda	*I think making sure that I pinpoint something that is truly useful. When you're conferring one-on-one, you can see it immediately. When I group them, is it something that they can all apply at the same time? Do they all need this lesson? And can they understand how to apply it?* *I haven't done many writing small groups, but I guess . . . it's too easy to turn into a conference with people watching. It feels worse versus when it's a whole group. Either I'm wasting my time, or I'm confusing things for you. It feels like I'm making things worse than better.*
Maren	*I think small groups are very effective. They are a great way to get to everybody without just conferring. I don't have any fears about small groups. When I worked in another state, I was mandated to write lesson plans for both whole class, every subject, and then small group for reading and writing. So right out of the gate, at 22 years old, I was used to it.*

science project. A few highlights from the literature review were helpful in the change ideas teachers employed in their own classrooms. Teachers were encouraged to identify the focus for improvement in their individual classrooms.

Van de Pol et al. (2011) wrote specifically about how scaffolds are a necessary component of running small groups within Writers' Workshop:

> Videotaping of and reflection upon teachers' own practice was a vital part of the current PDP because video can capture the complexity of classroom events, be watched several times, and enhance reflection and analyses that would not be possible during teaching. (p. 195)

Leading up to the first cycle, both Leona's and Jon's classes were videotaped during a Writers' Workshop. Student behavior in Leona's class caused students to be off task, whereas student behavior in Jon's class caused students to be focused and productive. The next day, Leona and Jon watched the videos of their small-group instruction, helping Leona strengthen her classroom management skills and help raise expectations for her own students and their work ethic.

In focusing specifically on Writers' Workshop and the Teachers College Reading and Writing Project, Rebora (2016) discusses the critical importance of allowing teachers time to collaborate: "The key is for teachers to be in study groups in their own schools, so that they're planning curriculum together and teaching a shared curriculum and are able to visit each other's classrooms together and study student work together" (para. 4). At the beginning of the improvement science project, the team of teachers calibrated their scoring of student writing. Each teacher scored the same piece of writing using the rubric from the Writers' Workshop model. Then scores were compared. Although it didn't fit precisely into the eventual focus of the project, the opportunity was empowering and meaningful. Amanda remarked, "This was extremely helpful. Can we do this again?"

Equity Audits

Three equity surveys were used to help better understand the scope of the project that focused on small-group work. Data were gathered from two different surveys administered to community members during our district's Student Success Night in early October 2019 in conjunction with the State of Oregon's Student Success Act. The surveys were picked because they included feedback from all members of the greater school community (staff, families, students), and the surveys were shared with community members that didn't come to Family Night. The *Academic Equity* survey was designed using the equity work of Smith et al. (2017). The focus of the improvement science team was on small groups but grew to focus on classroom management and, thus, student behavior. Smith et al. (2017) argue that "by broadening single-focus equity initiatives to comprehensive, schoolwide measures and approaches, we can make the practices that support equity standard practice" (p. 18). The improvement science team did just that; classroom management is a schoolwide and districtwide issue. It's not specific to one classroom. By working together, the teachers strengthened their classroom management skills over the course of this work.

Student Engagement Survey

The student engagement survey was composed of three Likert scale questions and two open-response questions. The Likert scale questions asked respondents to agree or disagree with three different statements. The options were *Strongly Disagree, Disagree, Neutral, Agree,* or *Strongly Agree.* For the purpose of averaging the results from this survey, and for the results of the Academic Equity Survey as well, numerical values were assigned to each response. *Strongly Disagree* was a 1 while *Strongly Agree* was a 5 (see Table 6.3).

The biggest takeaway from this survey is that overall, parents and staff members felt that students experienced quality core instruction. This was validating and reaffirming that the work done in school is of good quality.

The *Academic Equity* survey asked a variety of questions regarding facilities, access to resources, math curriculum, and challenges. Two questions had a strong connection to the focus of the improvement science project (see Table 6.4).

Table 6.3. Academic Equity Survey Results: Student Engagement

	Question		
	My student can select learning opportunities related to their interests.	My student experiences quality core instruction.	Grading and progress reports are focused on student growth and mastery.
Average score	3.7	4.2	3.8
Descriptor	Almost Agree	Agree	Almost Agree

Note: 1 = strongly disagree, 5 = strongly agree.

Table 6.4. Academic Equity Survey Results: Improvement Science

	Question	
	Students are encouraged to take on challenging classes, projects, and activities.	Teachers notice and meet students' individual instructional needs.
Score	3.9	3.3
Descriptor	Very close to agreeing	Neutral

Note: 1 = strongly disagree, 5 = strongly agree.

These results are important because they showed that there is room for improvement across the district, specifically in meeting students' individual academic needs. When teachers target writers' needs by working with them in small groups, students receive scaffolds and are encouraged to grow as a writer.

Teacher Surveys

In addition to the two surveys from the Student Success Night, a survey was designed and administered to the five teachers on the improvement science team seeking their input on small groups. Four questions specifically asked teachers to rank their comfort with small groups: (1) "Please rate your comfort level (scale of 1–5) with leading small groups before this school year"; (2) "Please rate your confidence level (scale of 1–5) when leading small groups before this school year"; (3) "Before this school year, how did you determine the focus of your small groups in writing?" and (4) teachers were asked to select statements about teaching small groups they agreed with. These data helped show that anxiety and uncertainty around small groups were quite present in their classrooms (see Table 6.5).

Table 6.5. Academic Equity Survey Results: Attitudes Toward Small Groups

Likert Scale Responses					
	Score of 1	Score of 2	Score of 3	Score of 4	Score of 5
Please rate your **comfort** level (scale of 1–5) with leading small groups before this school year.	0	2	2	0	1
Please rate your **confidence** level (scale of 1–5) when leading small groups before this school year.	0	2	1	1	1

Theory of Improvement

The rich conversation regarding Writers' Workshop challenges revealed the initial working theory of improvement: By strengthening teachers' classroom management skills, student behavior would improve, and small-group instruction would become more effective because teachers would not need to direct their attention to behavioral needs outside of the small group.

Fishbone Diagram

The finalized fishbone diagram shows the six major obstacles that teachers identified (see Figure 6.1). Now that we know more about improvement science, we know that the fishbone should have a problem of practice at the head of the fish. In our case, we identified our goal, which was to implement a writers' workshop. However, the next time we engage in a fishbone activity, we'll follow the improvement science concept that the work of the team is stronger when the problem is clear throughout the root-cause analysis stage.

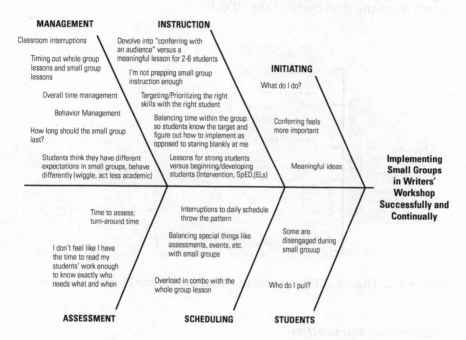

Figure 6.1. Fishbone

Driver Diagram

Before the first cycle was implemented in December 2019, primary drivers were identified as a team. The primary drivers that were identified were seating arrangements, language supports, equipment, expectations, attention span/energy, and bathroom protocol. Secondary drivers varied among the five teachers based on the students in their classes. Secondary drivers included short attention span, a need for attention, nervousness about mistakes, a need to share, students with attention-deficit disorder, preliterate students who could not read prompts, students with attention-deficit/hyperactivity disorder, a lack of independence, and a lack of knowledge. Each teacher then selected one primary driver to address based on the needs of their own classrooms. Because the driver diagrams were different for each teacher, Figure 6.2 is an example of one driver diagram from the first cycle of the PDSA.

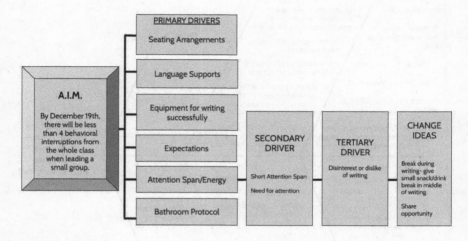

Figure 6.2. Theory of Improvement: Example of One Driver Diagram

Addressing Variability

The change ideas also varied based on each teacher's individual needs for their classroom, but they all centered on improving student behavior and, thus, strengthening classroom management. Change ideas, all supported by the research, included giving a break during writing, providing snacks, opportunities to share work, using privacy shields and/or headphones, preteaching expectations, using extensive language frames, reteaching using writing supports, spelling mini-lessons, and prepping more writing supports, such as graphic organizers and sentence starters.

Classroom management was resoundingly chosen as an area each teacher wanted to address when the fishbone diagram was initially made. However, each teacher chose a specific primary driver most pertinent to their own teaching, classroom management style, and environment. The five teachers identified a primary driver that they were most passionate about and, from there, created their own secondary drivers, tertiary drivers, and change ideas. For example, Jordyn's change idea included using privacy shields and headphones because Leona had already implemented those and they worked well. Maren noticed her students' behavior struggles primarily stemmed from a few students who always interrupted her for word-spelling questions.

Equity concerns were addressed through teachers' change ideas for their own classrooms. For example, Maren was struggling with students who needed help with spelling, so she implemented small groups focused on spelling strategies as one of her change ideas. Jon had four English Language Learners in his classroom and he decided to use language frames, such as sentence starters and prompts, to help them with their writing. Amanda's class consisted of several students identified for intervention support in the area of writing. She knew she had a lot of work to do to help her struggling writers produce and grow, so she focused on using writing supports in small groups with the hope that with this targeted instruction, they would gain more independence. In sum, practices were employed in individual classrooms based on the students' needs and necessary modifications. At the core of equity is ensuring that each child, of every background, is taught in such a way that they, as a unique learner, are successful.

Testing the Change

PDSA Cycle 1

The first cycle took place in mid-December. The second cycle was in mid-February and the third in mid-March. Below is a table summarizing each of the teacher's aim statements, change ideas, and results during the first cycle (see Table 6.6).

At the heart of this first cycle was the desire to improve students' independence in writing. All the teachers were frustrated that when they were administering a small group, they would have to pause

Table 6.6. Plan–Do–Study–Act Cycle 1: Results of Aim Statement and Change Ideas

	Name				
	Leona	Jordyn	Jon	Amanda	Maren
Aim Statement	By December 19, there will be fewer than 4 behavioral interruptions from the whole class when leading a small group.	By December 19, there will be fewer than 3 behavioral interruptions from the whole class when leading a small group.	By December 19, there will be zero behavioral interruptions from the whole class when leading a small group.	By December 19, there will be fewer than 2 behavioral interruptions from the whole class when leading a small group.	By December 19, there will be zero behavioral interruptions from the whole class when leading a small group.
Change Ideas	Break during writing—give small snack/drink break in middle of writing Share opportunity	Privacy shields Headphones Set up sharing times	Preteach expectations more thoroughly with the few students who need it (provide explicit reasons) More extensive language frames for preliterate students	Reteach using writing supports in small groups	Prep more supports Spelling Mini-lessons
Results	<4 interruptions	Average of 3.5 interruptions per day over the course of the cycle	The results matched the prediction. (I predict frequent meetings with those frequent transgressors will lead to fewer interruptions.)	At or below 3 interruptions per day of the cycle	Date and # of interruptions 12/4—2 12/5—2 12/6—1 12/9—2 12/10—2

repeatedly to redirect others. The frustration was both on student behavior and classroom management; several of the teachers knew they needed to improve their ability to manage the class. The change ideas were measured by keeping track of how many times their small group was interrupted.

An interruption was defined as a student walking up to the teacher, the teacher having to pause instruction to verbally redirect a student outside of the small group, pause instruction to physically redirect a student or students (get up and leave the small group), or anything else that interrupted the pace of instruction in the small group.

PDSA Cycle 2: Leona, Jordyn, and Maren

After the first cycle, Leona, Jordyn, and Maren modified their change ideas in an effort to improve their classroom management skills and, in doing so, strengthen students' academic behaviors when working independently in writing. As noted later, Amanda and Jon shifted gears completely. Leona, Jordyn, and Maren wanted to continue focusing on classroom interruptions, specifically decreasing the number of times they were interrupted when leading a small group. They looked at their original change ideas and decided what to modify and/or change and how to do this. Refinements were made to their change ideas in an effort to better meet the goal of the aim statement. By refining the change ideas after the first cycle in preparation for the second cycle, they were met with different degrees of success. This trend continued during the second cycle, and most important, she only had one interruption on 2 days and two interruptions on 2 other days. Jordyn's average increased by less than one interruption per Writers' Workshop while Maren's interruptions also increased. Leona expressed a feeling of success and noted that her change ideas paid off, whereas Jordyn and Maren both tried new steps but had an increase in the number of interruptions. They were certainly disappointed that the change idea had not worked. Maren noted in her PDSA, "I learned that my presence can definitely affect how they're behaving during writing, but that this will take some time to be 100% effective." However, one concept in improvement science is that it's possible you are implementing the wrong change idea and that, rather than trying harder or longer to reach a goal, consider adapting the change idea or abandoning it and trying another change idea. Jordyn noted in her PDSA, "It is much easier to apply expectations/accommodations to the whole class versus just one or two students." It's a common concept that change ideas may require an extended period for improvements to be observed, or efforts need to be continually modified for a change idea to work as envisioned. Table 6.7 displays the AIM statement, change ideas, and results of PDSA Cycle 2.

Table 6.7. Leona's, Jordyn's, and Maren's Plan–Do–Study–Act Cycle 2

	Name		
	Leona	Jordyn	Maren
Aim Statement	By February 21, there will be less than 4 behavioral interruptions from the whole class when leading a small group.	By February 21, there will be less than 3 behavioral interruptions from the whole class when leading a small group.	By February 21, there will be less than 1 behavioral interruption from the whole class when leading a small group.
Change Ideas	Review expectations daily—more so 1st day of the week. Give compliments using anchor chart expectations. Keep kids in for a "Work Snack or Lunch" to work that weren't on task	- Privacy shields - Headphones - Set up sharing times - Add bathroom time - Expand share to whole class: sticky notes to mark - Recess/snack work time	Circulate around the room for the first two minutes to make sure writers are settled in and writing Prep attainable, daily goals
Results	Date and # of Interruptions 2/10—1 2/11—1 2/12—2 2/18—2 2/19—4 2/20—3	Average of 4 interruptions per Writer's Workshop over the course of the second cycle	Date and # of Interruptions 2/18—4-5 2/19—4-5 2/20—4-5 2/24—2-3 2/25—2-3 2/26—2

During each cycle, teachers recorded the number of interruptions that occurred during small-group instruction. During the first cycle, Leona had four or fewer interruptions in each Writers' Workshop (see Figure 6.3).

PDSA Cycle 3: Leona, Jordyn, and Maren

The data were used to inform the change ideas in preparation for the next cycle while keeping in mind the nuances of classroom life that may or may not have affected the number of interruptions. Teachers kept track of the data in a table designed for each day of the cycle, noting how many interruptions occurred using tally marks. The

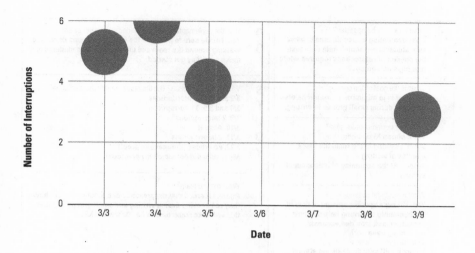

Figure 6.3. Leona's PDSA Cycle Data

number of interruptions was then organized into a specific type of graph for each cycle. As they planned for the third and final cycle, Maren stayed committed to her change ideas from the second cycle because she felt she could've done a better job implementing the change ideas. She added the importance of relocating students who were having a hard time working independently and initiating writing. Leona and Jordyn both modified their change ideas as shown in Figure 6.4.

In this third PDSA cycle, and similar to the results in the second cycle, results varied. Leona learned "that reducing the total amount of writing time did not increase their capability of working quietly." Jordyn shared,

> In reflecting on this process from Cycle 1 until now, I realized just how much progress we have made with our workshop time. Most interruptions during this cycle were absolutely minimal compared to interruptions during Cycle 1. Looking back on the fall I felt like I had to interrupt my small groups and conferences because many students were being disruptive/unproductive. By the time we got to this cycle it was always just a couple of students.

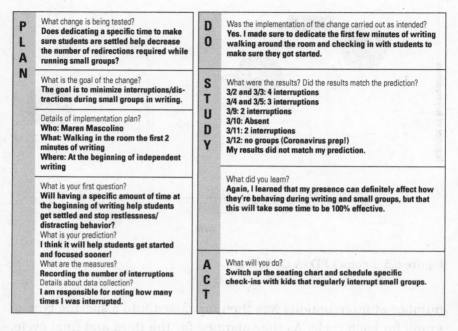

P L A N	What change is being tested? **Does dedicating a specific time to make sure students are settled help decrease the number of redirections required while running small groups?**	**D O**	Was the implementation of the change carried out as intended? **Yes. I made sure to dedicate the first few minutes of writing walking around the room and checking in with students to make sure they got started.**
	What is the goal of the change? **The goal is to minimize interruptions/distractions during small groups in writing.**	**S T U D Y**	What were the results? Did the results match the prediction? **3/2 and 3/3: 4 interruptions** **3/4 and 3/5: 3 interruptions** **3/9: 2 interruptions** **3/10: Absent** **3/11: 2 interruptions** **3/12: no groups (Coronavirus prep!)** **My results did not match my prediction.**
	Details of implementation plan? **Who: Maren Mascolino** **What: Walking in the room the first 2 minutes of writing** **Where: At the beginning of independent writing**		
	What is your first question? **Will having a specific amount of time at the beginning of writing help students get settled and stop restlessness/distracting behavior?** What is your prediction? **I think it will help students get started and focused sooner!** What are the measures? **Recording the number of interruptions** Details about data collection? **I am responsible for noting how many times I was interrupted.**		What did you learn? **Again, I learned that my presence can definitely affect how they're behaving during writing and small groups, but that this will take some time to be 100% effective.**
		A C T	What will you do? **Switch up the seating chart and schedule specific check-ins with kids that regularly interrupt small groups.**

Figure 6.4. Leona and Jordyn's PDSA Cycle 3

Maren stated, "Again, I learned that my presence can definitely affect how they're behaving during writing and small groups, but that this will take some time to be 100% effective." When coaching Maren on using improvement science principles, I wanted to coach her on how improvement science differs from other improvement efforts. Trying harder is almost never the answer. The context might mean that one change idea doesn't work and instead of applying more effort or taking more time, or increasing fidelity to the model, it's possible that Maren should adapt or abandon the change idea. This served as an ideal opportunity to learn about how improvement science does not mean more effort, nor does it mean more time. In Maren's situation, she learned that her presence alone can affect how students work productively. Thus, within the context of her focus and ultimate goal, rather than trying harder to make her change ideas work, Maren would have benefited from possibly creating a new change idea in this PDSA cycle (see Table 6.8).

Table 6.8. Leona's, Jordan's, and Maren's Plan–Do–Study–Act Cycle 3

	Name		
	Leona	Jordyn	Maren
AIM Statement	By March 10, there will be fewer than 2 behavioral interruptions from the whole class when leading a small group.	By March 10, there will be fewer than 3 behavioral interruptions from the whole class when leading a small group.	By March 10, there will be no behavioral interruptions from the whole class when leading a small group.
Change Ideas	Decrease the amount of silent writing time daily to 25 minutes. My goal is that I will have less than 2 teacher interruptions when I am doing small group work or meeting one on one for individual conferences.	Each time a student interrupts me, or I have to interrupt my small group to refocus them, they will get the signal that tells them they have to give me one of their beans (as opposed to saving it for the "party jar") and they will owe me 2 minutes of work time during their lunch recess.	Circulate around the room for the first two minutes to make sure writers are settled in and writing. Prep attainable, daily goals.
Results	Date and # of Interruptions March 3: 5 March 4: 6 March 5: 4 March 9: 3 March 10: absent	Date and # of Interruptions March 3: 4 March 4: 3 March 5: 5 March 9: 3 March 10: 3	Date and # of Interruptions March 2: 4 March 3: 4 March 4: 3 March 5: 3 March 9: 2 March 10: absent

PDSA Cycle 2: Jon and Amanda

After the first cycle was completed, Jon's and Amanda's classes had greatly strengthened their behavior. Both Jon and Amanda didn't feel that continuing with a focus on classroom management, and student behavior was meaningful for them in their own classrooms. Thus, their second cycle started anew; Jon shifted gears to focus on sight word acquisition with his struggling readers and Amanda decided to focus specifically on what type of small group she administers and with which students she works with in the small group.

This marked the biggest shift in the improvement science project, when one group chose to continue with the change idea and one group, having reached their goal, chose to focus on another problem of practice. Amanda and Jon chose new aim statements. Amanda stayed within the umbrella of Writer's Workshop to improve her small-group instruction, but Jon, who felt quite comfortable that his Writers' Workshop class was highly successful, changed focus completely and chose to home in on sight words with his struggling readers.

Table 6.9. Jon's and Amanda's Plan–Do–Study–Act Cycle

	Name	
	Jon	Amanda
AIM Statement	By February13, my lowest reading group will learn an average of 6 new sight words.	By February 21, I will use assessment scores and/or student-selected goals to determine small-group instruction at each Writer's Workshop.
Change Ideas	Adjust the structure of our reading group so that every day the kids have built-in time to assess sight words with me. Change independent time procedures to start with five minutes of sight word practice.	Create a goal chart with all students. Color code goals on sticky notes to match writing domains. Focus on one domain each day.
Results	Students improved by 7.25 words on average. However, some of them improved a lot, and others improved by just a few words or not at all.	During the week that I was best able to implement the change, I ran the most targeted groups. The following week, I still met with students, but was not nearly as efficient.

Jon noted an improvement in sight-word recognition, but the results varied. Overall, his change ideas led to more sight-word recognition; however, the number of sight words differed for each student.

PDSA Cycle 3: Jon and Amanda

Amanda went into the second cycle wanting to alter the instruction for small groups. Rather than haphazardly throw students into a small group in a way that felt like triage, she wanted a specific focus for her instructional strategies. Amanda took anecdotal notes on what she did each day during the cycle. These notes offer valuable insight into how she went about selecting students for a small group and the focus for instruction.

As Jon and Amanda began their third cycles, they slightly tweaked their change ideas in an attempt to better meet their goal. Table 6.10 shows their aim statements, change ideas, and results for the third and final cycle.

Table 6.10. Jon's and Amanda's Plan–Do–Study–Act Cycle 3

	Name	
	Jon	Amanda
AIM Statement	By March 10, my lowest reading group will learn an average of 6 new sight words.	By March 10, I will use assessment scores and/or student-selected goals to determine small-group instruction at each Writer's Workshop.
Change Ideas	Meeting with my sight words kids every day instead of every two days.	Continue to use the goals chart and have students refresh their goals during the upcoming writing project.
Results	The students improved by an average of 10.4 new words in the two weeks.	Results did not match prediction. Adapt or abandon the change idea.

The last cycle was very challenging for Amanda. In the third PDSA cycle, she stated,

> I started this cycle with the students on a computer program that many were unfamiliar with. The tech issues around this research project overshadowed the writing goals and skills for over half of the students. I learned that I need to do a tremendous amount of tech-preparation with the second and third graders who are still so new to using technology for writing in order to keep it from over-taking the writing process itself. When overwhelmed with their individual needs, I completely went back to my old habits of only working with the neediest students to solve their individual problems. It just wasn't as efficient.

Despite the frustration, Amanda experienced during the cycle, Amanda noted how making a color-coded goal chart with the class helped her home in on specific skills when leading a small group versus just deciding what to do at the last minute. Jon finished his third cycle pondering how to strengthen the reading skills of his lowest readers. He shared, "The students who appear to have a negative feeling about reading, and those that appear apathetic to learning, in general, still did not improve very much."

Lessons Learned

At the beginning of this project, that small-group instruction needed to be strengthened to reduce the academic disparities occurring between classrooms and to strengthen teachers' instructional skills was clear. What was not clear at the beginning was what was prohibiting the teachers from successfully hosting small groups within their Writers' Workshop. When the fishbone diagram was initially made in November, each teacher wrote down challenges they faced in their own classroom on sticky notes. As a group, the sticky notes were then sorted and categorized. As the challenges were verbalized and stories were shared, it became clear that classroom management and student behavior were overwhelmingly the biggest cause of anxiety for teachers.

The adaptation that teachers made after PDSA Cycle 1 marked a major turn in the team's work and shone a bright light on how the process promoted equity in the practices of the teachers. As the work evolved and teachers implemented changes in their classrooms, individualizing the focus for each student. Jon and Amanda needed to address a different topic that was meaningful and applicable to their classrooms and their specific skill set to grow as educators. What still needed to be addressed for Maren, Leona, and Jordyn was no longer the case for Jon and Amanda.

Biag (2019) notes the importance of user-centered design in improvement science work: "Educators who utilize user-centered design tools frequently immerse themselves in the lives of their users—interviewing, observing, and consulting with them so that they can fully understand their viewpoints and experiences" (p. 106). Jon and Amanda faced major problems every day in their classroom. Thus, each of them held the power required to solve the problems in their classrooms. For Amy, that meant attempting to determine which students to work with in a small group. For Jon, it was helping his struggling readers increase their sight-word recall (see Table 6.9).

As the project progressed over the course of the winter term, teachers made meaningful changes to their practices to strengthen their ability to host small groups. In doing so, teachers recognized strengths and weaknesses and what worked and what didn't, collaborated on what was happening in their classrooms, and supported each other in this journey of improvement.

Flashback to the end of the previous school year to before the improvement science project officially started. At the time, it was known that more student referrals for intervention services were coming from kindergarten/first-grade classrooms and from second- and third-grade classrooms. What was not clear was to what extent teachers implemented classroom-based intervention strategies before referring struggling students.

In his role as intervention specialist, the leader of the project was tasked with revising the Student Assistance Team note form used at each trimester meeting. An effort was made to streamline meetings by requiring teachers to complete the official note forms before the meetings, asking them to specifically include details such as what interventions were already being employed and how often struggling students were being assessed.

It became abundantly clear that a large equity issue was present; not all teachers were using small groups to effectively target struggling writers. A myriad of reasons as to why this was the case were hypothesized. Not until the empathy interviews were conducted did the intervention specialist begin to understand why teachers struggled with small groups, and the reasons were surprising.

Leading up to the project, classroom management was not viewed as an area that would be the most common obstacle blocking the teachers from hosting small groups. When the fishbone diagram was made, the conversation was dominated by classroom management and student behavior issues. As the teachers each shared their struggles with trying to host a small group while managing the rest of the class, it became clear that many lacked the confidence needed to simultaneously manage the class *and* lead a small group in a specific writing strategy. Of the five teachers, the ones who spoke with the most candor regarding student behavior and classroom management were the teachers with the least amount of classroom teaching experience.

Implementing the changes in the five different classrooms was easy and driven by the needs of each teacher and their individual classrooms. For all the teachers, the first cycle focused explicitly on interruptions. If a teacher was hosting a small group of writers in the meeting area, they would record how many interruptions occurred. Each teacher developed specific strategies that targeted the diverse needs of their student body. What worked for one teacher might not be needed for another teacher. After all, their classrooms and their students were not the same.

The beauty of the project is illuminated when you look at the experience through an equity lens. Not being required to adhere to the exact same change implementations or aim statements helped the process to be filled with meaning and authenticity for each teacher on the team. Compared with other processes that allow no wiggle room and that demand the same from each teacher, thus leading to a false sense of "equity," using improvement science created the most opportunity for equitable outcomes for children as each teacher was given the flexibility to do what worked for individuals in their classroom. As the project progressed, two teachers determined that focusing on classroom management and student behavior would not be beneficial to them because that wasn't a problem anymore. Those teachers could focus on other problems of practice.

Furthermore, although the process became specialized for each teacher and the needs of their classroom, the opportunity to collaborate, share concerns, and hear what others did in their classroom was rich, rewarding, and highly meaningful. This process was impactful because, as a group, the teachers were able to converse and share struggles as professional colleagues, collaborate on change ideas, and affirm the ability of each teacher to improve student outcomes.

Discussion Questions

1. What did you notice about how the teachers responded to variation in context promoting the improvement science principles of "adapt, adopt, or abandon" change ideas after short PDSA cycles?
2. What strategies would work in your school or grade-level team to reveal concerns about literacy models and delivering literacy instruction?
3. How could you use improvement science processes to improve your classroom management skills and increase academic success for your students while implementing small-group literacy instruction?
4. In what ways could ongoing assessments and student-created goals be used to guide small-group instruction?
5. During a time of budget cuts and strict financial restrictions, how can school districts support beginning teachers using improvement science processes to improve their ability to effectively manage instruction within the Writers' Workshop model?

References

Biag, M. (2019). Navigating the improvement journey with an equity compass. In R. Crowe, B. N. Hinnant-Crawford, & D. Spaulding (Eds.), *The educational leader's guide to improvement science: Data, design and cases for reflection* (pp. 91–125). Myers Education Press.

Rebora, A. (2016, June 20). Remodeling the workshop: Lucy Calkins on writing instruction today. *Education Week*. https://www.edweek.org/teaching-learning/remodeling-the-workshop-lucy-calkins-on-writing-instruction-today/2016/06

Smith, D., Frey, N., Pumpian, I., & Fisher, D. (2017). *Building equity: Policies and practices to empower all learners*. ASCD.

Van de Pol, J., Volman, M., & Beishuizen, J. (2011). Promoting teacher scaffolding in small-group work: A contingency perspective. *Teaching and Teacher Education, 28*(2), 193–205. https://doi.org/10.1016/j.tate.2011.09.009

CHAPTER SEVEN

Improving Gender Equity in Written Language

FRAUKE MEYER AND LINDA BENDIKSON

Context

"Nikau" Elementary School is situated in a relatively affluent suburb of Auckland, the largest city in Aotearoa New Zealand that attracts many new immigrant families. The school caters to about 450 students in Years 1 to 6 (approximately 5- to 11-years-old). The student roll has an almost equal gender split, with 51% girls, and is composed of mainly immigrant students from 39 different countries, with 39% Asian, 28% New Zealand European, 19% other European, 3% Indigenous Maori, and 2% students of Pacific Island descent (e.g., Tonga, Samoa, Cook Islands). Only a third of the students have English as their first language. Such diversity is not uncommon in New Zealand's urban schools. New Zealand is a small island nation with a population of approximately 5 million. Given its long immigration history, its population, particularly in its biggest city of Auckland, is highly ethnically diverse.

New Zealand schools and teachers have a high degree of autonomy relative to education systems globally (Hanushek et al., 2013). In 1989, individual schools became independent, self-managing administrative units, with schools being managed by a predominantly elected board of trustees (Wylie et al., 2016). The national curriculum provides a common framework of learning areas, values, and key competencies, but schools have the autonomy and flexibility to design, adapt, and assess the curriculum in a way that best serves their particular school community. Elementary schools are generally free to decide on the specific curriculum assessments they use. However, in 2010, overall teacher judgments (OTJs) were introduced to the elementary school sector. Teachers were asked to judge student performance in mathematics, reading, and writing as "well below," "below," "at," or "above" the "National Standard." Judgments were made based on evidence deemed most relevant by the student's teacher against a set of standards descriptors (Ministry of Education, n.d.). School-level OTJ data were published on the Ministry of Education website, and media agencies provided school league tables heightening public accountability. In 2017, a change in government saw the discontinuation of the requirement to report OTJs to the Ministry; however, most elementary schools still use OTJs for their own achievement monitoring and reporting to parents as can be seen in the case of Nikau School.

This case reflects on the last 2 years at Nikau School. It begins when Nikau School appointed a new principal, Poppy. She previously held a deputy principal (DP) position at another Auckland elementary school and had experience as a teacher and senior leader in a range of elementary schools in New Zealand and England. A couple years prior to her principalship, she completed a Master of Educational Leadership while on a fellowship with the university's Centre for Educational Leadership. Her fellowship provided her with a strong theoretical grounding in school improvement methodology, and her teaching experience in different schools had provided her with a depth of curriculum knowledge that she brought to Nikau School. Furthermore, she had a strong passion for equity and believed in the power of evidence and data:

> The knowledge and enthusiasm of [Poppy]. She came in with hands-on experience too and knowledge and not just "do this," "sort this out," and quite nice as well to actually have someone who knows a bit about it. (Teacher)

The Problem of Gender Equity in Writing

When Poppy arrived at Nikau School, she examined the school's performance data over the past years and concluded that the school was underperforming in writing compared to the other subjects and to schools of similar demographics. Furthermore, she found that boys performed considerably lower than girls, highlighting an equity issue that she set out to rectify.

Written language and gender differences in writing may often be overlooked in teaching as there is, typically, a stronger focus on reading and mathematics because these subjects tend to be seen as comprising the more important academic skills (e.g., Mitchell & McConnell, 2012; Reilly et al., 2019). In New Zealand, the Education Review Office (2019), which audits school performance, emphasized the teaching of writing as an important area for improvement in elementary schools due to a persistent decline in achievement, a decline in student attitudes to writing, and an increase in the gap between subgroups of students, including between boys and girls. However, the problem of gender equity in written language is not specific to New Zealand. Large-scale studies have shown a persistent achievement gap between girls and boys in writing internationally, with the gap growing over the schooling years (e.g., Mitchell & McConnell, 2012; Reilly et al., 2019). Reynolds et al. (2015) note that this gap is "the least mentioned achievement difference between boys and girls, despite some of the largest effect sizes" (p. 214).

In the following case, the journey of Nikau School is described over the course of 2 years (2018–2019), during which results in writing improved markedly and boys' performance came to match that of girls. We describe the school's progress using the Plan–Do–Study–Act (PDSA) cycle.

PDSA: **Planning for Improvement**

PDSA is a testing cycle that has three underlying principles (Langley et al., 2009). The first is that the trialing of an idea for improvement should be on a small scale initially, and knowledge should be built sequentially over time. Second, this relies on data being collected, collated, and communicated so that adjustments can be made in a timely way. The third is that a wide range of conditions should be trialed in a sequence of tests.

The following are leading questions in the plan stage of the PDSA cycle:

- *What are we trying to accomplish?* (i.e., what is the goal?)
- *How will we know that a change is an improvement?* (i.e., how can we measure improvement in the short term?)
- *What changes can we make that will result in improvement?* (i.e., what strategies will best address the root causes of the problem?)

The Goal

To answer the first question, "What are we trying to accomplish?" Poppy analyzed the school's past data in the core subject areas (mathematics, reading, and writing). Her analysis indicated that writing was the curriculum area that needed to be prioritized (see Figure 7.1), that performance in reading and mathematics was clearly higher, and that both of those subjects had been on an improvement trajectory over the previous 3 years.

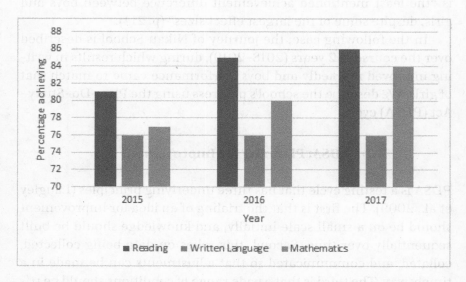

Figure 7.1. Nikau School Historical Achievement Data in Core Subjects

Although it seemed obvious to Poppy from looking at the data that writing should be a focus, staff was not immediately on board. They had been trying to improve their outcomes in that area for 6 years without making much impact on results. It seemed that teachers were suffering from fatigue in trying to raise writing achievement. Some also felt that, although the results were not as good as the other subjects, they were also not that bad and that the school had some huge challenges given its large number of new immigrants, many of whom did not speak English. Teachers also noted that in most New Zealand schools, writing was the weakest of the three subject areas and pointed to some students' foreign background as a potential factor in their underachievement:

> If it means that we are looking at boys who are "below" we need to move them to "at," have we looked at every reason why? In some cases, it is going to be really hard to move some of these kids from here to there yet the goal is they are going to move. (Teacher)

Poppy's approach to resistance to a continued emphasis on writing was to present the school's achievement data in comparison to data from other schools in the area that served similar communities. Teachers found these an "eye-opener," as the comparative data suggested their largely well-performing school was, in fact, underperforming in this curriculum area. This pattern was highlighted when new English Language Learners (ELLs) were omitted from the data providing a more accurate picture of how the school was performing for students who had been in the school for 3 years or more. This removed the opportunity for teachers to suggest that results were impacted by the new immigrants who could not yet speak English. It also heartened them when they reviewed students' progress during the 2 years without ELL student data muddying the picture:

> I think there have been some quite significant shifts that are really exciting. Things have been really well targeted and I think it is also really helpful that we have separated out the data so instead of it just being really depressing because it always stayed at this level you go actually because we have had so many ELL students coming in, if you take them out and look at it, we have actually made really

big shifts. But we are also not, how do I explain that, we are also not looking at it just without the ELL students. (DP Special Needs/ELL)

Initially, then, the answer to the first PDSA question, "What are we trying to accomplish?" (i.e., the goal), became clear: improve writing. Further analysis of the data clearly showed that boys were underperforming by a considerable degree (see Figure 7.2). The trend lines show not only that boys in the school were underperforming compared to girls but also that their results were declining and that the gap between genders was increasing over time.

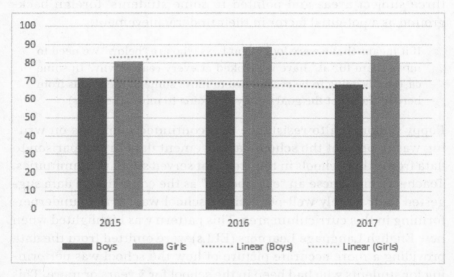

Figure 7.2. Nikau School Historical Writing Achievement by Gender (2015-2017)

The Measures

The second question in the PDSA planning stage is, "How will we know that a change is an improvement?" Clear measurement of success is at the heart of improvement science. Effective measurement of improvement requires both long-term success indicators (called "lag indicators" because by the time you get the results it is too late to impact them) and short-term indicators (called "lead indicators" or "quick wins" because these indicate whether the work is on track to deliver long-term results). In this case, the annual OTJs were used as the lag indicators. OTJs were set by teachers at the end of the year across the three main subject areas (reading, writing, and mathematics) and hence served to monitor the school's progress over the years and compare progress across subjects. OTJs were also used to report student achievement to parents. OTJs were already embedded into the school's system and hence an obvious choice as a "lag indicator."

However, formulating specific lead indicators and implementing a system to measure and monitor success were probably the most complicated parts of this initial stage of the PDSA cycle in Nikau School, because it meant designing and embedding new structures, processes, and artifacts. The school developed a "priority student" approach. Priority students were identified as those who could succeed but were at risk of not succeeding for various reasons. Each teacher identified six "priority" students in writing within their class. The students would not be those who had yet to gain fluency in English or who had special needs but, rather, students who were underperforming (e.g., who were performing at the upper end of the "expected level" and who teachers felt could be performing higher or those who were performing under the expected level), with a specific focus on boys.

The initial "quick wins" were goals of improving sentence structure and the independent use of high-frequency vocabulary. The performance of priority students toward these goals was used as the school's lead indicators. Student progress was monitored closely in weekly team meetings using rubrics that set out progression in these facets of writing. Teachers would bring the priority students' work to illustrate students' progress and challenges and collectively problem-solve with support from both external (e.g., a professional development provider) and internal experts (i.e., teachers with a strength in writing). Thus, priority students were the focus of teachers' inquiries into their own effectiveness and the subject of very close monitoring:

Each teacher knows where their children are at, where they moved to, and what we have done as an inquiry for ourselves to push our priority students. . . . Then, in our team meetings, we discuss our priority students and inquiry, and what we are doing to move them. At staff meetings, we discuss it as well and [the principal] reports back . . . where we are at, where we want to be, and if we are on track to get there. (Teacher)

This specific focus on named students, not numbers or statistics, helped build teachers' and middle leaders' collective responsibility. The weekly meetings based on data and evidence of student learning not only heightened accountability but also enabled teachers to see the significant impact of their explicit teaching and problem-solving on the progress of priority students within a short period, which was motivating for both teachers and students, as described by the DP:

So, there is something really exciting happening; they [teachers] know that there is a shift, you know, like the boy/girl thing, the balance shifted quite dramatically and that is quite affirming. We have taken risks and done things they didn't necessarily believe in or want to do but they wanted to make a difference. So they had a go and they saw some quite good shifts.

Strategies for Improvement

The third question in the plan stage is, "What changes can we make that will result in improvement?" In other words, what strategies will address the root causes of the problem? Poppy engaged staff in a "root cause" analysis which involved talking to students and staff, and close analysis of achievement data. Table 7.1 summarizes the teachers' hunches about what was going wrong in writing. This process was carried out over numerous staff meetings and was enhanced by the input of an external expert who, along with senior leaders, visited classrooms while teachers were working on writing with their students. Trends in teacher practices were summarized, and these data were discussed with each of the three teaching teams across the school (junior, middle, and senior). They were then discussed at staff meetings during which potential strategic approaches to resolving the issues that had been raised were decided on. Some identified causes and strategic responses are summarized in Table 7.1.

Table 7.1. Causes and Strategic Responses to Boys' Underachievement in Writing

Causes	Strategic Response
Lack of whole school approach to improvement	• Adopt a whole-school focus on writing • Identify lead indicators to measure "quick wins" • Implement improvement cycle at school level
Lack of specific leadership and goal-focused processes	• Deputy Principal appointed to lead curriculum • Literacy curriculum teams with representation from across year levels established
Lack of clarity about progressions	• Introduce new data management system to share, view, and monitor progression online • Introduce exemplars and rubrics
Inconsistent teaching approach across school	• Expert to provide long-term professional development • Expert to observe every teacher and provide feedback to teams of teachers • Year-level teams plan, review priority student data and problem-solve together • Across-school literacy curriculum team ensures whole school coherence
Topics not appealing to boys	• Student voice collected to inform writing topics • Students given more choice

This exercise was not finite. The problem and its causes, the goal, and the strategies were reflected on at staff meetings throughout the year. This process, however, led the school to formulate answers to the third question of the PDSA cycle: "What changes can we make that will result in improvement?" The identification and analysis of root causes, followed by the identification of solutions, ensured that these solutions or strategies for improvement were clearly linked to the causes of the identified problem and that the identified improvement strategies were implemented and reviewed on a regular basis over the 2 years.

PDSA: Doing the Improvement Work

In the following, we describe in more detail the strategies for improvement that Nikau School identified and their implementation. These include adopting a whole-school focus on writing, introducing new leadership structures and processes, introducing a new data management system, utilizing expert help and joint planning, and acting on student voice. These strategies were linked to the causes identified for boys' underperformance.

Lack of a Whole-School Approach to Improvement: Adopt a Whole-School Focus on Writing

One major departure from the way the school had worked prior to Poppy's appointment was the focus on one strong schoolwide goal of improving writing achievement. This meant that all staff were working on improving the same facets of writing that were identified by teachers and the invited expert, as a barrier to student achievement. Thus, an initial focus was on building students' ability to structure sentences and on raising competence with high-frequency words. Previously, different areas of the school had worked on improving different aspects of writing and even different teachers in a year-level team had different improvement agendas. This had not been successful as described by the DP:

> The year when it didn't work was when we looked at the data and said it is different for different year groups so we had different targets for different areas of the school for different year groups and there wasn't that same, you know, some had been trying to get the "ats" [students working at expected level] and the girls "at" in maths to "above" and then the something or others were trying to do this in writing and it all made sense, but it meant that it was very messy and nothing really happened.

Now a clear schoolwide focus and approach were established with pedagogical strategies aligned across the school, creating consistency in expectations. This new approach entailed all teachers assessing their priority students' progress on just these two facets of writing every 10 weeks and inquiring into whether they had made a difference for these students. As some students reached their competency goal, teachers would select new priority students to take their place and teachers would focus on improving their competency. In essence, the school completed the PDSA cycle every 10 weeks, as shared by the DP: "Writing teams and year groups meet so each year group was getting the same message and doing the same things, trying the same things, not just one or two pockets."

Although the school did not dictate details about how writing should be taught, over time, through discussion in staff meetings and team meetings, agreement was reached about some bottom lines. First, there was agreement at the school level that they did not want to use ability groups as their negative impact on some students was acknowledged. Some teachers were eager to implement more flexible grouping practices and did so for all their lessons while some took time to fully implement a totally flexible grouping approach. Overall, the expectation was, however, that teachers would not use fixed "ability groups." Another expectation was that learning intentions and success criteria would be used by teachers and shared with students so that teaching was more explicit about what the students were learning to do and when they succeeded in doing so:

> It is getting a bit more streamlined now so that we are all on the same page, we all know what we are doing in literacy which is a good thing whereas previously it was I'll do this and I'll do this. (Teacher)

Lack of Specific Leadership: Introduce New Leadership Structures and Processes

To support this whole-school focus and coherent approach, numerous changes needed to be made organizationally. First, there was only one DP in the school when Poppy was appointed, and this DP carried a large load. She was the school's special educational needs coordinator, which was a very large role in a school with such a diverse body of students, and she was also the leader of literacy. In response, this DP moved to a full-time focus on the many students with special needs in the school, including the large numbers of students with English as a second language. A second DP with a particular strength in literacy was appointed to lead the implementation of the literacy curriculum.

Second, a literacy curriculum team with representation from across year levels (with representation from the junior, middle, and senior areas of the school) was established to inform across-school planning and teaching. These three literacy leaders, along with the DP of Curriculum, also took instructional roles by, for example, providing one-on-one support for teachers, modeling pedagogy in classrooms, and supporting teachers in their problem-solving. By creating the literacy team, more sustainable leadership and ownership from across the school were ensured; the expertise did not reside in one person. The school had always had a strong culture built around the three area teams (junior, middle, and senior), but did not have a strong overall school culture. This creation of a literacy curriculum team was one of many deliberate acts aimed at breaking down the culture of three school sectors. The literacy leader shared, "There is unpacking as a whole school on 'What do we need to do to move them?' There is a lot of discussion about that. That is that collaboration."

Third, the role of the year-level team leader also changed in response to the new focus on data and priority students, from a largely administrative role to one of monitoring, reporting, and leading joint problem-solving in their team meetings. These team meetings became the "powerhouse" for the school's improvement effort. The school started to call team meetings professional learning groups (PLGs) to more accurately capture their new intent. Leading the PLG was not necessarily the role of the team leader. The PLG leader role was taken by one person in each team who had in-depth writing expertise, and additional expert guidance for the problem-solving was provided by a member of the literacy team when needed.

Lack of Clarity About Progressions: Introduce New Data Management System and Shared Planning Platform

It is impossible to gain consistency in practice if there is not a shared understanding of the outcomes to be achieved. So, although a spreadsheet was initially used to track progress against expectations, a more robust and permanent solution was sought. The school's original student management system did not lend itself to tracking student progress, so the principal moved to a new system almost immediately after her arrival at Nikau School to better enable staff to engage in data analysis and monitoring. This made students' progressions in literacy more visible and able to be monitored online.

Discussing and refining exemplars and rubrics were central to developing a shared understanding of expectations at each level of the school. The DP and principal invested time into supporting teachers to engage with the new system and showing its advantages. The clear progressions enhanced all teachers' understanding of "next steps" and eventually improved the staff's ability to accurately track student progress. One teacher shared:

> She [the principal] actually sat with me. She was my partner when we did the [assessment] so it was really good when I had a tricky child. I actually leveled him too high but she was really good. She went over, over and over it with me and we had discussions with other colleagues. It was good. It wasn't a judgment, it was done very nicely, very fairly.

Inconsistent Teaching Approach Across the School: Utilize Expert Help and Joint Planning

To address inconsistency in teaching, the school turned to an acknowledged expert for professional development in writing. She observed every teacher's writing lessons alongside members of the senior leadership team, so they developed a shared understanding of the current state of teaching. Then the expert provided explicit feedback to the three teams of teachers (junior, middle, and senior areas of the school). The feedback was not only personalized to some degree but also anonymized because trends were shown across the four or five teachers in each team. Based on these data, the expert developed a professional development program for the school that focused on

- improving students' ability to structure sentences and to read and write high-frequency words,
- acting on student voice by adjusting the choice of topic and genre, and
- embedding ways of accelerating progress.

The expert worked with the school for about 1.5 years and would come in for whole days to work with teams of teachers on planning and teaching practice or to lead whole-school staff meetings. Consistency in teacher practice was also enhanced by the ongoing leadership of the literacy curriculum team and the priority school leadership put on providing time for teams of teachers to meet and work together in the PLGs, often with the leadership and support of the year-level team leader, a member of the literacy curriculum team, or the principal. The PLGs' focus on joint problem-solving and planning encouraged teachers to support and learn from each other. A teacher noted early in Poppy's principalship that

> [Poppy] is trying to encourage a lot more collaboration through team planning and team assessment and team talk. She has come in and she's seen we are all squirreling away doing really good things but we are not sharing.

Topics Not Appealing to Boys: Act on Student Voice

As part of the ongoing effort to respond to the needs of boys, teachers gathered feedback from students about their likes and dislikes about writing. Feedback from students highlighted three areas for improvement: student confidence regarding surface features of writing, the choice of writing topics, and time spent on one writing genre. First, many boys were hampered by a lack of confidence and competence with surface features of writing, such as spelling and the ability to structure a sentence correctly. In response to and on the recommendation of the writing expert, the school put in place a phonics program so all teachers had a consistent approach to teaching spelling. As noted earlier, both of these facets of writing became lead indicators for student progress and rubrics and exemplars were developed to guide teachers in their teaching and assessment of these.

Second, teachers found that boys were bored with the writing topics they were often directed to such as "What I did on the weekend." They wanted to write about real but exciting experiences, including science experiments (older students), and shared experiences, such as what they had made out of Legos (younger students) at school.

Finally, the students also did not enjoy spending extended periods of time being locked into one genre of writing, which had been the school's approach previously (i.e., to spend 10 weeks exploring one type of writing such as narratives, before spending the next 10 weeks on report writing). One key response, therefore, was to provide for more choice on topics and abandon the genre approach but teach different genres as appropriate in context. Abandoning that approach made teachers more responsive to students' interests at a given time and allowed writing to be better linked to learning in other curriculum areas.

PDSA: Studying the Results

Nikau School studied results on different levels. First, lead indicators or "quick wins" of the priority students were monitored in weekly team meetings (PLGs) and then collated and examined by the senior leadership team after each 10-week term. Finally, lag indicators were collated and reported at the end of the school year. Monitoring and examining data on these different levels and at regular intervals ensured that expectations were clear across the school and built shared responsibility for results with a focus on improvement rather than blaming. This was achieved by the school's focus on joint problem-solving. The DP shared the following:

> Everybody in the team being part of that improvement and achievement and that means that it is more sustainable as well, because whatever good things have been learned and have been done that have helped that particular child, everybody is getting those same messages and learning those same things.

By the end of each term, teachers were excited at their impact and were asking, "How are we doing?" They wanted to see the larger data sets beyond their own class. A whole-school culture started to replace the previous team-based culture. At the end of each 10-week term, the Senior Leadership Team collated the data across the school and reported on the level of success gained to the governing board and the teachers. School staff meetings were then used to discuss what was working and why across the year levels. From this, teachers gained a sense of their shared success and were able to celebrate visible improvement in outcomes that were further confirmed when overall results of all students were assessed in the form of OTJs at the end of the year.

PDS*A*: Acting on the Results

The nature of the quick wins changed as students developed competence in the initial areas of focus (e.g., improving sentence structure, improving high-frequency words) to include other facets of writing (e.g., spelling, author voice). The writing focus itself was maintained until the leaders and teachers were happy with the overall results and confident that new processes and practices had been embedded and improvement would be sustained. This took nearly 2 years of intense focus. The academic year no longer drove the improvement agenda:

Interviewer: Are you on track to achieve the school goals?

DP: Yeah, but they will probably go over into the next year as well. They are not like you just tick them off, but we are definitely making good progress on them.

Furthermore, what was learned in one area was applied to the other learning areas. It became clear to all that what worked in one curriculum area could also work in others. The monitoring practices were readily applicable across the curriculum; thus, nearly 3 years on, monitoring of all subjects now occurs in PLGs; it has become the way they do things. Despite this, Poppy resisted the temptation to try to "do too much at once." For deep learning, the teachers needed to be able to concentrate their efforts on one curriculum area at a time. Thus, currently, the school is prioritizing improving mathematics achievement, but the quality of the monitoring will continue to ensure student success in all subject areas.

Timperley et al. (2020) describe this transfer of learning from a narrow "wedge" of the curriculum to other areas: "Opportunities to learn deeply in the 'wedge' lead to [the] transfer of professional learning to other aspects of teachers' work, thus creating a more comprehensive, but still focused, improvement agenda over time" (p. 23). In the case of Nikau School, the transfer refers not only to content and pedagogical knowledge but also to structures and processes. As Andreoli et al. (2020) point out, school leaders need to know "how to apply what is learned in one part of the school system to other parts" (p. 520).

Results

Nikau School steadily improved its results in writing over the 2 years, and importantly, they have the evidence to demonstrate that they have largely solved the gender equity issue in writing. The gap in achievement, which was the largest in 2016, with 24% fewer boys achieving than girls, had reduced to only 5% in 2019; see Figure 7.3.

The trend lines further show a decline in this gap. Not only did the writing results improve, but the school also improved results across all three core academic areas of reading, writing, and mathematics. Much of this success was attributed to the systems and processes that the school had developed.

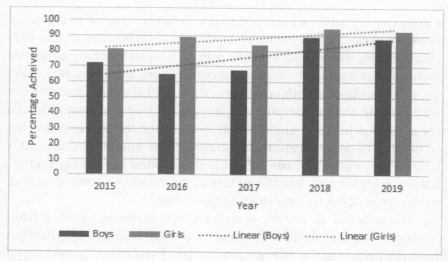

Figure 7.3. Nikau School Writing Achievement by Gender (2015-2019)

Discussion: Lessons Learned

The results attest to the effectiveness of rigorous implementation of the PDSA cycle to achieve improvement by setting goals, identifying causes and ways to improve, and implementing measures for evaluating change on an ongoing basis. In the case of Nikau School, several aspects of the implementation seemed important in creating this success.

First, Poppy, the principal, arrived at Nikau School with a deep knowledge of the improvement cycle and its tools. She then explored what needed to be the focus for improvement in the local context and involved staff early in a deep analysis of root causes. The root-cause analysis meant that strategic responses were aligned to the actual causes of the problem. Research has shown that too often, schools implement an array of improvement strategies that have little linkage to the problem to be solved; rather, schools get caught in so-called activity traps (Katz et al., 2009), or "quick fixes" (Bryk et al., 2015), or they implement preconceived solutions before analyzing the problem within the given context (Marcy & Mumford, 2010; Mintrop & Zumpe, 2019). The early involvement of staff ensured that contextual complexities were noted in the analysis (Andreoli et al., 2020; Tichnor-Wagner et al., 2017) and addressed the often problematic, top-down approach to school improvement (Cohen et al., 2007).

A second aspect that greatly impacted success at Nikau School was the focus on data and the attention to building systems, processes, and capabilities to collect, analyze, and use data for decision-making and problem-solving. Poppy had a strong background in working with data; she brought in a new data management system and, in collaboration with staff, developed lead indicators of student performance in writing. The new structures and processes around teachers collecting data, sharing, and examining data in team meetings built capabilities across the school and embedded this work in the day-to-day routines of the school. Poppy's approach addresses the discussion of Park et al. (2013), in which they note the requirement to have or build the capability of using evidence and the importance of establishing "disciplined processes for developing, testing, evaluating, and improving its core work streams and programs for building capacity" (p. 23). The role of the leader in guiding this overall process cannot be underestimated (Bendikson et al., 2020); Poppy had a deep understanding of the required process of improvement.

The regular feedback on progress via "quick wins" was motivational for teachers and enabled them to prioritize and persevere with their goal focus as they saw the impact of their teaching. Gaining feedback by seeing visible results in the short term has a significant effect on goal commitment (Klein et al., 1999) and the development of both student and teacher self-efficacy (Bandura, 2013). This was only achieved by the purposeful construction of rigorous systems and processes. For example, an important move that helped win teachers over and enhanced their ability to see their impact on student achievement was the effective management of the overall data of the school. Managing data well is a critical part of the PDSA cycle (Tichnor-Wagner et al., 2017). Nikau School was fortunate to have a principal who was highly data-literate. Her role in effectively collecting, collating, and communicating patterns in the data was a key to the school's success and to motivating teachers.

Third, the focus and systemized provision of time and space for teacher collaboration and joint problem-solving in team meetings speak to a central notion of a science-of-improvement approach to creating a "learning mindset" or learning culture in the school (Fullan, 2005). Collaboration and shared decision-making can break open cultures of isolation often seen with teams and departments in schools. Collaboration fosters dialogue and reflection among teachers and leaders and develops a culture supportive of learning and change (Drago-Severson, 2012). It allows trust to build which is necessary for risk-taking and fosters creative solution-seeking (Timperley et al., 2020).

Furthermore, although the principal took the lead role initially in setting the focus for improvement, setting up processes and structures, and developing the method of using data on priority students' progress as lead indicators, the embeddedness of these improvement strategies enables the sustainability of solutions as they become the way staff expect to operate. This has been built over time by seeing the positive results that have accrued and by their increasing role in owning and driving the processes. The processes are now maintained by the whole staff, not by the principal or one staff member. Thus, the processes have become a "self-sustaining" model of improvement as trust and capability are built (Bellei et al., 2020).

Finally, none of what has been depicted here should lead any reader to believe this is a simple process. Although one can interpret the PDSA cycle as logical and straightforward, putting it into action with a staff who have not operated in that way previously can be challenging as old ways of working are questioned and teacher collaboration is mandated. It is the results that start to drive the belief of teachers in their ability to make an impact, and it is the systems that enable progress to be sustained.

Discussion Questions

1. How does your school examine performance data on a regular basis to check where improvement is needed? Is there capability in the school to lead this process?
2. What are potential reasons for the gap in performance that you have identified? (Ensure you only consider causes within your direct control.)
3. What goals and targets have your school been working toward? How do you ensure everyone in your school is aware of and committed to these goals? What can you do to optimize conditions for improvement?
4. What are your quick wins that are indicators of your current academic goal? How does school leadership collate the data, communicate the data, and allow staff to engage with the data regularly?
5. How is progress, or the lack of it, communicated to the whole school on a regular basis?

References

Andreoli, P. M., Klar, H. W., Huggins, K. S., & Buskey, F. C. (2020). Learning to lead school improvement: An analysis of rural school leadership development. *Journal of Educational Change, 21*(4), 517–542. https://doi.org/10.1007/s10833-019-09357-z

Bandura, A. (2013). The role of self-efficacy in goal-based motivation. In E. A. Locke & G. P. Latham (Eds.), *New developments in goal setting and task performance* (pp. 117–148). Routledge.

Bellei, C., Morawietz, L., Valenzuela, J. P., & Vanni, X. (2020). Effective schools 10 years on: Factors and processes enabling the sustainability of school effectiveness. *School Effectiveness and School Improvement, 31*(2), 266–288.

Bendikson, L., Broadwith, M., Zhu, T., & Meyer, F. (2020). Goal pursuit practices in high schools: Hitting the target? *Journal of Educational Administration, 58*(6), 713–728. https://doi.org/10.1108/JEA-01-2020-0020

Bryk, A. S., Gomez, L. M., Grunow, A., & LeMahieu, P. G. (2015). *Learning to improve: How America's schools can get better at getting better*. Harvard Education Press.

Cohen, D. K., Moffitt, S. L., & Goldin, S. (2007). Policy and practice: The dilemma. *American Journal of Education, 113*(4), 515–548. https://doi.org/10.1086/518487

Drago-Severson, E. (2012). New Opportunities for principal leadership: Shaping school climates for enhanced teacher development. *Teachers College Record, 114*(3), 1–44.

Education Review Office. (2019). *Keeping children engaged and achieving in writing*. Education Review Office. https://www.ero.govt.nz/assets/Uploads/Keeping-children-engaged-and-achieving-in-writing3.pdf

Fullan, M. (2005). *Leadership and sustainability: Systems thinkers in action*. Corwin and The Ontario Principals' Center.

Hanushek, E. A., Link, S., & Woessmann, L. (2013). Does school autonomy make sense everywhere? Panel estimates from PISA. *Journal of Development Economics, 104*, 212–232. https://doi.org/10.1016/j.jdeveco.2012.08.002

Katz, S., Earl, L., & Ben Jaafar, S. (2009). *Building and connecting learning communities: The power of networks for school improvement*. Corwin.

Klein, H. J., Wesson, M. J., Hollenbeck, J. R., & Alge, B. J. (1999). Goal commitment and the goal-setting process: Conceptual clarification and empirical synthesis. *Journal of Applied Psychology, 84*(6), 885–896.

Langley, G. J., Moen, R. D., Nolan, K. M., Nolan, T. W., Clifford, N. L., & Provost, L. P. (2009). *The improvement guide: A practical approach to enhancing organizational performance* (2nd ed.). Jossey-Bass.

Marcy, R. T., & Mumford, M. D. (2010). Leader cognition: Improving leader performance through causal analysis. *The Leadership Quarterly, 21*(1), 1–19. https://doi.org/10.1016/j.leaqua.2009.10.001

Ministry of Education. (n.d.). *Making an overall teacher judgment*. https://assessment.tki.org.nz/Overall-teacher-judgment/Making-an-overall-teacher-judgment

Mintrop, R., & Zumpe, E. (2019). Solving real-life problems of practice and education leaders' school improvement mind-set. *American Journal of Education, 125*(3), 295–344. https://doi.org/10.1086/702733

Mitchell, A. W., & McConnell, J. R., III. (2012). A historical review of *Contemporary Educational Psychology* from 1995 to 2010. *Contemporary Educational Psychology, 37*(2), 136–147.

Park, S., Hironaka, S., Carver, P., & Nordstrum, L. (2013). *Continuous improvement in education*. Carnegie Foundation for the Advancement of Teaching.

Reilly, D., Neumann, D. L., & Andrews, G. (2019). Gender differences in reading and writing achievement: Evidence from the National Assessment of Educational Progress (NAEP). *American Psychologist, 74*(4), 445–458.

Reynolds, M. R., Scheiber, C., Hajovsky, D. B., Schwartz, B., & Kaufman, A. S. (2015). Gender differences in academic achievement: Is writing an exception to the gender similarities hypothesis? *The Journal of Genetic Psychology, 176*(4), 211–234. https://doi.org/10.1080/00221325.2015.1036833

Tichnor-Wagner, A., Wachen, J., Cannata, M., & Cohen-Vogel, L. (2017). Continuous improvement in the public school context: Understanding how educators respond to plan-do-study-act cycles. *Journal of Educational Change, 18*, 465–494. https://doi.org/10.1007/s10833-017-9301-4

Timperley, H., Ell, F., Le Fevre, D., & Twyford, K. (2020). *Leading professional learning: Practical strategies for impact in schools.* ACER Press.

Wylie, C., Cosslett, G., & Burgon, J. (2016). New Zealand principals: Autonomy at a cost. In H. Ärlestig, C. Day, & O. Johansson (Eds.), *A decade of research on school principals* (pp. 269–290). Springer.

CHAPTER EIGHT

Expressive Writing: Students With Disabilities

ADRIENNE STIMSON CLARK

Background

In the field of special education, teachers are tasked with providing instruction to students at different grades and ability levels. To provide instruction to all students, special education programs have consistently used paraeducators. Paraeducators are teaching assistants who work directly with students under the supervision of a licensed teacher. According to the Para2Education Center, from the University of Colorado, there are more than 800,000 instructional and noninstructional paraprofessionals in the United States (Chopra, 2018). Paraeducators are 95% female; 80% live in the community in which they work; 62% are employed to work with children in preschool and elementary level, with 71% working in special education (Chopra, 2018). Generally, most paraeducators have no formal training for their role.

In 2004, the Individuals with Disabilities Education Improvement Act was reauthorized and specified that school personnel who support children with disabilities, such as paraprofessionals, are provided the relevant training and are appropriately supervised to reach the goals of IDEA. The licensed teacher is legally responsible for creating and providing training and specific lesson plans for the paraeducator to deliver instruction.

Need for Improvement

In our improvement project, it became obvious that paraeducators knew how to follow a schedule that included who they would work with, what time they would work with the specific group or student, where their instruction would take place, and generally the topic of instruction. They did not, however, know how to deliver student-specific instruction.

This project began by looking at the training required for paraeducators to implement teaching practices with fidelity (Capizzi & Da Fonte, 2012). The initial improvement team consisted of the entire special education classroom staff, including two special education teachers and 10 paraeducators. To gather information about areas of instruction, the special education teachers created a survey that asked paraeducators to write a response to the following questions:

1. What are areas of difficulty with working with children or within a classroom?
2. Describe your past experiences with providing systematic instruction, delivering reinforcement, and collecting data?
3. What training have you had that has been job-specific?
4. Where would you like more support/information about doing your job?

After reviewing individual responses, a theme developed around a need for instruction in teaching literacy skills.

To further direct the area of instruction for paraeducator training, the special education teachers and staff looked at student individual education plan (IEP) goals for reading and writing and determined that four students had new writing goals with objectives to use speech-to-text technology to create phrases and sentences. These goals were new for all students, and no training had been provided to paraeducator staff to address how to instruct students in using speech-to-text technology.

Once the technology was set up on student accounts on all Chromebooks, a target group of paraeducators was chosen to work on teaching the specific speech-to-text skills to students. This target group was chosen based on the current school schedule and who was working with students who had goals for speech-to-text technology. The initial task was for paraeducators to instruct students to watch a person model opening the read-and-write technology to use speech-to-text. The paraeducator continued to use the current writing curriculum, Language for Writing by the Science Research Associates (SRA) to generate target sentences. The paraeducator collected data daily using visual observation to evaluate speech-to-text for errors. Errors were defined as incorrect words produced in the target sentence due to inaccuracies in voice recognition. Once students were on distance-learning instruction, the team had to develop other data collection methods for evaluating speech-to-text errors. Based on student growth and accuracy of the speech-to-text, the team would meet to determine the next steps for specific target phrases or sentences.

Theory of Improvement

Our team theorized that if we provided comprehensive training to staff on speech-to-text technology and subsequent data collection, we would see an increase in independent writing skills for students who experience significant disabilities (see Figure 8.1).

To teach students how to use speech-to-text software, the team determined that the staff must complete the prerequisite tasks first: equipment and staff training. The team made sure all equipment, including mice, headphones, and a quiet space, was available and ready for student use, and the voice rate was slowed on the device. Initially, the team provided very few visuals to support the students, including a graphic for the microphone and Google Docs.

Next, an assistive technology specialist came from the Education School District to provide training to all special education staff on how to use speech-to-text technology. The school district currently uses Google apps, and all students have access to Chromebooks. The training focused on teaching how to use Chromebook technology to

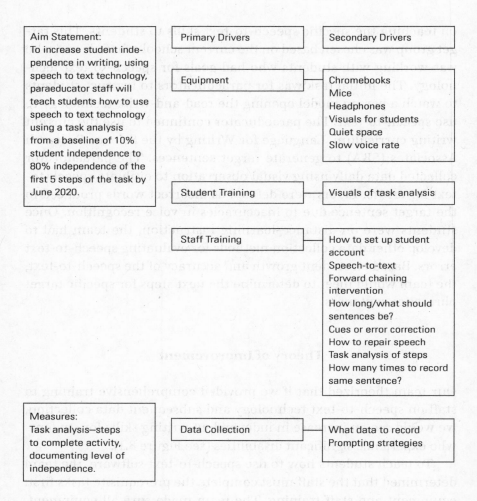

Aim Statement:
To increase student independence in writing, using speech to text technology, paraeducator staff will teach students how to use speech to text technology using a task analysis from a baseline of 10% student independence to 80% independence of the first 5 steps of the task by June 2020.

Primary Drivers

Secondary Drivers

Equipment

Chromebooks
Mice
Headphones
Visuals for students
Quiet space
Slow voice rate

Student Training

Visuals of task analysis

Staff Training

How to set up student account
Speech-to-text
Forward chaining intervention
How long/what should sentences be?
Cues or error correction
How to repair speech
Task analysis of steps
How many times to record same sentence?

Measures:
Task analysis—steps to complete activity, documenting level of independence.

Data Collection

What data to record
Prompting strategies

Figure 8.1. Theory of Improvement

turn on Google Read and Write, the speech-to-text technology for Chromebooks, and the steps for implementing the technology for students. Following the training, two paraeducators who would specifically be working with the focus students set up the individual student Chromebook accounts with Read and Write add-ons. The team also created a data collection tool and a task analysis of the steps to complete the task (see Table 8.1).

Table 8.1. Data Collection Tool

	Date					
Get Chromebook						
Get headphones						
Plug in headphones						
Locate Google Chrome icon						
Locate app waffle						
Locate Google Doc icon						
Use cursor to select typing spot on screen						
Click Record						
Record sentence						
Stop recording						
Play back recording						

Note: I = independent—1; VP = verbal prompt—2; G = gestural prompt—3; PP = partial physical prompt—4; FP = full physical prompt—5.

Student demographics are presented in Table 8.2.

Table 8.2. Student Demographics

Student 1	**Student 2**	**Student 3**
Female	Male	Male
Fine Motor: Able to write name and a few letters about 1 inch in size.	**Fine Motor:** Able to write name and a few letters about 1 inch in size.	**Fine Motor:** Able to write name and a few letters about 1 inch in size.
Typing: Can copy log-in information with minimal gestural prompts	**Typing:** Can copy log-in information with minimal gestural prompts	**Typing:** Can copy log-in information with minimal gestural prompts
Visual: Can identify and follow visual schedule/ sequence	**Visual:** Can identify and follow visual schedule/ sequence	**Visual:** Can identify and follow visual schedule/ sequence

We collected student baseline data as described in Table 8.3.

Table 8.3. Student Baseline Data

Student 1	Prompt	Baseline: 1/10
	Get Chromebook	vp
	Get headphones	vp
	Plug in headphones	g
	Locate Google Chrome icon	pp
	Locate app waffle	pp
	Locate Google Doc icon	pp
	Use cursor to select typing spot on screen	g
	Click record	pp
	Record sentence	vp
	Stop recording	pp
	Play back recording	pp

Student 2	Prompt	Baseline: 1/10
	Get Chromebook	vp
	Get headphones	vp
	Plug in headphones	fp
	Locate Google Chrome icon	g
	Locate app waffle	pp
	Locate Google Doc icon	fp
	Use cursor to select typing spot on screen	pp
	Click record	pp
	Record sentence	vp
	Stop recording	pp
	Play back recording	pp

Student 3	Prompt	Baseline: 1/10
	Get Chromebook	vp
	Get headphones	vp
	Plug in headphones	pp
	Locate Google Chrome icon	pp
	Locate app waffle	pp
	Locate Google Doc icon	fp
	Use cursor to select typing spot on screen	pp
	Click record	pp
	Record sentence	vp
	Stop recording	pp
	Play back recording	pp

Note: pp = ; g = ; vp = ; fp = .

Testing the Change

Plan–Do–Study–Act (PDSA) Cycle 1: Students Begin Using Speech-to-Text

The initial PDSA Cycle 1 in January began with a paraeducator guiding the students through the steps using verbal prompts. Our first question was, "Will giving the students the same verbal steps daily increase students' level of independence in completing the task?" The team predicted that by having consistent routines and expectations, the students would begin to gain increased independence. We collected data three times per week on the level of prompts it took for the students to access the speech-to-text technology and compose a phrase. Our aim statement and drivers are found in Figure 8.2.

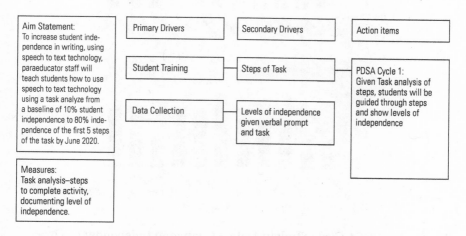

Figure 8.2. PDSA Cycle 1 Diagram

In a review of the students' progress, data indicated that all students made minimal gains toward independence. The team saw some independence in the first steps of the task to get a Chromebook and headphones and to plug in headphones. However, there was limited to no growth in accessing steps on the computer as described in Figure 8.3.

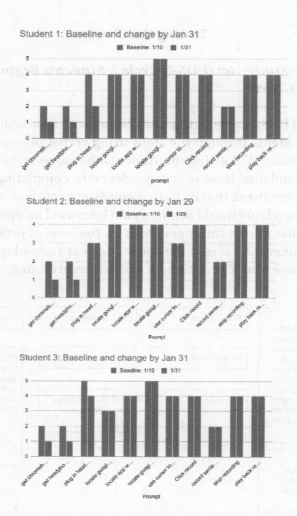

Figure 8.3. PDSA Cycle Student Data – Change in Independence Over Time

The Individual Service Plan (ISP) team learned that the students seem to have become verbally prompt-dependent and have shown little independence in using the technology. Therefore, the team decided to make a change for the next PDSA Cycle 2 by making a visual sequence of steps for students to follow to see if they gain more skills.

PDSA Cycle 2: Students Follow Visuals

The team began the second PDSA cycle in February by providing the students with visuals to represent each step of the previously created task analysis. The visuals were individually printed, laminated, and attached to a strip of cardboard pinned to the top of the students' computers. The students needed some help pinning the visuals. When initially prompted that it was time to write with their computers, a staff member handed them the visuals to begin the task. The team predicted that initially there would be an increase in gestural prompts as students learn to follow the visuals but that over time, they would show more independence in the overall skills required to complete the task. The aim statement and drivers for this cycle are displayed in Figure 8.4.

As the team used visuals, we learned that using Velcro to attach the visual prompt was very helpful as the visuals were able to be spaced about an inch apart, which helped students keep their place and not need a gestural prompt. According to the data, all the students were able to independently get their computer on and plug in their headphones by the end of the second PDSA cycle. Once visuals were attached (with adult help) to the computers, students were able to follow the visual prompts independently about 50% of the

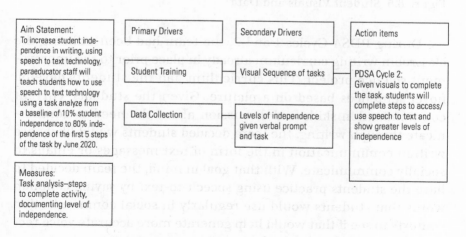

Figure 8.4. PDSA Cycle 2 Diagram

time to access all steps of the task. Although the students were all gaining independence in being able to access the technology, once the speech-to-text was turned on, the clarity of the students' articulation significantly affected the speech-to-text ability to understand what was actually being said (see Figure 8.5).

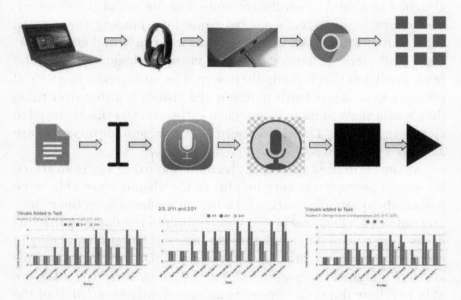

Figure 8.5. Student Visuals and Data

During PDSA Cycles 1 and 2, the team had been utilizing the classroom writing curriculum already in place prior to the improvement science project. This curriculum had the students develop novel sentences based on a picture. Given the students' current communication skills and discussion about the need to communicate through writing, the team decided students would likely use written communication in the form of text messages or emails to socially communicate. With that goal in mind, the team decided to have the students practice using speech-to-text by saying common words that students would use regularly in social communication contexts to see if that would help generate more accurate voice recognition and, therefore, readable text.

PDSA Cycle 3: Core Words for Speech-to-Text

In late February and early March, we discussed previous anecdotal data regarding the accuracy of the voice recognition of the students' speech. The team identified four target words for the students to practice saying: "Mom," the student's name, "hi," and "bye." All the students had articulation errors, with most of the speech previously spoken understood about 20% of the time. These phrases were all novel phrases about a picture they were writing about using vocabulary not generally part of the students' everyday vernacular. The students were given a list of words to say that they could practice beforehand, then go through the previous process of accessing the technology, and then record themselves saying practiced phrases.

Given the individual student articulation errors, the team began to question whether speech-to-text was going to be a viable communication option. The team predicted that words students used frequently would be clearer, but it would depend on the specific student and their articulation errors. The team began PDSA Cycle 3 by creating a new data collection tool to document the accuracy of the speech-to-text while continuing to monitor the increased independence in accessing the technology (see Figure 8.6).

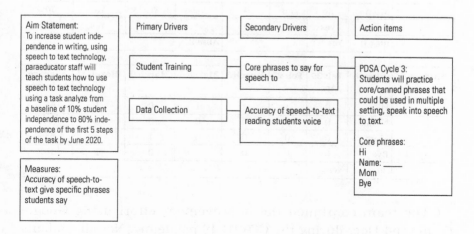

Figure 8.6. PDSA Cycle 3 Diagram

Students all began with a similar list of words that the team thought they regularly use now as well as in the future for regular written expression. The results indicated a difference in voice recognition based on individual articulation errors, although there was more accuracy than in the novel sentences students attempted before this change. Technology can be so helpful for the typical learner/user. However, a student who experiences a disability, whether fine-motor skills or speech delays/errors, may still struggle because the technology is not perfect yet, as shown in Table 8.4.

Table 8.4. Student Data: Voice Recognition Accuracy Using Speech-to-Text

Student 1	Phrase	Feb 25 Acc.	Feb 27	March 3	March 5	March 9	March 11	Average Accuracy
	Hi	0	1	1	1	1	1	83%
	Name	0	0	1	0	0	1	33%
	Mom	0	0	0	0	1	1	33%
	Bye	0	0	0	1	1	1	50%
	no = 0	Yes = 1						

Student 2	Phrase	Feb 25 Acc.	Feb 27	March 3	March 5	March 9	March 11	Average Accuracy
	Hi	no	Yes	-	-	Yes	Yes	75%
	Name	no	no	-	-	no	no	0%
	Mom	no	no	-	-	Yes	Yes	50%
	Bye	yes	no	-	-	Yes	Yes	75%
	no = 0	Yes = 1			Absent = -			

Student 3	Phrase	Feb 25 Acc.	Feb 27	March 3	March 5	March 9	March 11	Average Accuracy
	Hi	0	1	1	1	0	1	66%
	Name	0	0	0	0	0	0	0%
	Mom	0	0	0	0	1	1	33%
	Bye	0	0	0	1	0	1	16%
	no = 0	yes = 1						

The team continued the improvement effort using Google Forms and Docs during the COVID-19 pandemic. Not all students responded, but data we were able to gather indicated that given individual student progress, the team continued change ideas for Students 1 and 2 to include phrases containing previously practiced target words to describe individual-specific pictures of students with their moms or family members.

Student 1 had data for 10 trials as shown in Table 8.5.

Table 8.5. Student 1 Data for 10 Trials

Phrase (April 20-April 30)	Accuracy										Accuracy
Hi	0	1	1	1	1	0	1	1	1	1	80%
Name	0	0	1	1	1	1	1	1	0	0	60%
Mom	1	1	1	1	1	1	1	1	1	1	100%
Bye	1	1	1	1	1	1	0	1	0	1	80%
No = 0	Yes = 1										Total: 80%

Student 2 had data for 16 trials (see Table 8.6).

Table 8.6. Student 2 Data for 60 Trials

Phrase (April 20-April 30)	Accuracy																Accuracy
Hi	1	1	1	1	1	1	1	1	1	1	1	1	1	1	1	1	100%
Name	1	1	1	1	0	0	1	1	1	1	1	1	1	1	1	1	88%
Mom	1	1	1	1	1	1	0	1	1	1	1	1	1	1	1	1	94%
Bye	1	1	1	1	1	1	1	1	0	1	1	0	1	0	1	1	81%
No = 0	Yes = 1																Total: 91%

Student 3 had 2 trials (see Table 8.7).

Table 8.7. Student 3 Data for 2 Trials

Phrase (April 20-April 30)	Accuracy		Accuracy
Hi	1	1	100%
Name	0	0	0%
Mom	1	1	100%
Bye	0	0	0%
No = 0	Yes = 1		50%

Implementation and Challenges

Throughout this process of improvement science, the team changed based on who was working with the students. Initially, a large group was used to inform and help formulate a problem of practice whittled down to a small problem of practice and a group that would work specifically on that problem. A similar process is likely to happen in all school settings, but it seems important to not just start with a small group because the entire group perspective also was needed to find a valued problem of practice. In this instance, the team developed some large-group skills about using assistive technology that can be a basis for later training. The smaller subgroup of two paraeducators who implemented the changes and worked on the project daily gained valuable skills, and the students showed growth.

In the school setting, it seemed that students were gaining independence in skills based on the small changes to visuals practicing target words. It may have been helpful for a speech pathologist to be on the team to offer an additional perspective on target vocabulary and articulation errors. Based on the data collected from individual student progress, the team believed that the words and phrases collected were beneficial; however, we had serious conversations about the importance of research and the use of expert opinion. We all seemed to agree that in education, it feels like there are lots of times we start our improvement efforts without seeking to find prior experience or research to guide the process or we fail to consider our context before trying an improvement effort. What our team does not know is whether other target words would have helped our third student make more progress.

Another challenge the team experienced was the change in setting due to COVID-19 and distance learning. The goal of students being able to access all steps changed to just being able to speak clearly enough for Google Read and Write to create a correct dictation. It was interesting to note that both Students 1 and 2 quickly saw a significant increase in the accuracy of the voice recognition. The first student's data showed they went from saying *mom* accurately 33% of the time to 100%. The second student's data improved across the board from an average intelligibility of 33% of the time to an overall intelligibility 95% of the time. The team has wonderings about the data, whether the initial data were accurate as there wasn't a recorded response but rather just tabulated accuracy, whereas during the pandemic, there were Google response forms showing specific speech generated that showed a higher level of accuracy. We also considered that the change in accuracy could have been that the students were working with parents who may have practiced the response multiple times before attempting the task on the Google Doc, thus skewing the results. What was most important was that the students made progress. The added benefit to this project was that families also learned how to use the speech-to-text technology to further assist their students.

Discussion

In this improvement science project, the focus was largely classroom-specific with a very specific subgroup of students and staff. The team who implemented the instruction reported feeling competent in carrying out changes and understood how to manipulate and apply the technology and features of speech-to-text. The two paraeducators who actively worked on the project daily said that they felt that had gained valuable training and skills. In an informal survey, asking the entire classroom staff of 10 paraeducators who attended the training, 7 shared that they liked the initial training but that because they didn't actively use the skill, they didn't remember how to access the different features of the speech-to-text or Google Read and Write technology. This situation seems to continually happen: Large-scale training that provides cursory knowledge to the whole does not end up having a lasting impact or a positive effect on overall instruction (Ashbaker & Morgan, 2012). However, the specific training given to the smaller group of paraeducators proved to be highly valuable as there was a significant increase in the independence of skills for students from baseline to end product.

As a leader in education, the most important learning for me from this improvement science project, regardless of topic area, is the value of getting expert opinions, surveying a large portion of the population to get different perspectives, and knowing that in some instances, a change to instruction may only impact a small group of the population. In this instance, the training for paraeducators only had a significant impact on a few of the original team. However, the skill of knowing how to use speech-to-text technology and examining whether to adapt, adopt, or abandon a change idea, such as adding visuals or adjusting the instruction to focus on target vocabulary, can be applied to other improvement efforts.

Discussion Questions

1. Given your setting and achievement data, what questions would you like to ask (in a survey or an empathy interview) your students about their experience with writing?
2. What are the problems of practice you've experienced as a teacher or school leader helping children with IEPs and how could you apply the improvement science principles to identify improvement ideas to support students?
3. This chapter focused on paraeducators supporting students with IEPs in writing; how could you apply the improvement science processes to other professionals supporting students with IEPs in the classroom?

References

Ashbaker, B., & Morgan, J. (2012). Team players and team managers: Special educators working with paraeducators to support inclusive classrooms. *Creative Education, 3*(3), 322–327.

Capizzi, A. M., & Da Fonte, M. A. (2012). Supporting paraeducators through a collaborative classroom support plan. *Focus on Exceptional Children, 44*(6), 1–15. doi:10.4236/ce.2012.33051

Chopra, R. V. (2018). *Paraeducator Supervision Academy (PSA).* [Unpublished PowerPoint slides]. Clackamas Education Service District.

Individuals With Disabilities Education Improvement Act, 20 U.S.C. § 1400 et seq. (2004). https://sites.ed.gov/idea/statute-chapter-33/subchapter-i/1400

Part III:
Math and Science

CHAPTER NINE

Improvement Science Models Used for Achievement in Mathematics

JACLYN PEDERSEN, MICHAEL ODELL,
TERESA KENNEDY, KELLY DYER,
JO ANN SIMMONS, AND YANIRA OLIVERAS-ORTIZ

The University of Texas at Tyler established laboratory schools within the College of Education and Psychology in 2012. The schools serve two purposes: to design and deliver innovative STEM (science, technology, engineering, and mathematics) education to our K–12 students and to serve as a research and demonstration platform in teaching, learning, and assessment for faculty in the School of Education, providing training of future teachers, educational experimentation, educational research, and professional development. Administrators and teachers within the academy serve as adjunct faculty to the School of Education and partner to support educator preparation and research. The laboratory schools allow for longitudinal research and the testing of interventions to fidelity not always possible in traditional partner schools not managed by the university. A Network Improvement Community (NIC) has been established to implement improvement science practices and leverage the expertise of professors, content experts, school administrators, teachers, and students when appropriate. The school curriculum is co-managed by university faculty and district personnel. The NIC helps identify and guide school improvement priorities and research.

The University Academy Laboratory School District consists of three K–12 schools in East Texas. The schools are co-located on the main university and two university satellite campuses. The laboratory schools also serve different demographic populations. The University Academy (UA) Tyler is an urban campus and is designated as a Title I targeted assistance campus. The UA Palestine is a rural school and designated as a Title I schoolwide campus. The UA Longview is a school that serves a suburban demographic and does not meet the requirements of a Title I school. The academies provide an ideal research platform as school improvement interventions can be implemented and studied in different settings in schools with different demographics and designations.

The NIC is discussed in more detail in the companion chapter that highlights English language arts improvement interventions and outcomes using Plan–Do–Study–Act (PDSA) cycles over the last 9 years. This chapter focuses on improvement science cycles implemented in mathematics classrooms at one laboratory school over the course of nine years. The target school is the urban campus located on the main campus of the university. Each of the cycles presented is grounded in the use of disciplined inquiry to drive changes that lead to improvement. In *Learning to Improve*, Bryk et al. (2015) describe that

> all activity in improvement science is disciplined by three deceptively simple questions: 1. What specifically are we trying to accomplish? 2. What change might we introduce and why? 3. How will we know that a change is actually an improvement? (p. 114)

Three distinctive improvement science cycles are described, and each one focuses on the preceding questions by stating a problem of practice, describing the interventions and their primary drivers that took place to address the problem, and reviewing data to measure the effectiveness. The PDSA inquiry cycle was applied to each of the cycles, and often, multiple PDSA cycles were used in one larger improvement cycle. Figure 9.1 highlights the PDSA model used by the NIC and staff to drive improvement.

Was the intervention an improvement?
- Adopt, Revise or Reject

What are we trying to improve?
- Identify Goal(s)
- List expected outcomes
- Identify Measures and Research Design
- Operational Definitions
- Procedures and Methods Responsible Parties

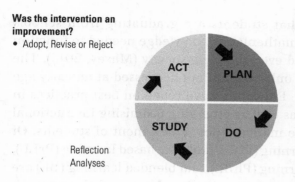

Implementation
Documentation
End User Support

Reflection
Analyses

Figure 9.1. The Plan-Do-Study-Act Model Approach

Literature Review

The achievement of students in mathematics in the United States has lagged behind other countries for years. According to some studies, the achievement of U.S. students in mathematics ranks around average (Desilver, 2017). In the most recent Program for International Student Assessment (PISA) in 2018, students in the United States performed below the Organisation for Economic Co-operation and Development (2019) member countries' average in mathematics. Mathematics scores have remained stable since 2006, with no significant improvement in results. However, other studies that include results from the Trends in International Mathematics and Science Study (TIMSS) show U.S. students, particularly fourth-grade students, to be ranked eleventh out of 45 countries (Provasnik et al., 2016). When reviewing the TIMSS study, Provasnik et al. (2016) found that although U.S. fourth graders had shown average progress over the five administrations of TIMSS, they have shown little to no progress from the 2011 administration to the last administration in 2015. An examination of the results of the 2019 National Assessment of Educational Progress (NAEP) results in mathematics shows that the average mathematics score for students in Texas was not statistically different from their average score in 2017. Only 30% of students in Texas performed at or above the NAEP proficient level as reported by the National Center for Education Statistics (2019).

There is concern that students are graduating from schools without the necessary mathematics knowledge needed to function well in our complex and ever-changing society (Maxey, 2013). The gaps from early grades only widen if not addressed at an early age (Provasnik et al., 2016). Educators have relied on best practices in teaching mathematics as well as emerging promising instructional methods to increase the mathematics achievement of students. Of these, project-based learning (PBL), problem-based learning (PrBL), phenomenon-based learning (PhBL), and blended learning (BL) are practices that are garnering attention in schools and the research literature. Each of these instructional methods is addressed separately for ease of presentation for their individual PDSA cycle.

PBL and PrBL are both inquiry types of instructional methods; however, they are not the same. These terms are sometimes used interchangeably, but there are clear distinctions in the methodologies. The foundational concept behind PBL and PrBL is to develop students who can manage their own learning (Odell & Pedersen, 2020). Students learn by designing, applying, and problem-solving while collaborating with other students and presenting their ideas and findings. PhBL shares similarities with both PBL and PrBL; however, PhBL extends learning to a global context through both topical and thematic instruction while focusing on real-world issues or phenomena (Drew, 2020; Finnish National Board of Education, 2016; Prakash Naik, 2019).

In the past several decades, there has been much support for the use of PBL, PhBL, and PRBL in STEM classrooms. Today's educators face the challenge of preparing students for jobs yet to be created and problems yet to arise (Bybee & Fuchs, 2006; National Science Teachers Association, 2011). Inquiry methods such as these could possibly be a solution to this problem in that both methods focus on 21st-century skills in addition to the standard content.

BL can be defined as any time a student learns, at least in part, at a supervised brick-and-mortar location away from home and, at least in part, through online delivery with some element of student control over time, place, path, and/or pace (Staker, 2011). A newer approach, which falls under the BL umbrella, is personalized learning (PL). A consensus on the definition of PL is not reached in the literature, but most research points to some aspect of customization, student groupings, and flexibility of instruction (Berry, 2018). The implementation of PL practices in American schools has increased significantly over the past several years (Pane et al., 2015) however, the variances in implementation range drastically from organization to organization (Staker, 2012) resulting in little research on the effect PL has on mathematics achievement.

When PL models utilize online content delivery, typically used to customize the learning for the student at their functional level, PL is one way to implement blended learning. While PL can be thought of as an instructional approach that focuses on the individual needs of students, it has often been implemented in such ways that either focus solely on the academic achievement of students or the interests and social impacts on students. When PL classrooms are inclusive of students' interests and their personal needs and goals academically, such programs have the potential to increase student learning and engagement (Pane et al., 2017).

The National Council of Teachers of Mathematics (NCTM) promotes eight practices that are considered to be best practices in mathematics, which were summarized in the *Personalized Learning and Mathematics Teaching and Learning* publication:

> Establish mathematics goals to focus learning, implement tasks that promote reasoning and problem solving, use and connect mathematics representations, facilitate meaningful mathematics discourse, pose purposeful questions, build procedural fluency from conceptual understanding, support productive struggle in learning mathematics, and elicit and use evidence of student thinking. (Berry, 2018, para. 5)

When reviewing and implementing PL practices into the classroom, the NCTM encourages educators to ask questions around each of the eight practices and how they are addressed in the PL model (Berry, 2018).

Setting

The setting is an open-enrollment public charter school in Texas made up of three K–12 campuses. The charter was written as a funding mechanism to support a laboratory school for the university and it is modeled after the 2015 T-STEM Academy blueprint (Texas High School Project, 2015). The district implements PBL, PrBL, and BL as the primary methods of instruction, with occasional opportunities for PhBL scenarios. PBL has been identified as an instructional model used to improve the achievement of students in STEM classes (Odell et al., 2019). The district is considered a high-performing district in the state, earning an overall rating of "A" on the most recent accountability ratings (2019), a rating only given to 10% of districts. However, the district received a "B" rating in the domain related to student progress. In 2019, 22% of students in the district not only did not meet progress, in mathematics, reading, or both but also declined from one standard to the next (e.g., from Masters in 2018 to Meets in 2019 or Masters in 2018 to Approaches in 2019 and so on) on the state assessment.

Even though the district is currently considered high-performing, it has not always been the case. Three major improvement cycles in the area of mathematics have led to the current performance rating, one of which is still in progress to make even more progress. The remainder of this chapter focuses on three distinct problems of practice: the need for overall improvement in mathematics achievement, the need to close the gaps, and the need for individual student progress. Each problem of practice is addressed with specific components of the PDSA cycles.

PDSA Improvement Cycle 1

Prior to the opening of the laboratory school, little was done curriculum-wise in terms of foundational systems to align the curriculum, instruction, and assessment. Instead, teachers completed six full weeks of professional learning focused on the best practices of PBL, the main instructional approach of the laboratory school. PBL was the only method of instruction and the only foundational system in place. Teachers created their own PBL opportunities with resources they found. Standards were taught in any order teachers deemed instructionally appropriate. There were minimal checks and balances for monitoring that all standards were taught. Practice assessments were not given prior to the state assessments. At the time, the belief was that teachers could plan the projects without a mandated scope and sequence in place and without any standardized assessments to test for mastery other than authentic assessment products such as PBL presentations or other products.

The theory in the early years was that students could be successful without testing and that projects could drive learning even if they were designed without a sequence of standards in mind. One of the goals was to provide teachers the flexibility to collaborate and integrate content from different disciplines. A standardized scope and sequence would minimize opportunities for collaboration and interdisciplinary projects. Projects were fun and engaging for students, and teachers were quoted as saying, "It was the most fun year I've had in my career." However, projects at this time could be described more as interest projects, and on reflection, they were not tightly aligned to standards.

Mathematics is tested each year in Texas starting in Grade 3. There is also a high school end-of-course exam in algebra required for graduation. As one might imagine, the academic results on state assessments in Year 1 were not only poor but also landed the charter in the bottom 5% of the state.

The problem of practice for PDSA Cycle 1 was clear: the need for overall improvement in mathematics achievement according to state assessment results. Academic achievement is Domain 1 of the state accountability system. Once the results came back and were analyzed internally, we realized that our students were well below the state average in every grade level in mathematics. Even worse, students who had transferred to us with test scores from the prior year had dramatically declined. The proposed intervention by the NIC was a better curriculum alignment to the state standards and the state assessments. Planning and implementing aligned instruction can be difficult when using inquiry instructional strategies.

The first improvement science cycle spanned over a period of two years. It's important to note that this is longer than a typical improvement cycle. However, it's technically made up of two major change ideas, each one needing its own time and space to be planned, studied, implemented, and tweaked. We believed it was necessary to start with one change idea that would eventually roll into a larger one to make one overall PDSA cycle rather than focusing on both right away. This was done intentionally considering how much needed to be done but trying to avoid overwhelming the teachers in the process that could ultimately lead to setbacks instead of gains. At this point in the school's development, structures from the college of education and the laboratory schools were not closely aligned.

The primary drivers of the low test scores in mathematics were the lack of a scope and sequence, the lack of assessments, standards not being tightly aligned to PBL opportunities, and overall alignment of curriculum, instruction, and assessment. Along with identifying the problem and root causes, users (teachers described in the case studies reviewed in this chapter) needed to be engaged in instructional decisions made thereafter. With the data in mathematics being drastically lower than the state average, overall systems had to be put into place for Year 2. Teachers were consulted and came together to make a plan for Year 2. The intervention would be simple: alignment of curriculum, instruction, and assessment; however, our question was, What would that need to entail since nothing was in place? The co-founding faculty members of the laboratory schools and school leadership developed an advisory structure to better support the school. This advisory structure would eventually become the foundation for the NIC that exists presently.

Change ideas were identified by a team of stakeholders which resulted in a scope and sequences for each grade level, revision of PBLs to align the standards, creation of standards-based classroom assessments, the use of a district PBL coach, and PBL content rubrics based on standards.

First, a team of teachers created scope and sequences and then revised PBLs from Year 1 as a team to tightly align them to standards. This same team of teachers created posttests for the PBLs (remember, no tests were given in Year 1). Second, a coach was identified who would travel to each of the three campuses to support mathematics for all schools districtwide to observe teachers, give feedback to teachers, co-teach lessons, and lead professional learning communities (PLCs) in the afternoons, embedded into the workday. Finally, content rubrics for each PBL lesson based solely on the standards included in the PBL were implemented. Thus, PBLs were now directly aligned to standards.

The changes were studied over the course of the year, with many revisions to the PBL model based on new scope and sequences, instruction of the PBLs based on feedback from observations, and different versions of the content rubrics to adequately assess student knowledge through PBL products. By the end of Year 2, the laboratory schools gained 11 percentage points in the area of mathematics on the state assessment. We knew we were on the right track after analyzing the data because we saw improvements, but we knew more improvements were needed. Even though the district had seen gains in mathematics, scores were still below the state average, which told us our focus still needed to be aligning instruction with state standards to state assessments.

Year 2 of PDSA Cycle 1 continued to focus on the primary intervention of alignment, but as the year progressed, additional drivers were identified through the PDSA process, such as the need for teachers to receive timely and relevant feedback directly tied to the content. In response to the primary driver, a mathematics content coach was hired for the district with the main responsibility of supporting teachers by writing model PBL lessons with and for teachers, coaching mathematics-specific strategies in the classroom, and modeling mathematics instruction for teachers while giving feedback and helping pull resources. Two extra interventions in Year 3 included the addition of district benchmark tests aligned to the state assessments and the purchase of a mathematics textbook (the first district-adopted resource in mathematics).

By the end of the third year of the school (the second year of PDSA Cycle 1), the laboratory schools again saw improvements in overall performance in mathematics increasing by 36 percentage points.

For the first time, the district mathematics score had exceeded the state average.

The main takeaway from the early years is that there is an incredible need for alignment among curriculum, instruction, and assessment. This may seem obvious, but keep in mind there were not readily available PBL curricula available for implementation. PBL and PrBL inquiry-based lessons are primarily developed and implemented by teachers to this day. To refine the model, in the context of PBL instruction, it is necessary to provide

1. a written scope and sequence and mathematics resources for teachers,
2. instructional feedback that is aligned to the curriculum, and
3. formative assessments based on the curriculum and state requirements.

Table 9.1 provides annual data by PDSA cycle. It should be noted that the trend in scores has been increasing annually and through each PDSA cycle. State averages have remained flat over time.

Table 9.1. Mathematics Achievement by Intervention Cycle

		PDSA Cycle 1			PDSA Cycle 2			PDSA Cycle 3	
	2013	2014	2015	2016	2017	2018	2019	2020	2021
State	79	78	81	76	79	81	81	82	N/A
District	48	59	95*	83	86	88	88	91	N/A

Note: PDSA = Plan–Do–Study–Act.
*New Texas Essential Knowledge (TEKS) requirements were implemented and tested this year. Fewer TEKS were tested, and scores of special education students were not included.

PDSA Improvement Cycle 2

At the conclusion of Cycle 1, mathematics scores were trending in a positive direction. Cycle 2 is characterized by the NIC and school personnel focusing on a related but finer grained problem of practice.

The identified aim for Cycle 2 was focused on equity in mathematics achievement and the improvement of mathematics achievement for all students. The problem of practice focused on closing the achievement gaps, Domain 3 of the state accountability system, among groups of students from diverse racial, socioeconomic, linguistic, and ability backgrounds. The proposed interventions included the following:

- Intervention 1: Data Tracking
- Intervention 2: PrBL and Mathematics Best Practices

Once improvements had been achieved in overall student performance, a new challenge became increasing equity and thus ensuring success among students of all demographic backgrounds. Clearly, gains had been made in mathematics achievement overall, but the state assessment data revealed significant achievement gaps by subgroups when compared to the overall score. For example, data for the end of Year 3 showed there was a 10 percentage point gap or higher when comparing the progress that Hispanic students made from the year before to the overall students and, in some cases, a 20 percentage point gap when comparing African American students to overall. In this second PDSA iteration cycle, two interventions were implemented simultaneously. This improvement cycle, which centered on closing the gaps, required a 4-year span with numerous adjustments to complete.

The first intervention was grounded in assessments and data tracking. As previously described, district benchmarks were implemented at the end of Cycle 1. However, data at that point were simply being tracked by overall student performance (percentage of students at each grade level who was having success on the state exams). During Cycle 2, a plan was made to track data by subgroups to measure the gaps by demographics. Stakeholders agreed that there needed to be a common system for tracking these data, and thus, a primary driver became district spreadsheets. For the first two years in this cycle, spreadsheets were used to track benchmark data and compare it to the state assessment data. It is important to note that these data were held at the leadership level. Occasionally, teachers were asked to review their data with the instructional content coach, but this was not a practice often utilized.

During this two-year span, some gaps were starting to narrow but not significantly. Based on the "study" component of the PDSA plan, a revision was required. The plan needed to be revised to keep narrowing the gaps. The district that started almost six years ago looking at no data at all had come to the realization that it didn't have enough data or a robust system to manage data.

A second driver was the introduction of common district assessments, which would be administered at the end of each nine weeks. These assessments were developed by the director of curriculum in conjunction with the mathematics instructional coach. The assessments would be modeled on the state assessments but would include more open-ended questions to assess deeper understanding. The purpose behind these types of assessments was to increase the rigor of the instruction in the classroom.

In her President's Message for the NCTM, Linda Gojak shared, "Rigorous teaching and learning require rigorous formative assessment throughout a unit so the teacher knows what the student has learned and can plan additional activities, or adjust them, to address student needs" (2013, para. 7). By increasing the rigor of assessments at the end of each quarter, teachers would need to increase the rigor in the classroom for students to be successful. The data at this point had variation by classrooms; while some classrooms were proving to close gaps more quickly, others were not having the same success. One major observation, and takeaway, was that the classrooms experiencing greater rates of change in their data were classrooms in which the level of instruction was higher in rigor and teachers were paying close attention to their data.

As a result, a final primary driver addressed under this category was more frequent data meetings and teacher empowerment. Teachers were now asked to keep their own data spreadsheets, which would include their classroom assessments, common district assessments, benchmarks, and state assessment data. Data meetings were called once per quarter, during which members of the curriculum team would work with teachers to help them analyze their data while paying attention to their subgroups. Bryk et al. (2015) describe one of the main principles of improvement science thus: "We cannot improve at scale what we cannot measure" (p. 87).

The second intervention during this cycle was a significant change to the mathematics instructional model and curriculum. Even though there were improvements to the overall mathematics scores, when examining the equity gaps related to progress and keeping the observational data in mind mentioned before, stakeholders attributed some of the gaps to the rigor and variances in mathematics instruction.

Two major drivers under this intervention were (1) mathematics instruction switched from PBL to PrBL, due to better alignment with mathematics inquiry, and (2) a larger range of mathematics resources were implemented to create a more well-rounded mathematics classroom.

After three years of PBL in the mathematics classrooms, district personnel recognized that mathematics was always an afterthought when it came to the planning of the PBLs. All PBL lessons up to that point had been interdisciplinary, and on analysis, mathematics was rarely the driving discipline for the PBL.

Many elements of best practices in mathematics were missing from the curriculum and from instruction in general. With inquiry-based learning still being the foundational model of the charter, the switch to PrBL was made. Problems were introduced at the beginning of units and used to drive the learning of the standards throughout. PrBL also doesn't take as long to implement as PBL; therefore, opportunities emerged for supporting best practices in mathematics to be included in the classrooms. Supporting instructional practices were included in the mathematics instructional model, such as spiral reviews and skills and drills practice, while other best practices, like mathematics discussions and questioning, were left in place. New resources were acquired, and teachers were provided intensive professional development on how to use each one in relation to each best practice. It is important to note that the role of the content coach in the organization of materials and the

176   *Improvement Science*

training of teachers was instrumental in these interventions, leading to eventual success in closing the gaps.

By the end of Improvement Cycle 2, the laboratory school saw the gaps narrow for subgroups as seen in the state assessment data for Domain 3, closing the gaps. The gap for Hispanic students when compared to all students, was narrowed to two percentage points, and the gap for African American students narrowed to seven percentage points in terms of students progressing. Even though both interventions were done simultaneously, each year, there were adjustments to the existing drivers and/or additional drivers added. The data used to inform these decisions were based on studying the intervention through observations and testing data both in-house and at the state level, as well as feedback from the users (teachers).

Table 9.2 provides data from 2013 to 2019 in terms of student progress as determined by the state. Student progress is measured from year to year with predetermined growth rates. The table is also broken down by demographic group to see how the gaps were closed in student progress from 2013 to 2019.

Table 9.2. Plan–Do–Study–Act Cycle 2 Student Progress

Student Demo-graphics	Students With Limited Growth From Prior Year 2013	Students With Limited Growth From Prior Year 2019	Students Meeting Expected Growth From Prior Year 2013	Students Meeting Expected Growth From Prior Year 2019	Students Showing Accelerat-ed Growth From Prior Year 2013	Students Showing Accelerat-ed Growth From Prior Year 2019
All Students	62	35	5	38	2	15
Hispanic	83	38	6	36	0	14
Asian	20	0	0	31	20	31
African American	83	49	0	29	0	14

Table 9.3 depicts the change in mathematical student progress by diverse demographic backgrounds from 2013 to 2019. The students' progress by subgroups grew at close to the same rate over the course of the seven years, and the change in the percentage of students making accelerated progress was almost the same for each subgroup. This table, however, is a preview of Improvement Cycle

3, which will be centered on student progress alone. As the data in Table 9.3 show, there is much need for improvement in overall student progress for students of all backgrounds.

Table 9.3. Plan–Do–Study–Act Cycle 2 Change in Student Progress from 2013 to 2019

Student Demographics	Students With Limited Growth From Prior Year	Students Meeting Expected Growth From Prior Year	Students Showing Accelerated Growth From Prior Year
All Students	-27	33	13
Hispanic	-45	30	14
Asian	-20	31	11
African American	-34	29	14

A comparison chart of the academic achievement in math of students from diverse demographic backgrounds from the end of Year 1 to the most recent accountability data is presented in Figure 9.2.

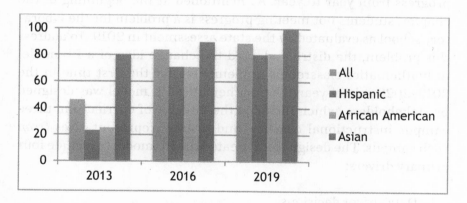

Figure 9.2. PDSA Cycle 2 Academic Achievement by Race and Ethnicity

Figure 9.2 also displays the end of the first year of Cycle 2 (2016) to the end of Cycle 2 (2019). It is important to consider how these data relate to data from the state. While the district began with a 21-point gap from all students to the lowest subpopulation, it narrowed this gap to 13 points in 2016 (which is the current average gap size in the state according to 2019 data reports) and closed it even tighter to an eight-point gap by the end of 2019.

PDSA Improvement Cycle 3

The latest iteration of the annual PDSA cycle resulted in the identification of a new problem of practice. It should be noted that the NIC and the Laboratory Schools have the goal of continuous improvement. Work from PDSA Cycles 1 and 2 is still underway, and refinements and adjustments are being made as needed to maintain and increase positive results. Cycle 1 focused on achievement for all students, while Cycle 2 focused on closing the gaps between groups of students. Cycle 3 is focused on improving individual student progress, Domain 2 of the state accountability system. The intervention is the implementation of PL.

As noted, the third and current improvement science cycle focuses on the problem of practice for individual students making progress from year to year. As mentioned at the beginning of the chapter, students not meeting progress is a problem for the laboratory school as evaluated by the state assessment in 2019. To address this problem, the district adopted the change idea of a PL model in mathematics classrooms implemented for the first time in the 2019–2020 school year. The mathematics PL model was designed by stakeholders, which included the director of curriculum, three campus instructional coaches, and teacher representatives from each campus. The design team created the PL model to include four primary drivers:

1. Data-driver decisions
2. Student reflection
3. Targeted instruction
4. Integrated technology

Stakeholders theorize that if students are provided a PL model in mathematics designed to meet students on their functional level and address their individual mathematics needs, then they will achieve academic growth from one grade level to the next and ultimately meet progress on the state assessment.

To support this intervention, an instructional coach is present on each campus to support the teachers to implement PL, a new instructional approach. Each teacher was placed at least on Tier 2 in terms of support level for Year 1.

It is important to note that due to COVID-19, there has been a disruption for a full year of implementation of the PL model. There are also limited data available since 2020 state assessments were canceled. The laboratory schools, like many other schools, were forced to implement remote learning in the spring of 2020. However, students and teachers were able to seamlessly transition from face-to-face BL to fully remote learning, which can be credited to the limited initial experience with the PL model.

The software programs and learning management systems were already in place to support students remotely. Students and teachers already had enough experience with the platforms to transition completely to an online environment. The district is currently in the process of evaluating the program. The following is a brief description of the data being collected and the theory behind the PL model.

The theory is based on three guiding principles:

1. Students met on their functional level will fill gaps more quickly.
2. Teachers making data-driven decisions (in short data cycles) to inform their instruction will help each student progress.
3. Students taking ownership in their own learning leads to academic growth.

A mixed-methods research design was identified as the best way to evaluate the mathematics PL program. Quantitative data will include functional-level scores of each student from the IXL database (chosen software), common district assessments, district benchmarks, and state assessment data. Qualitative data will include teacher surveys and observations, as well as two types of teacher forms: data-driven instruction (DDI) forms and meaningful learning experiences (MLE) forms done in PLCs.

All quantitative data will be stored in the teachers' data spread-sheets and collected throughout the year. Teachers are responsible for inputting the data into the spreadsheets, and the teacher and campus instructional coach will meet twice quarterly to review the data. IXL functional levels are placed in the spreadsheets as soon as the diagnostic is completed within the first few weeks of the school year. IXL is a personalized software program that calculates the students' functional levels. A student's functional level can be different from the student's actual grade level. For example, a student can be in the fifth grade, third month of the school year, which is denoted as 530. For the student to be considered on grade level, the student's functional level score would need to match. A higher functional level would indicate the student is above grade level, and a lower functional level indicates that the student is below grade level. The IXL functional level is updated at the beginning of each quarter for the remainder of the year and tracked to monitor student progression. Common district assessments are given at the end of each quarter and are based on the standards taught within that quarter. Teachers place the scores in the spreadsheets at the end of each quarter. District benchmarks are given twice a year, once in November and again in March. Scores from each benchmark will be placed in the spreadsheets after they are gathered. In addition, data from the state assessment will be collected to assess the long-term goals for the program once the scores are released.

Qualitative data will be collected throughout the school year as well. Teacher surveys will be administered three times during the year. Each of the surveys will contain identical questions and for-matting. The surveys will include closed- and open-ended questions related to the use of student goal setting and student data tracking. The surveys will also include questions related to the affective factors impacting how teachers structure support and empowerment in PL with relation to the success of their students. Teacher observations will be conducted throughout the year by campus instructional coaches and will be reviewed with the director of curriculum.

Coaches use a standardized district-created PL observation form. The purpose of the observations is to collect data on the use of stations, the implementation of the PL model, the self-directedness and engagement of students, flexible groupings of students, teachers helping students set goals, and students tracking their data. Observations will be done on a biweekly basis throughout the year.

Teachers will complete two separate forms throughout the year as elements of the overall design of the program. The first form is a DDI form, which is designed to help teachers shorten their data cycles by having them reflect on student data weekly. The DDI forms ask teachers to discuss a specific set of data from the past week of their choosing, reflect on insights from the data, make an action plan based on the data, and discuss the expected student outcome. Teachers will complete one form every week during the school year, beginning in September. The campus instructional coaches and the director of curriculum review the forms weekly. Teachers in PLCs complete the MLE forms monthly. This form is designed to help teachers reflect on the PL model in their own classrooms as well as share ideas about any of the four components of the PL model with one another. The campus instructional coaches and the director of curriculum review the forms monthly.

Conclusion

The UA laboratory schools have institutionalized improvement science principles and tools as part of their structure and operations. The NIC that helps guide the work of the laboratory schools leverages resources and expertise of the College of Education and Psychology, the School of Education, and its related research centers focused on STEM education and school improvement.

The iterative improvement cycles as described in this chapter provide evidence that implementing improvement science principles and tools to develop a learning culture can lead to continuous improvement and closing achievement gaps among historically underserved populations as measured by state assessments in the area of mathematics. As a laboratory school, our charge from day one was to be a model school for our surrounding districts and eventually a larger region. Closing the gaps was imperative for us in order to prove that our model works for all students, not just a select few. Our focus on continuous improvement using principles of improvement science has resulted in the district moving from one of the lowest achieving districts to of one the top-achieving districts in a relatively short period.

Discussion Questions

1. A focus for improvement is often identified by the central office or principal. As a teacher, how could you use the improvement science tools and processes discussed used here to increase math achievement in your class or school?
2. What problem of practice do you have in your class or school related to math, and what data would you propose be collected as a part of your improvement process?
3. What lessons can be gleaned from this experience regarding NICs and the sustainability of improvement efforts?

References

Berry, R. Q. (2018). *Personalized learning and mathematics teaching and learning.* National Council of Teachers of Mathematics. https://www.nctm.org/News-and-Calendar/Messages-from-the-President/Archive/Robert-Q_-Berry-III/Personalized-Learning-and-Mathematics-Teaching-and-Learning/

Bryk, A. S., Gomez, L. M., Grunow, A., & LeMahieu, P. G. (2015). *Learning to improve: How America's schools can get better at getting better.* Harvard Education Press.

Bybee, R. W., & Fuchs, B. (2006). Preparing the 21st century workforce: A new reform in science and technology education. *Journal of Research in Science Teaching, 43*(4), 349–352. http://onlinelibrary.wiley.com/doi/10.1002/tea.20147/epdf.

Desilver, D. (2017, February 15). *U.S. academic achievement lags that of many other countries.* Pew Research Center. https://www.pewresearch.org/fact-tank/2017/02/15/u-s-students-internationally-math-science/

Drew, C. (2020, March 3). What is Finland's phenomenon-based learning approach? *Teacher.* https://www.teachermagazine.com/au_en/articles/what-is-finlands-phenomenon-based-learning-approach

Finnish National Board of Education. (2016). *New national core curriculum for basic education: Focus on school culture and integrative approach.* https://www.oph. fi/sites/default/files/documents/new-national-core-curriculum-for-basic-education.pdf

Gojak, L. M. (2013, February 5). *What's all this talk about rigor?* National Council of Teachers of Mathematics. https://www.nctm.org/News-and-Calendar/Messages-from-the-President/Archive/Linda-M_-Gojak/What_s-All-This-Talk-about-Rigor_/

Maxey, K. S. (2013). *Differentiated instruction: Effects on primary students' mathematics achievement* (Publication No. 3573708) [Doctoral dissertation, Northcentral University]. ProQuest Dissertations Publishing.

National Center for Education Statistics. (2019). *Nation's report card: 2019 NAEP Mathematics Assessment.* National Center for Education Statistics, Institute of Education Sciences, U.S. Department of Education. https://www.nationsreport card.gov/highlights/mathematics/2019/g12/

National Science Teachers Association. (2011). *Quality science education and 21st century skills.* http://www.nsta.org/about/positions/21stcentury.aspx.

Odell, M. R. L., Kennedy, T. J., & Stocks, E. (2019). The impact of PBL as a STEM school reform model. *Interdisciplinary Journal of Problem-Based Learning, 13*(2).

Odell, M. R. L., & Pedersen, J. L. (2020). Project and problem-based teaching and learning. In B. Akpan & T. J. Kennedy (Eds.), *Science education in theory and practice* (pp. 343–357). Springer International Publishing. https://link.springer. com/chapter/10.1007/978-3-030-43620-9_23

Organisation for Economic Co-operation and Development. (2019). *PISA 2018 results (volume I): What students know and can do.* https://doi.org/10.1787/5f07c754-en

Pane, J. F., Steiner, E. D., Baird, M. D., & Hamilton, L. S. (2015) *Continued progress: Promising evidence on personalized learning.* RAND Corporation. https://doi. org/10.7249/RR1365

Pane, J. F., Steiner, E. D., Baird, M. D., & Hamilton, L. S. (2017). *How does personalized learning affect student achievement?* RAND Corporation. https://doi. org/10.7249/RB9994

Prakash Naik, Rajani. (2019). *Phenomenon-based learning in Finland* [Master's thesis]. University of Jyväskylä, Jyväskylä, Finland. https://jyx.jyu.fi/handle/ 123456789/64611

Provasnik, S., Malley, L., Stephens, M., Landeros, K., Perkins, R., & Tang, J. H. (2016). *Highlights from TIMSS and TIMSS advanced 2015: Mathematics and science achievement of U.S. students in grades 4 and 8 and in advanced courses at the end of high school in an international context.* U.S. Department of Education, National Center for Education Statistics. https://nces.ed.gov/pubsearch/pubsinfo .asp?pubid=2017002

Staker, H. (2011). *The rise of K–12 blended learning: Profiles of emerging models.* Innosight Institute. https://www.christenseninstitute.org/wp-content/uploads/ 2013/04/The-rise-of-K-12-blended-learning.emerging-models.pdf

Staker, H., & Horn, M. B. (2012). *Classifying K-12 blended learning*. Innosight
    Institute. https://www.christenseninstitute.org/wp-content/uploads/2013/04/
    Classifying-K-12-blended-learning.pdf
Texas High School Project. (2015). *Texas science technology engineering and mathe-
    matics academies design blueprint, rubric, and glossary*. Texas Education Agency.
    https://www.texasccrsm.org/sites/default/files/1_-_2015_Blueprint_Final.pdf

CHAPTER TEN

Access Versus Ability: Advanced Mathematics for Every Child

ANNE LARKIN AND COREY JENKS

A cademic tracking models are systems of oppression used to create and perpetuate perceived academic gaps (Kendi, 2016) among students of color, multilanguage learners, and students who are economically under-resourced when compared to their White, English-speaking, privileged peers. As Berliner (2006) said,

> if the educational opportunities available to White students in our public schools were made available to all our students, the United States would have been the 7th highest scoring nation in mathematics, 2nd highest scoring nation in reading, and the 4th highest scoring nation in science. (p. 963)

Gifted and Talented (GT) programming, as an example, is designed for economically resourced White children, while intervention programming models are designed to exclude non-White students from accessing grade-level instruction, maintaining their status as "below grade level" (Capper, 2019). Our school systems have fallen into a dangerous cycle of accelerating the advantaged and remediating those who are under-resourced.

Since the rise of standardized testing from the No Child Left Behind Act, students are categorized by proficiency bands. Standardized test scores are commonly used in identification processes for tracking systems such as Advanced Placement (AP), special education, English as a Second Language, and intervention groups. Intervention models have the potential to restrict access to rigorous instruction for some students while AP courses increase access to rigorous instruction for others. Many identification processes are based on a prioritization of White, Western school-readiness skills and knowledge. As early as kindergarten, students are predetermined to have "high aptitudes" and begin receiving "services" that boost and bolster the content areas in which they are already demonstrating strengths. In contrast, students who come to school without the White, Western skills are predetermined to be "behind" or in need of additional support. This can be seen in the disproportionate referrals for students of color to Multi-Tiered Systems of Support (MTSS) beginning, again, as early as kindergarten. The work of Shifrer et al. (2011) suggests that groups of students who are referred for services already have social disadvantages. These students are not a part of the dominant White culture, thus, the validity and reliability of the process for identifying learning disabled and placement in special education functions as a tool for discrimination (Shifrer et al., 2011, p. 246). As noted by Mansfield (2105),

> this tracking procedure became a type of property in that those from certain family stocks were destined to be segregated in "special" classes, which would ensure that the owners of the "low" label would receive less resources in terms of quality curriculum as well as earning potential as adults. Meanwhile, those owning the gifted label received special treatment that would "groom" them for important positions in society, resulting in an accumulation of material wealth that was just not possible for those not owning the gifted label. (p. 127)

Kendi (2016) equates standardized tests to racist weapons used to exclude Black students and defines a racist policy as "any measure that produces or sustains racial inequity between racial groups" (p. 18). Furthermore, Capper (2019) applies critical race theory tenets that present the U.S. education system as White property that continuously exercises the right to exclude. Pollack and Zirkel (2013) describe how those who are White defend the entire AP system and elaborate that special education identification reinforces this system. When daily teacher planning processes begin with standardized test data and classroom placement, a child's access to rigorous instruction has already been predetermined within a racist and oppressive system.

Developing lessons while relying on systemic tracking programs will continue producing inequitable outcomes. It must be an urgent priority to dismantle tracking systems to ensure that every child in the United States has frequent and repeated access to the highest level of instruction. The purpose of this improvement science study was to analyze the effects of an advanced-mathematics-for-all model to repair the harm produced by the GT, AP, and Honors tracking systems.

Background to the Study

The site for this study was an urban public elementary school located in a highly affluent, predominantly and historically White neighborhood in Denver, Colorado. With a population of roughly 460 students, the school consisted of a traditional K–5 program, a Deaf and Hard of Hearing Program, and a Highly Gifted and Talented (H/GT) magnet program. Due to an increase in neighborhood enrollment, in 2017, the school began to phase out the H/GT program. With an intent to ease the phase-out of the H/GT program, the school adopted a district-supported advanced math model for high-performing and/or GT-identified students. Through various data points and measures, students qualified for this advanced math program after their kindergarten year.

The H/GT classrooms at this school site mirrored the demographics of the current state and national data in relation to students who are over- or underrepresented in identification. In the largest urban school district in Colorado, Latinx students make up 52% of the total population and only 31% of students who are identified as GT. Black students make up 13% of the total population and only 5% of students identified as GT. Finally, White students make up 26% of the total population and represent 53% of students identified as GT (see Table 10.1). The under-identification of students of color in H/GT has and continues to be a systemic inequity in our educational system. Many schools, including the one in this design improvement (DI) project, utilize instructional models that are self-contained and prohibit other students from accessing accelerated content and advanced instruction.

Table 10.1. School Site Data for 2019–2020

Total School Population	GT-Identified Student	SPED-Identified Students
463 total students	97 total students	37 total students
• 5% Black	• 0% Black	• 24% Black
• 8% Latinx	• 7% Latinx	• 32% Latinx
• 3% Asian	• 7% Asian	• 5% Asian
• 8% Two or more races	• 8% Two or more races	• 3% Two or more races
• 76% White	• 77% White	• 35% White

Note: This is the school-level data that mirrors the district-level data that indicates systemic-level identification issues leading to inequitable access. GT = Gifted and Talented; SPED = special education.

At this school, a large majority of White kindergarteners qualified for the advanced math class beginning in first grade, while all other students were denied access to this rigorous instruction. In the spring of 2018, the DI team spoke to the first-grade teachers and began noticing a level of awareness raised around the inequitable experience for the nonqualifying students. Furthermore, the team began to question the process by which students were being referred for enrichment services leading to recommendations for the advanced math classes. The students in the advanced math class were achieving at high levels, and by second grade, many of them were formally identified as GT or H/GT. We knew that buried under the surface of the referrals was a system of inequity that was perpetuated by our own instructional models.

In May 2018, the DI team met with the first-grade team and GT teacher to review advanced math qualification data. The GT teacher presented the test scores from the end-of-year kindergarten assessment and the end-of-year first-grade assessment. We then compared these data with our standardized math assessment system iReady (Curriculum Associates, 2019). Figure 10.1 presents the student scores.

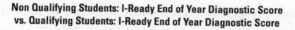

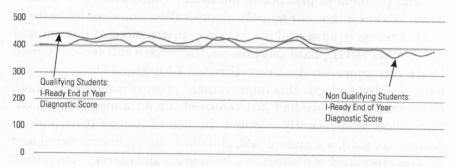

Note. Students who did not qualify based on GT teacher's recommendation scored similarly if not better than the qualifying students on I-Ready.

Figure 10.1. Qualifying vs. Non-Qualifying Student I-Ready Scores

The GT teacher placed each kindergarten student in a performance group with one group being recommended for the advanced class. All the students they had worked with in pullout groups throughout the year were recommended, in addition to a few others who had high proficiency on the end-of-year assessments. After considering the conversations with the first-grade teachers about the inequitable experiences and after seeing the data by which students were being placed into tracked classes, the principal made the decision that the first-grade advanced math class would be dissolved for the 2019–2020 school year, and there would be three evenly distributed classes who would all receive advanced math instruction.

Knowing the challenges and unanswered questions that lay ahead with the new implementation of advanced math for all first graders, the principal, principal intern, and a teacher leader launched an improvement science project with the hope of understanding the inequitable roots supporting the previous system and to discover the path forward to ensure success for every child.

Improvement Science Strategies

Aim Measures

To launch our project, the team came together to identify the over-arching problem of practice in addition to determining aim measures. We knew that our school's identification practices led to inequitable access to advanced mathematics instruction. At this point in the school's H/GT phase-out process, there were still self-contained H/GT classrooms in the third- through fifth-grade classes, so our team decided to focus this improvement process on the first-grade classrooms where we had just removed the advanced math class. The school had recently adopted the use of iReady (Curriculum Associates, n.d.), a standardized, standards-based instructional and progress monitoring platform for both math and literacy. Therefore, our aim measure looked to increase the percentage of first graders meeting grade-level benchmarks from our beginning of the year report of 51% to 80% by June 2020. We knew that we needed to better understand the user experience within the advanced math model to help us clarify the problem and develop change ideas so we created a driver diagram (see Figure 10.2).

From this initial draft, we narrowed in on two essential questions. The first question we needed to consider was, "How might we ensure that our students who struggle with math are able to access advanced math content?"

The first primary driver focused on instructional coaching via a unique equity-based framework called Reparative Teaching. For the purposes of this project, it is important to understand the development and framework of Reparative Teaching and how it related to the implementation of the work. Developed by Anne Larkin and Corey Jenks, Reparative Teaching is a framework that utilizes an accelerated approach to instruction rather than a remedial approach to getting students caught up (Larkin & Jenks, n.d.). Reparative Teaching, a form of educational reparations, was created to redefine equitable access to instruction by developing an instructional model that utilizes strategic skill and knowledge-based leverages for

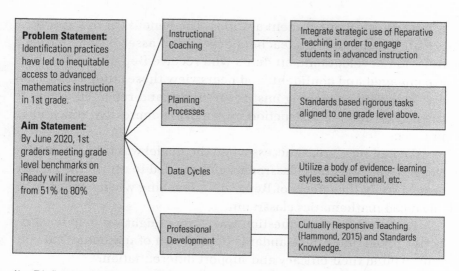

Note. This diagram explains the structures that the school intended to use in order to meet the Aim statement goal.

Figure 10.2. Driver Diagram

students *prior* to their whole group or first-time instruction. After applying critical race theory to analyze current school systems, the developers evaluated how systems of oppression have built barriers to students of color, multilanguage learners, and students who are under-resourced. In turn, the developers have created systemic reparations for these students.

Traditionally, within data and planning structures, teachers determine students who need a reteach based on concepts they missed during whole-group and first-time instruction. In addition, these same students are often referred to intervention groups, which lead to restricted access to core grade-level instruction and focus on remedial, foundational skills. Through this new lens of Reparative Teaching, teachers are no longer spending data meetings asking, "Who didn't get it, and who needs a reteach?" Teachers are now discussing "who might benefit from a preteach that targets specific skills so that they can access this lesson **at the same rate or faster than their peers**." This not only shifts experiences and outcomes for students, but it also shifts teachers' mindsets (Claro et al., 2016) when talking about student abilities. The benefits of this approach are all-encompassing: Teachers develop an asset-based approach to lesson development, students who receive Reparative Teaching are engaged and confident, and peers view these students as leaders. Reparative teaching ensures frequent and repeated access to the highest level of instruction by removing oppressive educational practices.

We had seen great success when the model was implemented in the general education classrooms and decided to utilize the DI process to study the effects of Reparative Teaching when applied to an advanced mathematics classroom.

The next essential question was, "How might we help teachers better understand the standards progression of mathematical content to build their efficacy and support differentiation?"

To answer this question, we needed to begin the discovery phase of our DI project.

Discovery

The team began the discovery phase of the project by collecting empathy interview data from students, teachers, and families. Our goal was to understand not only the experiences of the students in the advanced math class but also those of students in traditional classes. We also wanted to understand the teacher's perspectives on the implementation of this model in addition to their own efficacy in teaching mathematics and challenging students with standards above their grade level. Finally, we wanted to better understand what families prioritized in their students' learning experiences with math and what their hopes were for their children in developing mathematical identities. We conducted all empathy interviews one-on-one, in person, using a note-taking format. The teacher leader met with seven total teachers representing every grade level from kindergarten to Grade 5 and multiple programs (traditional and H/GT). There were 15 students interviewed ranging from Grades 1 to 5 and, again, representing experiences in the traditional classrooms, advanced math classes, and in the self-contained H/GT classes. The team also met with four families to conduct the interviews, capturing notes for their responses (see Table 10.2).

Table 10.2. Empathy Interview Questionnaire

Empathy Interview Questions	
Students	How do you feel about math? What do you like? What do you not like? Have you ever wanted to go to the advanced class for math? What do you wish was different about math?
Parents	What do you hope for your students as mathematicians? How do you want them to get there? What role should the school play in developing mathematicians?
Teachers	What are your thoughts on the current model for teaching mathematics? What would you change? Are there students who would benefit from this model (compacting/accelerating) who do not yet? How would you rate your comfort in teaching math? What about advanced math or above standards math?

Note: To ensure consistency, one interviewer completed all interviews.

Empathy Interview Findings

After conducting the interviews, the team collaboratively analyzed the student, teacher, and family responses. We looked for common themes in student responses and compared student perspectives of those in the advanced or H/GT math class and those in the traditional class.

When asked about going to another class for math, some students expressed that they wished they could go to the advanced math class while others felt content where they were:

I actually have wanted to go, but the only time I've been to someone else's class is when I went to the [first-grade H/GT] class for second-grade math. I think other kids leave because maybe they're smarter. The [second-grade H/GT teacher] teaches third grade so the people who go there are really, really smart [and] get to go. Sometimes I actually think I should go, I do want to, sometimes I think I should because I know times and divided. My friend asked if I knew times tables, and I said, "Of course not, I'm not in that class so I wouldn't know." But if I was, I would have learned them probably. (Second Grader)

Some students assumed their peers were leaving to go to a different class because they were smarter than the others or because their parents had signed them up for these classes:

> I did not get to go with [GT Teacher] for math. I guess it feels fine.
> I think they go because I think their parents signed them up to go
> with [her]. I wish I could go. I think they do math problems and
> numbers. (First Grader)

There were students who expressed a strong interest in math; these same students were typically the ones interested in being more challenged. Some students who expressed that math was difficult for them did not have any interest in leaving to be more challenged. Some even expressed that they wished they were in an easier class that went slower.

When looking at the teacher responses, the team followed the same process of looking for common themes or trends articulated through repeated words and phrases. The teacher empathy interviews demonstrated that our H/GT and advanced math teachers all had high efficacy and interest in teaching math. Many of these teachers had their own experience as advanced mathematicians and felt confident in their abilities to challenge students and push them to their full mathematical potential. The teachers interviewed who taught in the traditional classes expressed lower efficacy and felt that they were challenged to meet the needs of all the students in their classes based on behavior management challenges and a wide range of mathematical skills.

Finally, in looking at the family empathy interviews, the team looked for where families were feeling confident and supported by the current model and what families were hoping to see change or improve. The family empathy interview responses indicated that several families hoped for their student to be performing above-grade-level standards in mathematics before leaving elementary so that they would be better prepared to succeed in middle school.

The next component to our discovery phase was to investigate the identification process to qualify students to the advanced math class in both kindergarten and first grade. For this, the principal intern met with the school's GT teacher who is responsible for all testing, data collection, monitoring, and development of advanced learning plans. This process investigation utilized an open-ended interview approach with note-taking and clarification questions. The process outlined by the GT teacher for identifying students for the advanced math classes is displayed in Figure 10.3.

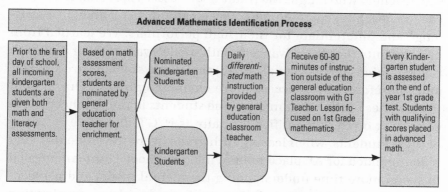

Note. The identification process uncovered that students were nominated for math enrichment *prior* to their first day of school. Students who had exposure to mathematics before kindergarten received GT instruction which furthered their access to advanced mathematics while all other students were restricted access to content that they would be assessed on at the end of the year for advanced math placement.

Figure 10.3. Kindergarten Advanced Mathematics Identification Process

The final component of the discovery phase was to analyze local data and current research related to inequitable identification processes. Our team investigated the processes the feeder middle school utilized for placement into the AP mathematics track and examined current research on the inequities in identification practices specifically for H/GT, AP, and Honors programs in the United States.

The team took away some key understandings from the discovery phase of the project. From a user perspective, the advanced math model seemed to be based on adult needs and behaviors rather than students' needs. The system of identification of students for the advanced math class began with adult perspectives of students' aptitudes before their first day of kindergarten. It was then perpetuated by giving these students regular access to accelerated math content and was finalized at the end of the year through a data analysis process, whereby students were categorized into "ability groups" for first-grade math. Furthermore, teachers who taught the advanced math or H/GT classes demonstrated higher efficacy in their ability to teach these students based on their background in mathematics instruction and ability to teach to groups at similar skill levels. The teachers who taught the traditional classes expressed lower efficacy in teaching mathematics, specifically in their ability to challenge and differentiate for their high performers. We learned from our students that the advanced math model was creating a mathematical mindset (Claro et al., 2016) that some students are smarter and, therefore, get to access more challenging math. Our system perpetuates itself in that many of the students in the advanced math class went on to be identified formally as H/GT, and more so, many of these students, when leaving fifth grade, were the students being recommended for AP placement in middle school. Our team needed to spend more time understanding the mental model and perspectives of the adults in our building and to analyze how our planning and professional development systems were related to our problem of practice.

Interpretation/Ideation

The team utilized several tools to begin the process of maintaining our user-centered approach while analyzing what we were learning about our problem of practice (see Figure 10.4).

The team created the affinity diagram by writing sticky notes with the key takeaways from the discovery phase. The team then organized the sticky notes into groups based on similarities or common themes and, finally, titled each category. The four main themes from the notes were mindset and beliefs, opportunity and access within systemic inequities, biases within data and testing, and maintaining identity. The team used the four themes from the affinity diagram and completed a fishbone diagramming process (see Figure 10.5).

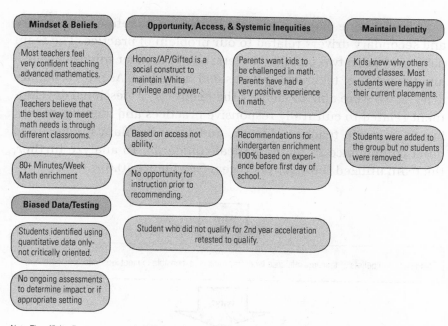

Note. The affinity diagram was completed during a collaborative meeting and sticky notes were used to develop themes.

Figure 10.4. Affinity Diagram

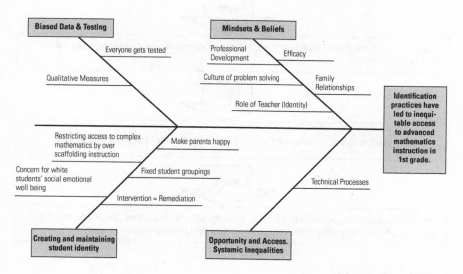

Figure 10.5. Fishbone Diagram

The fishbone diagram process allowed us to refine our primary and secondary drivers related to our problem of practice. The team narrowed in on two primary drivers: one of teacher mindset/beliefs and the other of technical systems and behaviors. As our secondary drivers, we were able to identify the needs for professional development related to culturally responsive practices and identity, coaching to increase teacher efficacy, and planning/data processes to build competence in mathematical standards. To analyze further, the team utilized the 5 Whys process (see Figure 10.6).

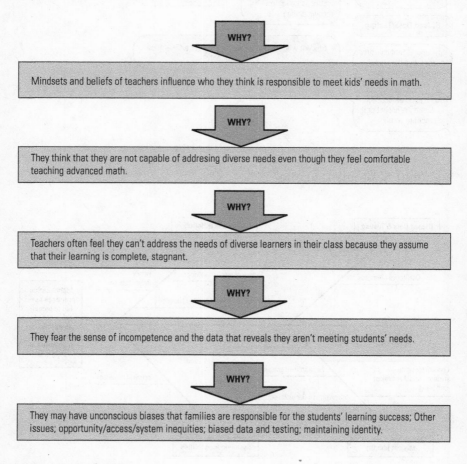

Figure 10.6. 5 Whys

Through the use of these tools, the engagement in conversation, and the analysis of data, our team had to make a difficult decision. We asked ourselves: Do we focus on the adaptive primary driver of beliefs and mindsets first and then hope the behaviors follow? Or do we focus on the technical second primary driver and disrupt the current system, change the behaviors, and allow the space for mindsets and beliefs to follow as a result of seeing the growth of students and teachers? The team ultimately decided the system needed to be addressed and changed. The team drafted the theory of action and then began brainstorming various change ideas to address the secondary drivers (see Figure 10.7)

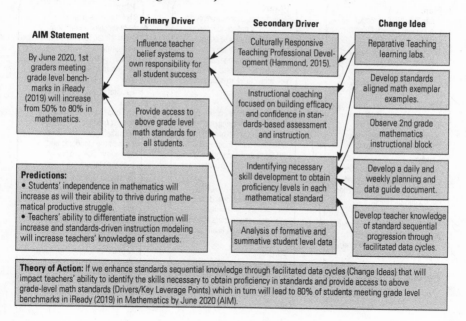

Figure 10.7. Theory of Improvement Diagram

Experimentation

Between September and December, the team completed Plan–Do–Study–Act (PDSA) cycles, specifically focusing on planning and data processes including daily planning, weekly planning, and facilitated data cycles. We began with the weekly facilitated planning and data protocol and asked for feedback from teachers about what they needed and what might change to develop instruction to 1 year above-grade-level standards. We went through three iterations of the planning and data protocol in response to feedback from the first-grade teachers in addition to classroom observations of math lessons and a review of student data (see Figure 10.8).

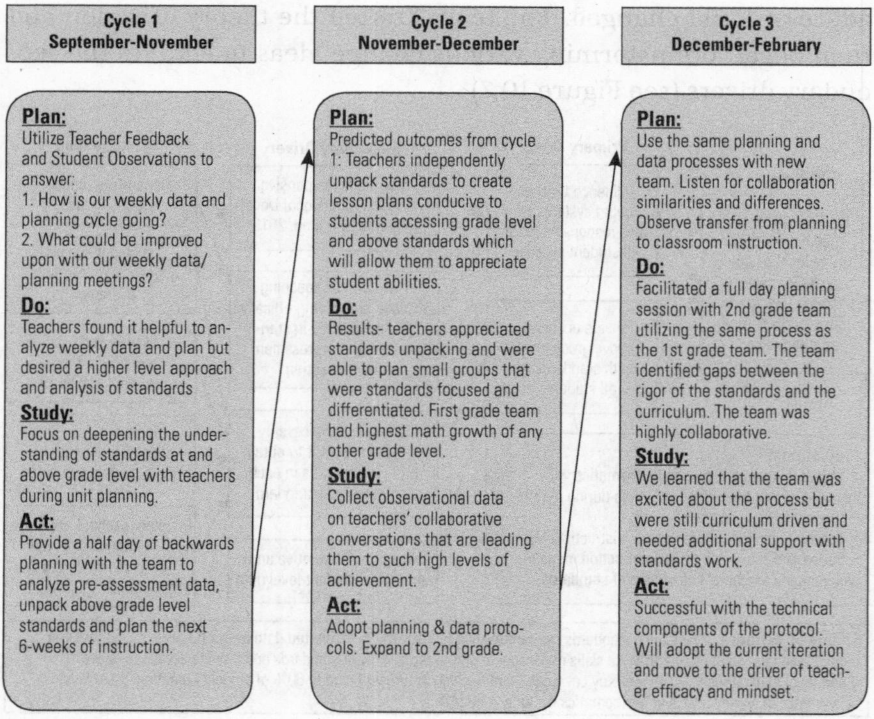

Cycle 1 September-November	Cycle 2 November-December	Cycle 3 December-February
Plan: Utilize Teacher Feedback and Student Observations to answer: 1. How is our weekly data and planning cycle going? 2. What could be improved upon with our weekly data/planning meetings? **Do:** Teachers found it helpful to analyze weekly data and plan but desired a higher level approach and analysis of standards **Study:** Focus on deepening the understanding of standards at and above grade level with teachers during unit planning. **Act:** Provide a half day of backwards planning with the team to analyze pre-assessment data, unpack above grade level standards and plan the next 6-weeks of instruction.	**Plan:** Predicted outcomes from cycle 1: Teachers independently unpack standards to create lesson plans conducive to students accessing grade level and above standards which will allow them to appreciate student abilities. **Do:** Results- teachers appreciated standards unpacking and were able to plan small groups that were standards focused and differentiated. First grade team had highest math growth of any other grade level. **Study:** Collect observational data on teachers' collaborative conversations that are leading them to such high levels of achievement. **Act:** Adopt planning & data protocols. Expand to 2nd grade.	**Plan:** Use the same planning and data processes with new team. Listen for collaboration similarities and differences. Observe transfer from planning to classroom instruction. **Do:** Facilitated a full day planning session with 2nd grade team utilizing the same process as the 1st grade team. The team identified gaps between the rigor of the standards and the curriculum. The team was highly collaborative. **Study:** We learned that the team was excited about the process but were still curriculum driven and needed additional support with standards work. **Act:** Successful with the technical components of the protocol. Will adopt the current iteration and move to the driver of teacher efficacy and mindset.

Figure 10.8. PDSA Cycles

Evolution and Results

In March 2020, our DI process was suspended due to COVID-19. Remote instruction began in April, and the first-grade teachers continued to provide access to advanced mathematics for every student.

We were unable to assess students at the end of the year; however, the midyear assessment data allowed us to interpret the impact of this model. The student outcome data collected indicated that the implementation of Reparative Teaching and strategic backward planning in an advanced math setting had a significant positive impact on student achievement. At midyear, 63% of first-grade students were on or above grade level, and 76% were on track to make yearly growth while 70% were on track to make stretch growth (the growth recommended to put below-grade-level students on a path to proficiency and on-grade-level students on a path to advanced proficiency levels) according to i-Ready. In addition, the first-grade students had the highest math growth scores in the school. While the outcome data were significant, the outcomes for individual students and the themes uncovered in teacher practice were more significant. Three of the students who were identified by the GT teacher as "too low" to be able to take the AP test were outperforming the peers who had qualified to be placed in the advanced math track by midyear. If we hadn't dismantled this system, these children wouldn't have had the ability to learn alongside their peers and accelerate their growth.

After implementing the advanced math for all model utilizing the strategic, standards-based backward planning protocol combined with Reparative Teaching, teachers described changes that occurred within their instructional practice. First, the teachers developed strong content knowledge of mathematical standards and the skills needed to master the standards. This increased their self-efficacy with being able to precisely differentiate instruction at advanced levels. Prior to this study, teachers developed lessons based on the curriculum pacing guides, which were not rigorous enough to engage students. This study shifted their planning and instructional processes to be fully aligned to standards, more specifically grade-level standards 1 to 2 years above first grade. Understanding the progression of learning allowed the teachers to adjust instruction in the moment based on a child's development of skills. Second, they began to utilize multiple factors, not just numerical data, to determine differentiated grouping structures. This was a result of their standards and skills knowledge development. They were able to determine a child's strengths and areas of growth at the skill level within a standard in which, prior to the study, students were grouped solely based on summative, numerical test scores. Finally, teachers recognized the constraints that the previous tracking model had put on their ability to teach. By granting themselves permission to break out of traditional lesson progressions and curriculum, they were able to accelerate growth for all students. Most important, teachers acknowledged that trusting relationships were the most important factor that resulted in great success. Teachers believed that all students could achieve at standards above grade level and the students trusted their teachers' beliefs in their abilities.

Equity Challenge

Although we saw tremendous success with the implementation of this DI project and the advanced math for all model, it is important that we tell the story surrounding the project regarding the process of dismantling inequitable systems within a community of power and privilege. The DI process was thorough and backed by research and data. One might think that this model would create excitement within the community because we had developed a model that positively impacted all students and all data exhibited that students were growing and thriving at the school. What we learned most through this process was that leading for equity is incredibly difficult. Our DI work was met with fierce resistance by the GT families, more than 90% of whom identified as White. Had we anticipated this resistance, we might have been able to plan for what happened next.

As we walked down the hallway to present our findings of this study to the school accountability committee, we were surprised to hear a buzz of conversation coming from the meeting room. Typically, these meetings consisted of the principal, the principal intern, three teachers, four parents, and one community member; occasionally, a few additional parents might attend depending on the topic. The topic of this specific meeting was to review the school's midyear data, present the positive outcomes from our study, and review the staffing and budget model that needed to be submitted the following week. We were well prepared and excited to share the results of our outstanding school growth, more specifically, the growth from the new advanced math for all model that we implemented in our first-grade classrooms. As we entered the room, everyone became silent. We were surprised to see that every seat was occupied and several parents were standing in the back of the room. A sinking feeling began to settle in our stomachs because we knew that the audience was not there to hear about our equitable instructional model but instead to fiercely oppose our path forward. After all, we developed this model to intentionally dismantle systems of inequity, which meant we were effectively chipping away at their power and privilege.

The audience at this meeting was packed with White parents, aggressively demanding to have the tracking model restored. It was their expectation that the school segregate their children into an advanced classroom in which only the elite could participate. We presented all our data findings and disaggregated the data by GT and non-GT to explain that even when the isolated advanced model was no longer implemented, GT students were maintaining the highest levels of growth and achievement. Our recommendation was to maintain the current budget and staffing model to continue to sustain the growth we had created over the last 2 years. The meeting lasted 3 hours and was the most intense and contentious meeting we had ever encountered. Every fact that we presented was met with debate while our expertise was questioned, even belittled, by White men who had no experience in the field of education. The meeting adjourned without a finalized budget. Ultimately, the families and community members refused to approve the budget unless the advanced math self-contained model was reinstated and allocated additional budget and staffing solely dedicated to identified students:

> Privilege confers a sense of entitlement in which those who have
> power are often unwilling to support changes that increase equity
> but that they perceive to increase their competition. This plays
> out in numerous ways, including a resistance to ending academic

programs that enhance the opportunities of the privileged or to providing additional resources for those who need it. Consider, for example, the outcry when resources for gifted programs are being decreased. (Shields, 2018, p. 55)

The DI team left the school at the end of the 2020 school year to expand Reparative Teaching to new school campuses and districts. It is our understanding that this model is still contested by the community, and multiple meetings have occurred in an attempt to reinstate the self-contained gifted classroom model, a model that historically included primarily White students.

Conclusion

The findings in this study concluded that when the DI team dismantled the tracking system, student growth scores exceeded the growth of all other grade levels. More important, dismantling the tracking system while implementing Reparative Teaching changed the way in which teachers differentiated instruction and led to a shift in their mindset while also increasing student self-efficacy. Providing access to all students and utilizing the Reparative Teaching method was beneficial to all stakeholders in the process. Future research should analyze the effects of Reparative Teaching in other settings, the challenges principals face when dismantling tracking systems, and how the Reparative Teaching model benefits students' social-emotional health.

Discussion Questions

1. When working to end systems of oppression, what could leaders and teachers do before beginning the improvement effort to address potential obstacles, hurdles, or roadblocks?
2. How did the teachers' individual and collective efforts contribute to the success of this improvement effort?

3. In what ways did the empathy interviews create strong evidence for improvement efforts?
4. Given your school and your context, what contextual considerations would you include if you were to engage in such an improvement effort?

References

Berliner, D. (2006). Our impoverished view of educational research. *Teachers College Record, 108*(6), 949–995. https://doi.org/10.1111/j.1467-9620.2006.00682.x

Capper, C. A. (2019). *Organizational theory for equity and diversity: leading integrated, socially just education.* Routledge.

Claro, S., Paunesku, D., & Dweck, C. (2016). Growth mindset tempers the effects of poverty on academic achievement. *Proceedings of the National Academy of Sciences, 113*(31), 8664–8668. https://doi.org/10.1007/s11256-012-0231-4

Curriculum Associates. (n.d.). *i-Ready.* https://www.curriculumassociates.com/products/i-ready

Kendi, I. X. (2016, October 20). Why the academic achievement gap is a racist idea. *Black Perspectives.* https://www.aaihs.org/why-the-academic-achievement-gap-is-a-racist-idea/

Larkin, A., & Jenks, C. (n.d.) [Resources for equity-based framework for accelerated instruction.] Reparative Teaching. http://www.reparativeteaching.com/

Mansfield, K. C. (2015). Giftedness as property: Troubling whiteness, wealth, and gifted education in the US. *International Journal of Multicultural Education, 17*(1), 121–142. http://dx.doi.org/10.18251/ijme.v17i1.841

Pollack, T. M., & Zirkel, S. (2013). Negotiating the contested terrain of equity-focused change efforts in schools: Critical race theory as a leadership framework for creating more equitable schools. *The Urban Review, 45*(3), 290–310. https://doi.org/10.1007/s11256-012-0231-4

Shields, C. M. (2018). *Transformative leadership in education: Equitable and socially just change in an uncertain and complex world.* Routledge.

Shifrer, D., Muller C., & Callahan, R. (2011). Disproportionality and learning disabilities: Parsing apart race, socioeconomic status, and language. *Journal of Learning Disabilities, 44*(3), 246–257. https://journals.sagepub.com/doi/10.1177/0022219410374236

Increasing Fourth-Grade Math Achievement for Historically Underserved Populations Utilizing Targeted Intervention Groups

DR. HOLLY ALTIERO

Background

Pacific Public School District (PPSD) is one of the largest school districts in Oregon and includes more than 50,000 students. The demographics in each school vary extremely based on both location and income bracket. PPSD is easily divided into geographic quadrants; Eagle Elementary School (EES) resides in the northwest quadrant and is the focus school of this research. The schools in the northeast and southeast quadrants tend to have higher numbers of historically underserved (HU) students as well as higher numbers of students receiving free and reduced-price lunch services. Additionally, the school district allocates budgets based on enrollment size and not based on need, so schools with low enrollment but high needs are often denied funding for counselors, mental health, educational assistants (EAs), or secretaries. This school has historically served some of the wealthiest families in the city, but as of the 2018–2019 school year, EES enrollment boundaries were changed to include three large transitional housing complexes assisting historically homeless families. Many of the children who were transitioning from homelessness struggled immensely in classes both academically and behaviorally, and the school was severely under-staffed. For the 2019–2020 school year, school counselors were cut from two to one, all kindergarten EAs were cut, and the school secretary was reduced to a morning half-time schedule. These reductions created an extreme equity issue for students with significant behavioral needs transitioning in, as well as significant access issues for parents who needed secretarial help in the afternoon and who could not come to ask questions before school. The reductions also proved to be a significant safety concern as there were not enough leaders in the building able to respond to crisis situations.

Since 2011, PPSD projected to both staff and community members that they operate through a racial equity and social justice lens. More recently, in 2018, policies were updated to include specific mission and vision language for these policies; specific goals for closing achievement and opportunity gaps for students of color and HU students were written. In reviewing these policies and the language in the mission and vision statements, and after considering achievement data, I chose to use improvement science to focus on the racial and economic disparities in math achievement at the fourth-grade level.

The following were the members of the improvement science team:

- Vice principal: oversees student responses and discipline as well as coordinates some of the professional development (PD)
- Principal: is the school leader and mentor, instrumental to the creation of this Improvement Science Project
- Trauma-informed coach: newly hired due to increase in behaviors that have accompanied the influx of previously homeless students who transitioned to EES during the 2019–2020 school year
- Union advisor/librarian: has historically helped lead efforts in the district around equity
- Special education (SPED) teacher/case manager: knowledgeable about student interventions in general, as well as interventions specific to students receiving specialized instruction
- Fourth-grade teachers: chosen level of focus for intervention

Equity Audit

To gather information regarding math achievement and student demographics specific to the EES site, I chose to utilize several sections of the Frattura and Capper (2007) Equity Audit for its extensive categories involving and related to opportunity and access for HU populations. Specifically, this template encompassed sections about achievement data disaggregated by demographics including race and socioeconomic indicators. I completed more than three sections of this specific audit just to get a good sense of potential disparities at EES. Based on the equity audit results, I discovered that 100% of the Black students in fourth grade who took the Smarter Balanced Assessment Consortium (SBAC) test in spring of 2019 had cumulative math scores at Level 1, 2, or 3 (the lowest quadrants), with no Black students ranking in the Level 4 quadrant (the highest quadrant) (Smarter Balanced Assessment Consortium, 2020). Similarly, Latinx students had 75% of their cumulative math scores rank within Levels 1 to 3, and only 25% ranked at Level 4. The educational disparities are significant, as 35% of White students scored at Level 4, and 80% percent of Asian students scored at Level 4. Although these data are based on only one achievement test, the Measures of Academic Progress (MAP) testing data for EES seemed to corroborate that students identifying as Black, Latinx, multiracial, and low-income and those receiving SPED services were all achieving at significantly lower rates than their White peers during the 2018–2019 school year.

In addition to the achievement disparities, the school itself had experienced a visible and disturbing act of racism in the fall of 2019, when a noose was found in the building. White power symbols began to be graffitied on the playground. "White lives matter" signs were hung around the neighborhood. A large group of understandably upset parents created social media pages both in support of and outraged at these acts of explicit racism against the Black population at EES. At a school where students of color had historically been underserved in a variety of ways, addressing the math academic disparity seemed a valuable use of the Improvement Science Team's time and of my time. The data from the equity audit can be seen in Table 11.1.

Table 11.1. Smarter Balanced Achievement Data—Fourth Grade 2018–2019 School Year

Score Ranges	Level 1: <2,411	Level 2: 2,411–2,484	Level 3: 2,485–2,548	Level 4: >2,548
Cumulative	Level 1: 23%	Level 2: 13%	Level 3: 31%	Level 4: 33%
Gender				
Female	Level 1: 25%	Level 2: 30%	Level 3: 29%	Level 4: 18%
Male	Level 1: 24%	Level 2: 24%	Level 3: 28%	Level 4: 23%
Nonbinary	Level 1: 22%	Level 2: 33%	Level 3: 22%	Level 4: 22%
Ethnicity				
Multiple	Level 1: 28%	Level 2: 15%	Level 3: 29%	Level 4: 29%
White	Level 1: 19%	Level 2: 9%	Level 3: 38%	Level 4: 35%
Latinx	Level 1: 50%	Level 2: 17%	Level 3: 8%	Level 4: 25%
Black	Level 1: 0%	Level 2: 50%	Level 3: 50%	Level 4: 0%
Asian	Level 1: 0%	Level 2: 0%	Level 3: 20%	Level 4: 80%
Special Populations				
FRPL	Level 1: 42%	Level 2: 19%	Level 3: 25%	Level 4: 14%
SPED	Level 1: 51%	Level 2: 7%	Level 3: 25%	Level 4: 17%
TAG	Level 1: 0%	Level 2: 0%	Level 3: 9%	Level 4: 91%
ELD	Level 1: 24%	Level 2: 12%	Level 3: 31%	Level 4: 34

Note: Data have been modified to increase anonymity. FRPL = free and reduced-price lunch; SPED = special education; TAG = Talented and Gifted; ELD = English Language Development.

When I shared the information gleaned from the equity audit with the Improvement Science Team, they agreed that there needed to be a closer look at this data in order to break it down more specifically by accessing the school MAP data for fourth grade. MAP assessments occur three times each year, so those assessments were ideal to utilize for the improvement science project in terms of both implementing an intervention and then assessing the effectiveness. In examining MAP data with the improvement science team, it was clear that roughly 40% of fourth-grade students were not meeting standards on MAP in math during the 2018–2019 school year. Of this 40%, a majority were students of color, students living in low-income homes, and students qualifying for SPED. These data compelled the team to create a set of questions for the purpose of conducting empathy interviews to gather additional qualitative data to support the need for and to formulate an intervention.

Empathy Interviews

In an effort to gain a deeper understanding of the issues at hand, the improvement science team conducted several empathy interviews with teachers and other school staff. Empathy interviews are interviews conducted with stakeholders that help bring personal anecdotes and stories to the table to help structure an intervention that has meaning for the community (Carlile & Peterson, 2019). In the case of this improvement effort, the improvement science team interviewed several teachers of color and several EAs who worked in a variety of classrooms and, thus, saw a variety of teaching styles. Before conducting the empathy interviews, the improvement science team created the following list of questions to structure the interviews, although questions were subject to change or expansion depending on interviewee responses and storylines:

1. Describe your thoughts on our school's overall climate. Why do you feel that way?
2. What do you feel may be contributing to our students of color achieving at lower rates in math and reading on the SBAC exams? Why?
3. What supports do you feel are in place to help decrease achievement gaps for our students of color? How could we improve them?
4. What do you feel we are doing well as a school to help our students of color achieve academically? To help our students receiving special education achieve academically?
5. How do you feel our school addresses academic disparities in student achievement?
6. When have you noticed teachers or interventions that work well for our struggling students? What do you feel made them successful?

In reviewing the empathy interview data, it was clear that the individuals interviewed felt that students of color did not feel safe at school due to both new and ongoing incidents of racism. Additionally, there were pervasive themes: that teachers, the majority of whom were White, did not know how to relate to students of color, that they were often less inclined to reach out to families of students of color, and that there were frequent incidents of microaggressions on campus. The interviewees all expressed that some teachers did a great job of differentiating learning so that all students received targeted interventions and that other teachers were not particularly skilled at this. A lack of consistency in teaching strategies and interventions was another key emerging theme that seemed important to address further.

Supporting Literature

A variety of literature is available on both the topics of math achievement gaps and HU populations, as well as targeted math interventions in the elementary grades. In particular, a literature review composed by Same et al. (2018) was conducted at the request of the Midwest Achievement Gap Research Alliance in an attempt to inform potential policy and policy stakeholders of effective interventions being utilized nationally in public schools for marginalized populations. The improvement focus we sought to address was "What interventions have been shown to be associated with improved academic achievement of Black students according to evidence tiers 1 (strong evidence), II (moderate evidence), and III (promising evidence) from the Every Student Succeeds Act?" Results from this literature review indicated that successful interventions targeting marginalized populations included allocating funding toward specialist positions to focus on creating interventions that were effective and sustainable, cultivating student–teacher relationships centered on trust and equity, utilizing highly qualified teachers and staff members to work with students during interventions, and increasing parental involvement (Same et al., 2018). Additionally, research provided by Yates and Collins (2006) that focused specifically on how elementary schools could increase math achievement scores indicated that a primary need was on analyzing and reanalyzing data to measure whereby math interventions were successful and efforts needed to be focused. These studies, as well as others, helped us look at how the improvement science team could address the math achievement gap for our HU student groups, students from low-income families, and students receiving SPED services in accordance with best practice. The improvement science team's proposed intervention is detailed more in the following pages.

Theory of Improvement

The improvement science team focused on math achievement scores for fourth graders as measured by SBAC and MAP testing. To best understand the barriers to math achievement for our students we first constructed a fishbone diagram as can be seen in Figure 11.1.

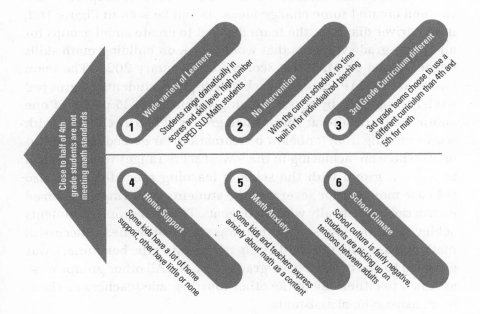

Note. Numbers in Figure 1 correspond to potential causalities contributing to the identified concern "close to half of 4th grade students are not meeting math standards".

Figure 11.1. Fishbone

Fishbone Diagram

Barriers identified by the improvement science team as impacting student success and math achievement were as follows: (1) a wide variety of skill levels, (2) no current math interventions, (3) variations in grade-level math curriculum, (4) varying levels of home support, (5) math anxiety, and (6) an overall negative school climate. Of these barriers, several stood out as ones that the improvement science team may be able to influence and measure to reduce math achievement gaps for students not meeting benchmarks on math MAP testing. The barrier the team chose to focus on first was the fact there were no active interventions in place for math that targeted students' skill levels and/or needs for improvement. The improvement science team brainstormed how to address that specific barrier and created some change ideas. As can be seen in Figure 11.2, in the driver diagram, the team decided to create small groups for all fourth-grade students that would work on building math skills needed based on MAP test scores from January 2020. The team looked at the MAP scores for each fourth-grade student and grouped students together by scores ranging within 10 to 15 points of one another. The result was seven small groups of 6 to 21 children, with scores ranging from far below benchmark to far exceeding. The students who were achieving in the lowest score ranges were assigned to a small group with the school's learning specialist, who also the case manager for several of the students requiring specialized instruction, specifically with math goals. The next group of students achieving in the low-score range was assigned to me, a successful math teacher, and the third group not meeting the benchmark was assigned to one of the fourth-grade teachers. All other groups were assigned to either one of the other fourth-grade teachers or classroom instructional assistants.

The goal of this small-group intervention as a change idea was to interrupt the learning pattern of little to no targeted interventions for students struggling the most with math achievement; this group was primarily composed of Black, Indigenous, and people of color (BIPOC) students, students from low-income homes, and/or students receiving SPED for learning disabilities. The small groups were to run for 4 weeks and would cover materials specific to lagging skills as assessed by the MAP assessments taken in January 2020, specifically focusing on partial product multiplication. During the initial intervention group, all students were to be given a 2-minute timed multiplication assessment and again at the conclusion of the fourth group. Data yielded from comparing these assessments were intended to help the team determine if additional modifications should be made to the intervention groups/method of group instruction to further increase learning. MAP assessments were to be administered again to students in May 2020, and scores were to be assessed for all students in Groups 1 through 3 to determine if a noticeable increase in achievement scores was present. Figure 11.2 is a visual representation of the driver diagram that led to the improvement science team's decision to focus on this particular intervention to address the issue identified.

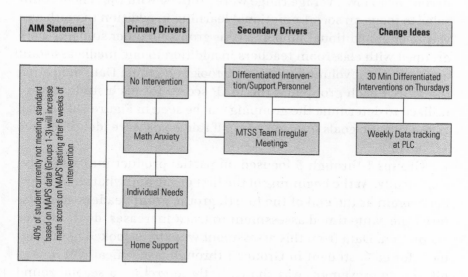

Figure 11.2. Driver Diagram

Testing the Change

The small group interventions described above ran for three weeks in February and March 2020 on Thursdays from 8:15 a.m. to 9:00 a.m. at EES. The final group was to take place in mid-March, but due to the COVID-19 school closures, this final group was not able to commence. Each small group had a specific goal and focused on specific skill sets of math identified as lagging per the MAP testing data. As previously mentioned, student MAP testing data from January 2020 was reviewed by the improvement science team, and students were put into seven small groups that corresponded to a 20-point range in scores. After students were grouped, they were assigned to small-group leaders based on the leaders' area of expertise. For example, all students identified as needing support for specific learning disabilities via specialized instruction with math goals were grouped with the SPED case manager. All students who scored in the low to low-average range were grouped with the school counselor to focus on social-emotional learning in addition to math as a way to offer additional support to this group. All other students were grouped with classroom teachers in addition to one media assistant and one parent volunteer who each took one group. Data indicating the size of each group and the MAP scores for each student were utilized to determine the grouping can be seen in Figure 11.2 as well as the specific goals for each group if said goals were identified (see Table 11.2).

Groups 1 through 3 focused on partial product multiplication specifically. At the beginning of the first group and what would have been again at the end of the fourth group, group leaders administered the same timed assessment to track increases, decreases, or stagnation. Data from this assessment were to be looked at individually for each student in Groups 1 through 3 specifically. If no significant improvement was shown in these groups, a second round of small groups was to begin on May 7, 2020, and run for 3 weeks with modifications in additional cycles of interventions determined by the team after analyzing the first cycle of data. The full outline of topics covered per group sessions follow:

Table 11.2. Fourth-Grade Pilot for Multi-Tiered Systems of Support Math Enrichment Group—Priority Standard

Staff Name	Tammy	Heather	Jane	Lynn	John	Georgia	Conner
MAP Score Range/ Special Considerations	SPED	Low 150–170	Low Average 170–190	Average 191–210	High 211–230	High 231–250	TAG Students
Goal by Student #	Individualized	For students to be able to use the partial product model with # less than 20 (with visual support)	For students to be able to use the partial product model with # less than 20 (with support)	For students to be able to use the partial product model	Compare and contrast a minimum of 2 models for multiplication	Compare and contrast a minimum of 2 models for multiplication	Individualized
Starting Score							
1	175	180	No Test	188	202	231	225
2	162	No Test	195	No Test	210	228	238
3	158	No Test	No Test	210	214	216	225
4	180	188	216	195	No Test	221	212
5	No Test	193	192	193	205	224	218
6	170	No Test	No Test	188	212	215	233
7	176		No Test	199	No Test		232
8	160		196	No Test	No Test		No Test
10			NS	216	212		
11			200	206	211		.
12			199	197	198		
13			188	206	213		
14			No Test	209	207		
15			191	209	209		
16			189	204	205		
17				206	217		
18					199		
19					No Test		
20					196		
21					219		

Note: Scores have been modified slightly for additional anonymity.
MAP = Measures of Academic Progress; SPED = special education;
TAG = Talented and Gifted.

- First Session: Team created preassessment; 2 minutes timed. Team-building activities, time spent discussing how we best learn math and what we feel we do well. Decorating math folders and some getting-to-know-you activities
- Second Session: Breaking down partial product for numbers under 10. Discussion of what we learned last week, what we can do if we don't understand how to set up a partial product
- Third Session: Breaking down partial product for numbers over 10. Using grid paper to set up partial product equations for numbers greater than 10. Teacher uses whiteboards to let each student practice setting up equations. Discuss that the timed test will happen again next week
- Fourth Session: The team created an assessment tool: postassessment—2 minutes timed. Discussing how we felt about doing the test for the second time, what felt easier/harder/the same, and why that might be. How do we feel about the group and about meeting together each week? Has that been helpful? Why or why not?

Implementing the Change

Data from this pilot intervention were to be shared with the rest of the MTSS team at monthly meetings before school closures ensued. If the intervention proved to be effective, the team planned to propose a schoolwide implementation of an "Intervention Hour" to first focus on schoolwide math achievement and comprehension and eventually move on to target additional academics. Creating a master schedule that would allow all teachers similar time in their day to conduct an intervention hour would be a crucial part of implementing this change schoolwide. Additional needs would include administrative and teacher buy-in. This would be particularly difficult given that culminating data for this intervention were not able to be collected due to school closures. The intervention team has discussed restarting the previously outlined intervention at the beginning of the next school year, although members of the Improvement Science team, including myself, will change. Although the leader of the original Improvement Science team may not be present for the continued implementation of interventions in future school years, the interventions are not difficult to replicate or build on. The key element will be communication from the leader to the rest of the team that the improvement effort was showing promise and that to continue building on the foundation of what was started will be critical to helping address the achievement disparities. Ensuring that all data are shared and that teams in PPSD continue to focus on targeted interventions that build on these shared data is essential, especially to maintain focused attention of HU and BIPOC demographics. This particular improvement effort was largely community-driven; keeping momentum for continuous, necessary improvement with an equity focus must continue to include the community. Improvement science urges small but powerful moves and the need for continued assessment and reassessment of the data to see what is working and what needs to be changed. In the years to come at EES, this need for continued data collection and analysis for change will show the students, community, and educators that improvement is not only possible but also probable no matter the attrition or other obstacles that may arise.

Discussion

In summary, the need to do better by our Black students has never been more apparent. Current events and the Black Lives Matter movement have garnered the rightful attention of both the news media and educators alike across the nation. We must do better. This equity-focused improvement project was directed at both addressing and minimizing the achievement gaps that exist among Black, other BIPOC students, those experiencing poverty and homelessness, and their more affluent and White peers in the elementary grades. These gaps pervade and persist throughout our HU students' K–12 educational careers, and the first way we can help combat that is by looking at the data, acknowledging that these enormous disparities exist, and finding ways to do better by our populations of students who need more support and advocacy. In the case of EES, the sudden change in racial and socioeconomic demographics within the school boundaries incited an increase not only in low SBAC and MAP test scores for students of color but also a stark increase in hate speech and racist attacks both overtly and covertly via overt acts of racism and microaggressions. The next steps for this project are to adapt the lessons learned in the PDSA cycles for this specific academic subject and this specific grade level and create a plan of action that could ideally be replicated across all grade levels if shown to be effective. It was truly disheartening to not be able to see this project to fruition due to the COVID-19 pandemic and unprecedented school closures in March 2020. What was more disheartening, however, was coming to understand and know a community of students and families felt targeted and marginalized repeatedly in an environment they were supposed to feel safe in and from adults they should have been able to trust.

Although the groups that were able to run were perceived by the group leaders as effective and helpful, these perception data are not tangible results that can be taken to school staff and utilized as evidence of an effective intervention strategy. However, the experience of each group leader is not without merit, and thus moving into the next school year, I suggest that the improvement science team create a presentation for the school staff that documents the journey of the improvement science project that was started and challenge the staff members to finish collectively by choosing to look at their own data and make their own efforts, however small, to improve the academic and social-emotional climate for the Black students at EES.

In closing, this project was a profound experience. It was a process by which I set out to use improvement science to impact educational disparities. I uncovered a deep-rooted fear and racial aggression within a community. It helped me see even more clearly how much racial oppression in education needs our attention, how we are utterly failing our BIPOC students, our students from low-income homes, our students with trauma, our students who don't fit into the White middle- to upper-class mold. I know that by engaging in improvement science processes, I am empowered and changed.

I will continue to lead improvement efforts to ensure every child in our schools succeeds and I will continue to encourage others to do that same.

Discussion Questions

1. What are all the types of data elementary school teachers and administrators could collect and analyze to assess racial disparities in your school?
2. How can elementary school leaders help decrease racial disparities in academic achievement?
3. When thinking about improvement science, what stands out to you about the concepts of opportunity and equitable access for all students?
4. Why might it be important to look regularly at data correlations regarding achievement and race?

References

Carlile, S. P., & Peterson, D. S. (2019). Improvement science in equity-based administrative practicum redesign. In R. Crowe, B. N. Hinnant-Crawford, & D. Spaulding (Eds.), *The educational leader's guide to improvement science: Data, design and cases for reflection* (pp. 197–216). Myers Education Press.

Frattura, E. M., & Capper, C. A. (2007). *Leading for social justice: Transforming schools for all learners.* Corwin.

Same, M. R., Guarino, N. I., Pardo, M., Benson, D., Fagan, K, & Lindsay, J. (2018). *Evidence-supported interventions associated with Black students' educational outcomes: Findings from a systematic review of the literature.* Regional Educational Laboratory at American Institutes for Research. https://files.eric.ed.gov/fulltext/ED581117.pdf

Smarter Balanced Assessment Consortium. (2020). *Our system.* http://www.smarterbalanced.org/assessments/

Yates, H. M., & Collins, V. K. (2006). How one school made the pieces fit. *National Staff Development Council, 27*(4), 30–35. https://peabody.vanderbilt.edu/docs/pdf/tl/Jackson_Wilson_2012_UrbanEd_Supporting_AA.pdf

CHAPTER TWELVE

Improving Math Growth Indicators for Elementary Students With Disabilities

SHANE BROWN

Background

Pacific Meadows Elementary School (PMES) is located within a rural district located 15 miles outside of a small town in the Pacific Northwest. PMES is unique in that it is not located in a city, town, or village. There is no post office, no store, and, except for the school itself, no community buildings of any kind. The school lies at the heart of the community and is surrounded on all sides by large farm fields. There are a few homes clustered a short distance from the school, but most students live on large farms. The PMES District is contained on one K–12 campus that serves 300 students, with an average of 25 students per grade level. Because there are not enough students in the district to offer the level of classes and services the residents want the school to offer, the district is allowed to accept students living outside the district's boundaries; about 40% of the school population is comprised of students living outside the district boundaries (Oregon Department of Education, n.d.).

Recent professional development at the school has focused heavily on social-emotional learning (SEL). Team members have attended conferences and training on the use of SEL instruction, and they have, in turn, shared what they have learned at various staff meetings. Team members have also received training on inclusive practices, specifically regarding LGBTQ+ students. The school has recently had two students transition from the gender they were assigned at birth. The school has adjusted expectations for bathroom use, eliminated classroom instructional strategies that only allowed for students to identify as male or female, and a number of other issues related to the experience of transgender students. Math instructional improvement has also been a topic of focus this year, albeit to a lesser degree than SEL.

Current initiatives at the school include increasing the amount of career and technical education (CTE) class offerings available to the students and increasing math achievement scores throughout all grade levels. As the team began allocating funds available to schools through the Student Success Act, we identified areas to address that included the disparity in math growth, increasing the number of instructional aides, increasing the level of SEL training for staff members, and monitoring the implementation on SEL instruction. The district also examined proposing a bond to upgrade the school facilities, including the construction and/or renovation of current building space to provide additional classroom space and areas for physical education and recess time.

Improvement Science Team

Our improvement science team included 10 team members: the team leader; the elementary principal, who also serves as our district superintendent; our district special education director; our special education instructor; our third-, fifth-, and sixth-grade teachers; and three instructional aides who work with students receiving special education services. Each member was invited to the team based on their daily interaction with the students we are targeting in our improvement project.

Need for Improvement

Equity Audit Data Collection

The greatest challenge to the equity audit process was the limited
number of students available to us due to the small, rural nature of
our school. We eventually settled on using a condensed version of
the Frattura and Capper (2007) Equity Audit. Our intention in con-
densing the audit was not to ignore various groups of students that
the audit invites one to examine. Rather, we needed to condense the
audit because the district simply did not have enough, and, in some
cases, any data on a number of the students described in the audit.
PMES is more than 95% White, and culturally and linguistically
diverse students compose less than 5% of our student population.
Two students receive English Language Learner (ELL) services in
the district, and they are performing at the same level as their classmates. As indicated, we have two transgender students at the school.
Despite the small number of students, we wanted to meet the needs
of all students and address any disparities in their equitable access to
a successful education experience at our school. For the purpose of
this improvement project, however, we sought to meet the needs of a
group that represented a larger sampling of our student population.
Disparities among genders did not indicate disparities between the
two groups in any of the categories we examined. Graduation rates,
growth levels in math and English language arts, and graduation
rates were all within 1 to 2 percentage points among diverse groups
of students. There is one area of concern in the Math Growth category, but for the most part, our equity audit did not identify significant equity disparities based on gender, race, ethnicity, or home language, although this information should certainly inform teacher
practices to address the disparities, however small.

However, two groups of students did emerge as being underserved: students with special education accommodations and those
from low-income households (see Table 12.1). The data for these
groups were obtained via the state department of education and our
school records.

Table 12.1. Achievement Data Economically Disadvantaged

Economically Disadvantaged		
	Free/Reduced-Price Lunch	All Students
Students receiving free/reduced-price lunches	92	300 Total Students
Regular attenders	85%	85%
On track to graduate	92%	97%
Level of math growth	Level 3 out of 5*	Level 5 out of 5*
Level of ELA growth	Level 4 out of 5*	Level 4 out of 5*
Ninth grade on-track graduation	89%	93%
Four-year graduation rate	91%	96%
Five-year completion rate	96%	99%

Note: Level 3 is at or above state average but not on track; Level 4 is on track to meet state target by 2025; Level 5 meets state target for 2025. Data have been slightly adjusted to protect identity. ELA = English language arts.

Students With Disabilities

The area of our equity audit of most concern for our team, and that led us to focus on the students represented, is in the category of Students with Disabilities. It should be noted that there are only a few students at the school who fall under this category, most of whom receive services for a learning disability, some of whom receive services for physical disabilities, and all of whom receive services outlined in their individualized education plans (IEPs; see Table 12.2).

The findings of this area of our audit were alarming to members of our team. As a school, math improvement had been an area of focus for the two previous years as we struggled to improve the number of students meeting the state standards. As a staff, we had taken pride in the fact that, although the number of students meeting the state standard had only displayed minimal improvement, the level of math growth indicated that we were doing what was necessary to reach that goal in the coming years. However, our students receiving special education services were failing to display growth at all, being rated at the lowest level. For this reason, our group chose this as the primary area of focus for this project. In addition, the number of students was large enough to collect meaningful data using the improvement science process.

Table 12.2. Achievement Data, Students With Disabilities

	Students With Disabilities	All Students
Students with disabilities	34	300 Total Students
Regular attenders	85%	87%
On track to graduate	Data Unavailable	95%
Level of math growth	Level 1	Level 5
Level of ELA growth	Level 2	Level 4
Ninth grade on-track	Not rated	92%
Four-year graduation	86%	97%
Five-year completion	88%	99%

Note: Level 1 is bottom 10% statewide; Level 2 is below state average; Level 3 is at or above state average but not on track; Level 4 is on track to meet state target by 2025; Level 5 meets state target for 2025. ELA = English language arts.

When discussing our goal to increase math growth, we realized we should not compare the achievement of students based on the Smarter Balanced Assessment Consortium (SBAC) standardized test. Focusing on that area would be futile, as our students with disabilities are usually one or more grade levels behind in their math comprehension and skills. Instead, we measured math growth based on the IEP math goals, measuring the performance of students from one year to the next. Students might still fall short of the state standard for their grade level but could still receive high marks regarding the growth they have displayed. Our team's initial thoughts regarding the root causes of the growth disparity in math were (1) inadequate or ineffective IEP accommodations or (2) inadequate time spent on math interventions for students on IEPs.

Empathy Interview Questions

Our team devised empathy interview questions tailored to those we wanted to interview: students, family members, and teachers. Student empathy interview questions included the following:

- Do you like math? Why or Why not?
- Tell me about your favorite math lesson. What made it so great?

- If 1 was *not confident at all*, and 5 was *completely confident*, what number would you use to rate your confidence in math?
- What do you do when you are working on math problems and you aren't sure how to complete them?
- If you could change one thing to make math class better, what would it be, and why?

Family members' empathy interview questions included the following:

- How would you rate your student's interest in math on a scale of 1 to 5, 1 being the lowest?
- What do you see with your student that leads to your rating them at that level?
- What do you think is your student's greatest challenge with math?
- On average, how much time per week do you spend on math at home?
- How confident are you in the math accommodations outlined in your student's IEP?
- If you could implement one thing in our school program to support math instruction, what would it be?

The empathy interview questions for the special education director, special education teacher, and general education teachers were as follows:

- What practices do you currently have in place to support special education math instruction in your classroom?
- What can the district do to better support your math instruction for our special education students?
- In your experience, how effective are the accommodations outlined in the students' IEPs at addressing math achievement?
- What are the biggest challenges you see in addressing math growth and achievement with our special education students?
- Are there any practices that you aware of that could support math instruction for our special education students that have worked at other schools/settings?

- Describe your comfort level with trying new techniques or routines related to math instruction in your classroom.

Empathy Data Narrative

Our empathy interviews revealed that about half the students like math and half do not. This perspective was an interesting contrast to the family members' rating of their student's interest in math. Parents were convinced that their child did not like math. The most significant takeaway was that all the students who claimed they enjoyed math pointed to engaging projects as the driving force for their enjoyment; they wanted more instruction like that, while those who claimed they disliked math said they needed fewer problems to work through. A second takeaway is that most of the students indicated they gave up on or skipped problems with which they struggled. Finally, several students were frustrated by having to leave their classmates for pullout services during math time.

Nearly every family member indicated that their students did not like math and that their student was frustrated because they did not understand the concepts being taught. Family members echoed the students by stating that students are frustrated with being pulled out from the general education classroom. Notable also is that family members overall routinely accepted the school's recommendation for IEP accommodations, but follow-up did not seem to be a priority. Cognitive ability and frustration with not understanding the material were also constant themes among the family members interviewed.

The most significant revelation from the teacher interviews was that none of the general education teachers could report on any special education practices they had recently heard of or on which they had received professional development. There seems to be a reliance on the special education staff to bring these practices to the teachers. The general education teachers focus on the general student populations, often excluding special education students. The cognitive ability of the students receiving IEP accommodations was identified as the greatest obstacle to math growth and achievement. Teachers also consistently pointed out that staffing was an issue when it came to providing optimum student supports. Many teachers also felt as though students were not taking full advantage of the accommodations laid out in their IEPs, although they did not recognize their own role in actualizing the accommodations.

Supporting Literature

Owen and Fuchs (2002) indicate that the students who received a full method instruction in the classroom, as well as ample opportunities to transfer their knowledge to problem-based tasks, achieved growth results at a higher rate than any of the other groups that either did not receive as much math instruction or who were not given tasks that required knowledge transfer. In fact, those with problem-based tasks achieved growth that was nearly double that of groups that received partial instruction paired with opportunities to transfer. Having opportunities to transfer method instruction to practical application was the critical component to increasing achievement in the study group. In addition, students working with general education partners indicated far more confidence working with the mathematical concepts.

Similar research by Bottge et al. (2004) reinforces the preceding findings. As part of a larger "enhanced anchored instruction" (EAI) strategy, focus students were given tasks in which they applied mathematical concepts to project-based and real-world applications. Bottge et al. note,

> Results of the transfer test showed that EAI students remembered the central concepts they had learned in the math classroom better than TBI [text-based instruction] students did. Posttests administered after instruction on the hovercraft construction showed that instruction in the technology education classroom closed the achievement gap between EAI and (text-based learning) students. (2004, p. 9)

Further support for these results is illustrated by the results of research by Bottge et al. (2015) in which students with math disabilities displayed four times the growth as their counterparts in traditional classes after their instruction was paired with problem-based enhanced instruction.

Theory of Improvement

Empathy interview data and observational data from the teachers informed the fishbone diagram that illustrated the primary causes of our problem of practice (Figure 12.1).

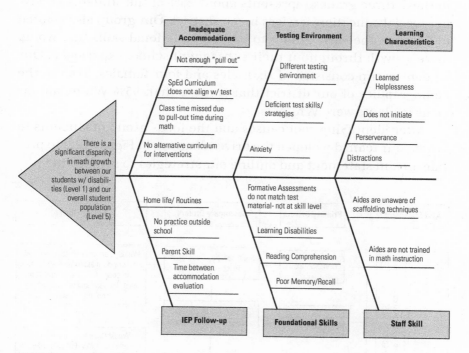

Figure 12.1. Fishbone

The primary barriers to growth among our special education students were grouped as inadequate accommodations, a lack of IEP follow-up and follow-through, testing environment, foundational skills, learning characteristics, and staff skill and knowledge. After discussing these root causes, our team selected the root causes to focus on during the project. Upon review of the themes illustrated on the diagram, we determined that supporting our families at home would be the focus of our intervention strategy as that would address multiple contributing factors. In addition, we decided we also needed to track confidence levels in math as empathy data revealed most students are not confident and give up on problems that they do not quickly comprehend.

We developed a focus group of students in third, fifth, and sixth grades to target with our interventions. Focusing on the 10 children in these three grades represents about 25% of the students receiving special education services in our district. Our group also wanted to focus on the early grades to build foundational skills that would drive growth throughout their subsequent school experience. Our student group consisted of six males and four females. True to the demographics of our district that is more than 95% White, all our focus students were White.

After identifying root causes and the focus group of students to target, our team developed the driver diagram in Figure 12.2 to provide an aim statement and outline our strategies to support them.

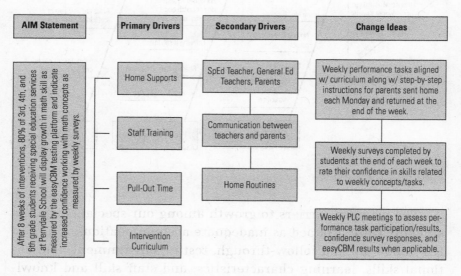

Figure 12.2. Theory of Improvement

Our strategy provided additional math supports while simultaneously increasing access to problem-based learning. Problem-based learning (PBL) was identified by several of our focus students during empathy interviews as the teaching practice that engaged them the most and made math more enjoyable for them. PBL also provides families with the tools necessary to better support math growth at home, something that parents expressed frustration with not being able to do with current practices.

The goal of this intervention strategy was to give students additional time to practice math concepts that they have worked on in the classroom at home. It was our belief that doing so would reinforce classroom instruction, increase the comfort level of students working with these concepts, increase math confidence, and drive math growth.

Testing the Change

Our first Plan–Do–Study–Act (PDSA) cycle was scheduled to run for 2 weeks in March and was designed to test whether providing families the opportunity to work on performance tasks at home drives improvement in growth indicators and increases the level of math confidence that our students identify within themselves. We hoped to measure these changes by collecting the performance tasks at the end of each week, recording who completed them and whether they were completed correctly, surveying students on their confidence level each week, and, finally, assessing growth via the easy-CBM math assessment at the end of 3 weeks.

Implementing the Change

The plan was that each week the team would meet as a professional learning community (PLC) to assess which students completed the tasks, who completed them correctly, and how they rated their confidence with the math concepts. Every 3 weeks, we anticipated also assessing the results of the easyCBM testing to determine whether math growth occurred. Alterations to our strategy would have been planned during these meetings if the data indicated we were not achieving our desired outcome of increasing math growth for our focus students.

Discussion

Unfortunately, our team was not able to complete our first PDSA cycle due to the school closure associated with the COVID-19 pandemic. Although the team gave some thought to sending home the project guidelines during the quarantine, we determined that this was not feasible for three reasons. First, the projects were intended to build on classroom instruction, allowing students extra time to practice concepts they had learned in the classroom. Because the amount of instruction time for elementary students was drastically cut short per directives from the State Department of Education, we could not make any expectations as to the pace with which math concepts would be taught through the distance-learning model.

Second, the premise of our change concept was to offer families an opportunity to work with their student on a project that could be completed at home after school hours, with the assumption that there was not a significant amount of other homework to be completed. Given the immense burden the school closure has placed on families, in particular families with students receiving services, asking them to complete another math project on top of the other work now being competed at home through distance learning was not an option our team felt was appropriate.

Finally, the inability to test students using the easyCBM platform during the closure would have made measuring math growth nearly impossible and could not have been done in a way that was consistent for each student. Some participants are meeting online for instruction, while those without access to the internet are completing packet materials with family members assisting them. Given the focus on the social and emotional needs of our students at this time, math growth simply was not the priority while our students and their families navigated the current challenges that the

COVID-19 closures presented to them. While leading this change in a rural community during a pandemic was challenging and we didn't finish the project as expected, using improvement science strategies helped us understand that meeting the needs of our students and families had to be our top priority, and we'll apply what we learned to future improvement efforts, remembering that the students and their families need to guide our improvement efforts. We also built capacity among our teacher leaders and within our system to engage in continuous improvement on a problem that directly impacts the experience of our students and families, guided by the input of our students and families.

Discussion Questions

1. In what ways could your grade-level team or school use empathy interview data to inform your classroom or grade-level math instruction?
2. What empathy interview questions would be helpful to ask in your setting with your problem of practice in math instruction?
3. How could this improvement strategy be expanded to include all students receiving special education services in our district?
4. What would be your strategy for taking this improvement strategy to scale in the general student population?
5. What professional development opportunities would be needed for your team to implement this improvement strategy?

References

Bottge, B. A., Heinrichs, M., Mehta, Z. D., Rueda, E., Hung, Y., & Danneker, J. (2004). Teaching mathematical problem solving to middle school students in math, technology education and special education classrooms. *Research in Middle Level Education Online, 27*(1), 1–17. http://www.nmsa.org/Publications/RMLEOnline/tabid/101/Default.aspx

Bottge, B. A., Toland, M., Gassaway, L., Butler, M., Griffin, A. K., & Choo, S. (2015). Impact of enhanced anchored instruction in inclusive math classrooms. *Exceptional Children, 81*(2), 158–175.

Frattura, E., & Capper, C. (2007) *Leading for social justice: Transforming schools for all learners*. Corwin.

Owen, R. L., & Fuchs, L. S. (2002). Mathematical problem-solving strategy instruction for third-grade students with learning disabilities. *Remedial and Special Education, 23*(5), 268–278.

Oregon Department of Education. (n.d.). *At-a-glance school and district profiles*. https://www.oregon.gov/ode/schools-and-districts/reportcards/Pages/default.aspx

CHAPTER THIRTEEN

Equity in STEM Programs

KEITH GROSSE

Background

Lake High School (LHS) is a 4-year public secondary school located in a suburban community, with more than 1,000 students. LHS offers a challenging course of study aimed at meeting the needs of a predominantly college-bound student body. LHS is accredited through the Northwest Association of Schools and Colleges. An alternating day schedule with four 90-minute classes daily is offered to all students. Extensive student activity programs include athletics, drama, music, dance, speech, clubs, and student government. More than 70% of LHS students participate in athletics, activity groups, and/or student government. LHS has a dual and concurrent credit program that provides students with the opportunity to enroll in rigorous college-level courses while attending LHS. These classes are taught by LHS teachers with advanced degrees in their respective fields. Students earn college credits that are accepted by our local community and state colleges.

Since 2017, Lake School District (LSD) has endorsed including an equity and inclusion lens in their work. More recently, in 2019, policies were updated to include a specific mission and goals for these policies to close achievement and opportunity gaps for students of color and historically underserved students. In reviewing the district strategic diversity plan and initiatives, this improvement science project was designed to focus on incorporating equity and inclusion into its vision for the Secondary STEM (science, technology, engineering, and mathematics) Program. Our improvement science team consisted of our superintendent, our assistant superintendent, the executive directors of the elementary and secondary schools, two high school principals, one elementary principal, and four teachers.

Need for Improvement

To gather information regarding STEM achievement and student demographics specific to LSD, three sections from Frattura and Capper's (2007) equity audit were chosen. This tool disaggregates achievement data by demographics, including race and socioeconomic indicators. It was clear from the data that Black students, economically disadvantaged, and disabled students scored significantly lower on their college admissions and state achievement tests. Students with disabilities who also receive free and reduced-price lunch (FRPL) services score almost 25% lower on standardized tests in eighth grade and on their college entrance examinations have a graduation rate of almost 20% lower than other students. When examining state achievement scores, a similar trend can be seen; economically disadvantaged students scored about 18% lower and students with disabilities about 52% lower. Graduation rates show that students who are Black have a 5% lower graduation rate, students receiving FRPL have a 15% lower rate, and students with disabilities have a 14% lower rate than the all-student population. Additionally, the middle and high schools recently experienced several acts of highly public racism, specifically racist graffiti in the bathrooms and racist comments on social media. Black and other historically underserved students have come forward to say how they have had to endure racist and discriminatory remarks from other students while in school. The data seem to indicate that students of color and historically underserved students have been underserved in a variety of ways; addressing the academic disparities would be valuable.

When the equity audit data were shared with the improvement science team, also known as the Vision Team, they said that they were aware of the standardized test data and agreed with its findings. They were interested in seeing how the standardized test data compared to those same groups in current high school STEM classes. Semester grades from teachers who taught the high school STEM engineering classes over the last 3 years were collected, averaged, and disaggregated by race, gender, and other groups. Vision Team members were also interested in these classes because their pedagogy is similar to STEM schools being considered as models for the new secondary STEM program. The STEM classes rely heavily on the engineering process, problem-based learning, are student-centered, and allow for multiple trials to show proficiency. In examining the STEM engineering data, the Vision Team identified that students with disabilities and English as a second language (ESL) students performed very similarly to White students. Unfortunately, no data were available for Black students or students receiving FRPL. These data compelled the Vision Team to do more site visits to top STEM schools for the purpose of gathering additional qualitative data about how they use STEM to increase equity and inclusion while closing both achievement and opportunity gaps.

Equity Audit Data

As a part of completing the equity audit, we examined the district demographic data (see Table 13.1).

Table 13.1. District Demographic Data

Race/Ethnicity		Number of Students
	Asian	1,000
	Black	800
	Hispanic	1,000
	Multiracial	1,000
	Native American	Too small for data to be reported
	Pacific Islander	Too small for data to be reported
	White	1,000
Disability	All students	800
Gender		
	Female	1,000
	Male	1,000
	Nonbinary	Too small for data to be reported
English as a second language		900
Free and reduced-price lunch		1,000

In addition, the equity audit included an analysis of data from the Oregon Assessment of Knowledge and Skills (OAKS) tests (see Table 13.2).

Table 13.2. 11th-Grade OAKS Scores for Lake School District, 2018–2019

Demographic		Average % Proficiency	Difference Between White Average Score
	Asian	95	+15
	Black/African American	*number too small to report	*
	Hispanic/Latino	75	-5
	American Indian/ Alaskan Native	*	*
	Multiracial	78	-2+
	Pacific Islander	*	*
	White	80	0
	Economically Disadvantaged	60	-20
	Female	75	-5
	Male	88	+8
	Students with disabilities	30	-50
	Talented and gifted	95	+15
	Total population all students	80	NA

Note: OAKS = Oregon Assessment of Knowledge and Skills.

Additional data collected as a part of the equity audit included data from STEM engineering enrollment (see Table 13.3).

Empathy Interview Data Narrative

To better understand what makes a STEM program successful, the Vision Team went on site visits to top STEM schools. After the first site visit, the Vision Team completed the equity audit. Analyzing the results, it was clear the team became enthusiastic about developing a vision for the STEM program that reflected an equity and inclusion lens that could potentially support historically underserved in LSD. Additionally, the team saw several common barriers that would

Table 13.3. STEM Engineering Classes 3-Year Enrollment and Grade
Averages

Demographic		3-Year Enrollment	% and Grade
	Asian	20	90% have a grade of A
	Black/African American	*number too small to report	*
	Hispanic/Latino	<5%	90% have a grade of B+
	American Indian/ Alaskan Native	*	*
	Multiracial	<20%	90% have a grade of A
	Pacific Islander	*	*
	White	60%	90% have a grade of A
	Female	20%	90% have a grade of A
	Male	80%	90% have a grade of A-
	Students with disabilities	<10%	90% have a grade of A-
	English learners	15%	90% have a grade of A-
	Talented and gifted	25%	95% have a grade of A

need to be addressed in the vision statement so students, teachers, and parents clearly saw themselves reflected in the mission of
the STEM program. Team members initially had a variety of visions
for the STEM program and varying expectations as to what the program should accomplish. We then conducted empathy interviews to
understand what teachers, students, and principals in those schools
thought about the STEM program, potential barriers to developing a program, their vision, and ideas for the future of the program.
During a follow-up discussion, all the interviewees expressed interest in doing more site visits to other top STEM schools so they could
better understand how they have helped each student become more
successful.

Supporting Literature

Initially, the Vision Team researched basic questions about STEM
programs. What kind of STEM schools are there? What makes
a STEM school successful? The team wanted to build a common

vocabulary and ensure everyone had a solid foundation about STEM before developing a vision. In 2011, the National Research Council (NRC) on Highly Successful Schools assembled a panel of experts to (1) develop criteria identifying successful K–12 STEM schools, (2) explore models of best practices, and (3) analyze the factors that evidence indicates lead to success. The NRC concluded that there are three main types of STEM schools: selective, inclusive, and career and technical education (CTE) STEM schools. None of the models is better than the other. The key to their success was to build a STEM program that fits the needs and interests of the students. However, the schools did have some common traits such as being project-based, focusing on problem-solving or the engineering design process, collaboration, adequate instructional time, and equal opportunity to STEM learning opportunities. Kasza and Slater (2016) conducted an extensive literature review on best practices and key learning objectives of successful STEM schools. Their results supported the NRC findings that successful STEM schools can be (1) selective, inclusive, or CTE as long as they fit the needs and interests of the students; (2) use PBL; (3) focus on problem-solving/design thinking; and (4) stressing soft skills, such as student collaboration, communication, and presentation skills.

Gender, racial, and economic inequities in STEM education and in STEM professions have been documented by many studies. Data do show modest gains for historically underrepresented groups in STEM programs. The Committee on Equal Opportunities in Science and Engineering states in its 2011–2012 biennial report to Congress that they are "working toward full inclusion of persons from underrepresented racial and ethnic minority groups (African Americans, Hispanics, and Native Americans), persons with disabilities, and women" (p. 1). However, action must be taken now:

> Effective action must be taken now to ensure that the large and rapidly growing population subgroups are empowered to participate and contribute to scientific and technological advances. If not, our democratic society faces a grave economic, intellectual and scientific disadvantage in an increasingly globalized competition for talent and innovation. (p. 2)

Many articles describe the need for more equity and inclusion in STEM education, and although a few programs have shown gains, there seem to be even fewer data showing how to make improvements. The Vision team wondered if there were data (outside or within the district) showing what the needs and interests of the students are, which practices would increase equity and inclusion and whether a model could be applicable across the district.

Theory of Improvement

For the purposes of this improvement science project, my team focused on creating a ubiquitous vision that has concrete pathways, support for teachers, and connects to the community. To best understand the barriers to our vision, we first identified our problem of practice: The LSD does not have a vision for its secondary STEM program. We next constructed a fishbone diagram that identified root causes for this problem, which included funding, location, grade level (high school, middle school), staffing, curriculum, and inclusion of all students. Of these root causes, two stood out as potentially having the biggest impact: curriculum and vision. Curriculum stood out as one that had the most potential to address the problem of practice. The Vision Team began by brainstorming how to address this specific barrier and create some change ideas. The Vision Team decided to observe and collect data on successful STEM programs by doing site visits. Each team member took notes on each school's practices and procedures. The unique lenses of the central administrator, superintendent, building administrator, and teacher from all three levels were represented on the team. Overall, five schools were visited in a 3-month period: an elementary school; a high school; a STEM center in a school district about an hour outside of Denver, Colorado; a career and technical education high school adjacent to Portland, Oregon; and a tech-focused high school in San Diego, California. At each site, the Vision Team made observations, took notes, and talked to students, teachers, and administrators about their experiences, both good and bad, and insights. Data gathered were shared in follow-up meetings during which Vision Team members discussed what they saw, how it applied to our situation, and the importance of that item to being part of the secondary STEM vision.

The goals of these site visits were (1) to see how accurate the initial fishbone and driver diagrams were and (2) to decide which action item to do first. As expected, modifications to both diagrams were needed as some items were deleted while others were added. However, it did allow the Vision Team to develop a decision matrix so qualitative data could be quantized and team trends more easily seen. A list of action items was created and ranked by each Vision Team member. The rankings were averaged in a final decision matrix with "design thinking" receiving the highest ranking with 23 points, "equity" receiving the second-highest ranking with 21 points, and "student-centered" and "community connections" tying for the third highest ranking with 19 points. "Strong professional development" and "an emphasis on technology" each received 17 points, and "targeted interventions" received 15 points. "Hiring industry experts" received only 8 points.

Next, the Vision Team decided to investigate how partnering with a specific software company could help with professional development, curriculum, and awarding certificates. To do this, the Vision Team spent a day at Apple's headquarters learning about their educational philosophy, resources, and support. They decided to investigate Apple first because LSD elementary students are currently using iPads and therefore would come into the secondary program already having a firm understanding of the technology and pedagogy being used in the secondary STEM program. Currently, this type of alignment is missing in LSD as elementary students use Apple products but middle and school students use PCs and mostly Google software. Another important factor in going to Apple first was that its educational curriculum is based on design thinking. A concern was that partnering with Apple would require the use of their products.

For the third and final Plan–Do–Study–Act (PDSA) cycle, the Vision Team decided to divide into two groups. One would investigate the alignment of current and future STEM classes to community college courses while the other group tackled the final action item of developing a plan for incorporating community partnerships. Both were found to be important in the literature reviewed, were evident during all the site visits, and scored high (3rd and 4th) on the decision matrix as keys to building a strong successful STEM program. The Vision Team also valued high school–community college dual-credit programs because they support equity goals. Dual-credit programs give students who are not going to a 4-year institution a smoother transition from high school to college, firsthand exposure to college-level work, and a chance to finish their degree earlier. This added concrete pathways for students who historically have struggled in LSD. The Vision Team also felt that a strong connection to the community and local businesses was crucial to add authenticity and credibility and to build support for the STEM program.

Testing the Change

After doing an extensive literature review, the Vision Team felt that a number of site visits would be necessary to better understand why certain traits were successful in a particular STEM program but not used in others. Also, site visits would allow members to better apply what they saw to LSD's situation. These immersive site visits lead to collecting a wealth of information and a lengthy analysis as team members discussed what they saw, the importance of it, and how it would translate to LSD. To better understand trends in what we were learning, the Vision Team decided to use the decision-matrix method (also known as the Pugh method or Pugh concept selection). A basic decision matrix consists of establishing a set of criteria/trait options that are scored and summed to gain a total score that can then be ranked. Importantly, it is not weighted to allow for a quick selection process. The advantage of the decision-making matrix is that subjective opinions about one alternative versus another can be made more objective. The Vision Team successfully used a decision matrix to quantify each member's observations from each site visit. During post–site visit meetings, the team worked cooperatively to design the decision matrix and come to an informal agreement about the meaning of the numeric scoring. For example, some discussion was needed to clearly define what a five (5) meant. Eventually, it was decided that to be scored a 5, the trait (i.e., design thinking or career education) was both observed often in the classroom and mentioned by administrators, teachers, and students. Once team members understood and agreed on the decision-matrix scoring, all nine traits were quickly agreed on and scored. The decision matrix helped give the Vision Team members clarity as to what traits they wanted their STEM program to have and which ones were not as important. The vision started to take shape.

The Vision Team was picked to investigate how partnering the secondary STEM program with Apple could move the vision forward by providing identified supports such as (1) curriculum professional development for teachers, (2) technology training for teachers, and (3) access to a variety of already made innovative lessons based in (4) design thinking and (5) could allow or lead students to have authentic learning experiences. This action item, which came from the driver diagram, was the next logical step in developing the vision because all five supports listed earlier could be accomplished through this one action. First, Apple's educational curriculum incorporates design thinking in a variety of innovative ways through PD for teachers, access to innovative curriculum, and for students to construct their own learning. Apple has both online and in-person PD for staff and LSD already has a teacher on special assignment (TOSA) who specializes in training staff on Apple products. Currently, LSD doesn't offer PD online; however, staff does do mandatory yearly training online. The Vision Team was hopeful that it would not be too difficult for teachers to expand their online training. Apple has also agreed to hold workshops at the district's annual midyear PD. This is 2 full days of training for all staff in the district. Workshops can be as large as 500 and as small as 5 participants, so there is a lot of flexibility as to what Apple trainers could offer. Another advantage to partnering with Apple is that it offers students the opportunity to earn a variety of Apple certificates (i.e., to become an Apple Genius) that could be used to help students find employment or internships with local businesses. During the site visits, Vision Team members observed students from middle school and high school doing online certificate work and, at the high school level, student-maintained school computers and/or worked at Apple Stores. During the Vision Team's visit to Apple, members worked in small groups with Apple trainers to get an idea of what teacher curriculum and hardware PD would be like. At the same time, we were asked to evaluate how innovative the curriculum was and how well design thinking was integrated into the curriculum. All Vision Team members were impressed by the trainers, knew how their curriculum is being used in schools, and thought that many of the example lessons presented would work well in the district. However, many of the non-Mac teachers found using the iPads difficult to navigate. Because the majority of secondary teachers do not use Apple products, Vision Team members agreed that this would be a hurdle for many staff members. The Vision Team felt that the majority of the lessons involved design thinking and constructivism. The novel way technology was used in the lessons made the lessons innovative. Prior to visiting Apple, the Vision Team had decided to say technology is only innovative if the activity cannot be done without it. For example, using a computer to read a book is not innovative technology because you could just read a book. However, using a computer to help students learn to read because it sounds words out is innovative. Many of the Vision Team members were very enthused with what they saw and heard at Apple, but one third were not convinced that using a curriculum so dependent on technology was a good idea. They are worried that teachers and students who are not so tech-savvy may struggle with this curriculum. They wanted to know how students who receive special education services, who receive free and reduced-price lunch services, or who are students of color, precisely those who are often underserved in a traditional classroom, did in classrooms that used the Apple curriculum. The Vision Team decided that until these questions were answered, no final decision would be made and that a visit to Google or Microsoft is needed to better understand what they have to offer. That being said, the decision was made to test the impact of Apple training on a small scale over the summer. The Vision Team created a chart to summarize the pros and cons of partnering with Apple (see Table 13.4).

Table 13.4. Pros and Cons Summary of Partnering With Apple

Pros	Cons
Curriculum based on design thinking	Curriculum always involves the use of an Apple device
Curriculum already exists	Secondary students and staff currently use Android devices (i.e., Chromebook, Dell, and Google Software)
Curriculum supported with in-person and online professional development	Could be expensive
Curriculum could lead to authentic learning experiences	Could be difficult to support
Teachers believe curriculum shows promise	

For the final PDSA cycle, more concrete progress was made when aligning current and possible future STEM classes with local community colleges. Currently, LSD works with two community colleges for dual credit, and the community college faculty agreed to keep the six classes that are currently dual credit and considered adopting three new classes. The community college faculty rejected three other classes. Table 13.5 summarizes the dual-credit classes LSD discussed with the community colleges.

Table 13.5. Lake School District (LSD) Current, Proposed, and Denied Dual-Credit Classes

LSD Class	Community College Class
**Automotive fundamentals	Automotive fundamentals
**General auto repair	General auto repair
**Small engine repair	Small engine repair
**Intro programming	Programming systems
**Computer programming	Programming systems
**Engineering and design	Engineering
*Food systems	Foods & nutrition
*Biology	Biology
*Anatomy and physiology	Anatomy and physiology
Architecture construction & engineering	**Architecture**
Digital media	**Digital video edit/post production**
Engineering concepts	**Electrical circuit analysis**

Note: **Bold** = denied dual-credit classes; * = dual-credit classes under consideration; ** = current dual-credit classes.

Although Vision Team members saw the increase in dual-credit courses as a positive step forward, they were discouraged at the community colleges' lack of flexibility in giving partial credit for courses that met most of the criteria of the community colleges' course. For example, LSD's Engineering Concepts syllabus mirrors more than half of Electrical Circuits Analysis I offered at the community college, but because 2 of the 10 units didn't align with the community college course, the high school class was denied any dual credit. This means that LSD must redesign its classes to meet the specific classes offered at the community college. Vision Team members questioned if this strategy was best for LSD students. Another issue was that the community colleges were not willing to offer more than one day for a high school teacher to work with one of the community college teachers on the curriculum. Eight hours may not be enough collaboration time and might become problematic during implementation. Finally, in addition to the usual paperwork the community colleges require for dual-credit certification, they added an annual observation. LSD agreed to this additional requirement but thought it might be difficult to do since high school class schedules, and vacation calendars, are often quite different from college. It was clear to many on the Vision Team that at least a part-time position may be needed to help LSD teachers align their class(es) to the community college, become dual-instructor-certified, create new pathways, and manage funding.

Finally, the Vision Team was able to generate a list of almost 25 local community individuals, businesses, or organizations that expressed interest in helping support current or new STEM classes. The list included engineers, health professionals, technicians, fabricators, programmers, mechanics, and more. It was clear from the community's response that every class could have one or more community members to support it. Volunteers who contribute their time and talents to LSD are valued assets and make significant contributions in helping the district accomplish its educational mission. However, because there is a formal process that all volunteers must go through before they are able to work with students, the Vision Team thought that the part-time position for dual credit could also be used to recruit volunteers and make sure they meet district guidelines before working with students.

Implementing the Change

The Vision Team found the site visits to other top STEM programs very successful because they were able to define the criteria/traits for their Secondary STEM Program. It also allowed them to prioritize their actions and gave them a clear target. According to the Vision Team, the most important criteria in order from most to least important were (1) design thinking, (2) equity, (3) community connection, (4) career education, and (5) emphasis on technology. The Vision Team believes that these criteria/traits are the future of LSD's Secondary STEM Program giving it real direction. As the ancient Roman philosopher Seneca observed, "if a [person] knows not what harbor [they] seek, any wind is the right wind." If you don't have a common, agreed-on destination, then everyone is left to their own devices to imagine one—a scenario that results in unharnessed and unfocused efforts, with everyone believing that what they are doing is right. A common understanding of the destination allows all stakeholders to align their improvement efforts. By the end of this process, the Vision Team had considered numerous ideas, research, and perspectives, incorporating more than 25 administrators and teachers in the improvement process while collecting data from almost 500 parents and students. The Vision Team believes that they have created a shared vision by listening to and validating stakeholders' thoughts and that this will help them cope with the change and create buy-in. Using this method of a shared vision will be tested by having teachers and building principals start working with other staff members on developing lessons that are built around these five criteria/traits. Before this work can begin, the Vision Team must decide if they are going to partner with Apple or another company that will supply the necessary supports.

After much discussion, the Vision Team is set on adopting a curriculum rather than building one in-house. The reasons given by the team were a lack of time, a lack of STEM expertise, and a desire for a clear instructional vision. The majority of STEM funds are coming from a capital bond and must be spent in 2 years so the Vision Team thought it may take teachers longer than that to develop curriculum and then order equipment. Also, LSD has no STEM experts on staff, only teachers who have expressed an interest in teaching STEM classes and have done some limited PD. However, the Vision Team does believe that the vision they developed gives a clear instructional direction to find a ready-made curriculum that fits those criteria. The Vision Team also reflected on past success and challenges when adding programs to LSD and felt that when they adopted the Project Lead the Way (PLTW) curriculum to start their engineering classes was a good example of how adopting an already made curriculum worked well. If Apple's curriculum is implemented, a cascade of effects would happen over the next 6 months. School leaders will have to establish elements for continuous innovation that include culture, team, capacity, community, finance, and measurement. Most Vision Team members see the current Vision Team teachers forming a PLC with other STEM teachers to (1) go through Apple's curriculum to look for lessons that they could use in their class, (2) do online training to become a certified Apple Teacher, and (3) set up a summer workshop whereby STEM teachers and Apple trainers can work together (virtually). It is believed that this will help build teams, capacity and take into account school and community cultures. Also, over the summer, the central office will make sure the necessary technology is ordered. Then it will be up to teachers to incorporate the lessons they developed over the summer into their classes. However, a system of measurement will need to be implemented that takes into account all five of the criteria/traits—(1) design thinking, (2) equity, (3) community connection, (4) career education, and (5) emphasis on technology—specified by the vision. Teachers, administrators, and Apple Trainers will utilize Apple's already vetted tools to assess how lessons are meeting these five criteria and more. It will also be important to collect student data by doing both pre and post surveys to see how students' perceptions, knowledge, skills, and personal attributes change or impact their future aspirations. The Vision Team understands that as important as the vision is, keeping it alive throughout the year is not an easy task. Supporting a school's vision is an ongoing process that requires thoughtful planning, practice, and improvement along the way.

To get more of the classes dual credit at community colleges, LSD is looking to hire a half-time teacher on special assignment to work with STEM teachers and community college professors to assist in aligning curriculum, to get STEM teachers dual-credit- and CTE-certified, and to work with administrators to apply for and allocate state and district funding for these classes. They could also help find PD for these teachers outside Apple, specifically in using tools such as CNC (computer numerical control) machines, laser cutters, and Vex Kits, tools that require special training. It is also hoped that this position could continue to grow and develop community connections. Although LSD's initial ask for community help was well received, these types of relationships need constant attention if they are to be sustained over time. The Vision Team is hoping to grow the current advisory board that LSD has had since the beginning of their STEM program 5 years ago. This board currently is composed of about 10 members, which include STEM teachers, parents, robotics club members, building administrators, and local business owners but no students. It is hoped to double the number of participants, increase diversity, and increase the opportunity for students to do internships or work for local businesses. Each of the efforts will include an equity focus.

Discussion

The purpose of this project was to work with LSD stakeholders to create a shared, ubiquitous vision that has concrete pathways and support for teachers and connects to the community. This vision will be the compass for the district's secondary STEM program. A guide to help close achievement and opportunity gaps by increasing equity and inclusion while empowering students. The Vision Team decided that STEM classes needed to be grounded in design thinking to reach students who have historically been underserved in the LSD. They also believe this pedagogical approach has many positive attributes such as developing a growth mindset; important problem-solving, analytical skills; and spatial thinking skills that will benefit all students in the LSD. Their vision combines design thinking with strong community connections, career education, and an emphasis on innovative technology.

LSD used improvement science to create this shared vision. In the first PDSA cycle, three site visits were used to help give the Vision Team important insights into what makes a STEM school successful, and it allowed them to go back and make changes to the fishbone and driver diagrams that were done using the background literature. Although the literature review was helpful and gave LSD a place to start, the Vision Team agreed that this alone would not have been enough to create a STEM vision for LSD. The site visits brought the literature alive and really allowed Vision Team to better understand why some criteria/traits are important at one school we visited but weren't at another and which would (or wouldn't) work for LSD. It was particularly important for non-STEM Vision Team members to actually see what students and teachers were doing in these classrooms so they could better understand challenges and successes in this area. This iterative process is really what improvement science is about as each site visit refined drivers and actions. This was also energizing the Vision Team as they were able to see some outstanding STEM programs, and it allowed them to dream big for their program and students. Although the Vision Team feels that they have correctly identified five important criteria/traits for their Secondary STEM program, these will have to be revisited after the lessons are taught and data are collected by teacher(s), Apple Trainers, administrators, and students.

In the second PDSA cycle, the Vision Team went to Apple to see if they could supply both supports for teachers and an innovative, empowering curriculum for students. The goal was to see if Apple could supply the supports to implement the vision. The Vision Team was pleased enough with Apple's curriculum and PD that their trainers will begin working with some LSD STEM teachers this summer in person and online. Lessons/units developed by these teachers will be tested in the fall of 2020. They will be closely assessed by teachers, administrators, Apple Trainers, and students. The Vision Team expects teachers to use improvement science to refine these lessons/units and hopes the process and the lessons will become a model for all teachers. The Vision Team understands that this is a change in pedagogy and will require a shift in culture. However, administrators are optimistic that this can occur because all the teachers exposed to this curriculum and the vision criteria/traits were enthusiastic and believe students (especially those who have historically struggled in LSD) will benefit. Eells's (2011) meta-analysis of studies related to collective efficacy and achievement in education demonstrated that the beliefs teachers hold about the ability of the school as a whole are "strongly and positively associated with student achievement across subject areas and in multiple locations" (p. 110). On the basis of Eells's research, John Hattie (2016) positioned collective efficacy at the top of the list of factors that influence student achievement. A school staff that believes it can collectively accomplish great things is vital for the health of a school, and if they believe they can make a positive difference, then they very likely will. Another positive indicator for implementing this new curriculum is that this was done in the past using PLTW when LSD implemented their engineering pathway. The PLTW curriculum is very similar to Apple's but is specific to only engineering. One of the main obstacles to the Apple curriculum being adopted is that it requires many secondary teachers and students to switch from their Google platform to the Apple platform. Most likely this will be less of a challenge for the students than for the teachers. It will also be challenging for LSD's technology support department because currently, they don't have any personnel that specializes in iOS which means either current employees will need training or new hires must have this expertise. This is a legitimate concern for LSD because they, as do many other school districts, have struggled to find and retain highly qualified computer technicians. For example, over the previous 4 years, computer technicians had an 80% turnover rate.

Examining district student achievement with an equity lens shows that students from historically underserved populations, those from low-income households, and those who have disabilities are achieving significantly below their peers in math and science but not in engineering classes. Engineering classes use a curriculum very similar to the one envisioned for the entire secondary STEM program. However, only about 10% of LSD engineering students fall into those demographics. This is a problem across the nation, as less than 20% of students enrolled in high school STEM classes are in these demographics (Means et al., 2017). To ensure equitable opportunities and access for every student to become a part of this inclusive innovation program LSD will need to encourage and actively recruit students in these demographics, to take STEM classes, ensure placement into these classes, provide them with the necessary support to be successful, continue to grow their elementary STEM program, and provide STEM extracurricular activities. The COVID-19 crisis has highlighted the social justice issue of schools getting STEM into low-income and underrepresented communities. All students, of all income levels, ethnicity, or gender, deserve the opportunity to be prepared with 21st-century skills for future occupations. This disparity is why LSD school leaders were—and school leaders everywhere should be—compelled to take action and provide STEM learning opportunities in all K-12 classrooms and communities. The group dynamics on the Vision Team made crafting this vision both productive and enjoyable as group members worked cooperatively and stayed focused, especially as deadlines approached. Parents, business owners, and community college representatives were also easy to work with, and each brought a wealth of talent and knowledge to the project. By working together, LSD has set up the secondary STEM program for success. It will be several years before this vision work can be evaluated, but if LSD stays committed to the improvement science processes, in particular abandoning change ideas that are not working, adapting those showing potential, and adopting change ideas that work, the LSD Secondary STEM Program will positively impact the lives of many students, in particular historically underserved students.

Discussion Questions

1. How would partnering with Apple or another technology organization add or detract from credibility to the Secondary STEM Program vision?
2. What other action(s) should be taken next to ensure students of color, low-income students, and girls are equitably enrolled in and successful in this program?
3. What are all the ways to measure the success of the Secondary STEM Program?

References

Committee on Equal Opportunities in Science and Engineering. (2011–2012). *Biennial report to congress: Broadening participation in America's STEM workforce.* https://www.nsf.gov/od/oia/activities/ceose/documents/CEOSE-Recom mendation.pdf

Eells, R. (2011). *Meta-analysis of the relationship between collective efficacy and student achievement* [Unpublished doctoral dissertation]. Loyola University of Chicago, IL.

Frattura, E. M., & Capper, C. (2007). *Leading for social justice: Transforming schools for all learners.* Corwin.

Hattie, J. (2016, July 11). *The current status of the visible learning research* (Keynote address). Mindframes and Maximizers, 3rd Annual Visible Learning Conference, Washington, DC.

Kasza, P., & Slater, T. F. (2016). A survey of best practices and key learning objectives for successful secondary school STEM academy settings. *Contemporary Issues in Education Research, 10*(1), 53–66. doi:10.19030/cier. v10i1.9880

Means, B., Wang, H., Wei, X., Lynch, S., Peters, V., Young, V., & Allen, C. (2017, September). Expanding STEM opportunities through inclusive STEM-focused high schools. *Science Education, 101*(5), 681–671. https://www.ncbi.nlm.nih.gov/pmc/articles/PMC5575480/

National Research Council. (2011). *Successful K–12 STEM education: Identifying effective approaches in science, technology, engineering and mathematics.* The National Academies Press. https://doi.org/10.17226/13158

Part IV:
Health, Wellness, and
Physical Education

CHAPTER FOURTEEN

Physical Education and Indigenous Youth: Middle School Physical Education and Indigenous Youth

JAROD MILKO

Youth aged 5 to 17 who are physically active have an array of health benefits related to growth and development. Health benefits include more favorable measures of bone health, cognitive functioning, academic achievement, anxiety, metabolic health, motor competence, and physical, mental, emotional, and social functioning (ParticipACTION, 2018). To meet the goals of the physical education (PE) curriculum, opportunities for students to be physically active must be provided in various environments every day. In all public elementary schools in Central Canada, there is a Daily Physical Activity (DPA) policy that all schools are mandated to follow. This policy mandates that every Grades 1 through 8 students must receive 20 minutes of moderate-to-vigorous (i.e., heart-pumping) exercise during instructional time every day. At Silver Maple Middle School (SMMS; a pseudonym), there are three areas where physical activity can occur (Ontario Physical and Health Education Association, n.d.): (1) curricular (i.e., during the instructional time), (2) interschool (i.e., school-sponsored competitions between other schools), and (3) intramurals (i.e., school-sponsored recreational activities during student breaks). Many students either refuse to participate or participate minimally in physical activity within instructional time, interschool sports, and intramurals. Typically, the same students are physically active in the various opportunities provided at SMMS, and the same students are inactive across various contexts. The DPA policy is not being met regarding the moderate-to-vigorous physical activity (MVPA) requirements. MPVA can be identified as "heart-pumping" exercise, whereby students appear to be breathing heavily (ParticipACTION, 2018). Indigenous students avoid engaging in physical activity more than non-Indigenous students and have difficulty expressing barriers that may be hindering their physical activity experience. Achievement levels are lower, and tardiness and absenteeism are higher with Indigenous students compared to non-Indigenous students in PE, physical activity opportunities (i.e., team sports, intramurals, clubs), and across all subjects.

This chapter shares the experiences of SMMS, which is part of the Forest District School Board (FDSB, a pseudonym) in Central Canada and spans more than 75,000 km². Several students are from neighboring communities and commute up to 1.5 hours to school. There are 28 schools in the FDSB, with a total student population of 7,500 students comprised of 53% self-identified Indigenous students. SMMS consists of students in the 7th and 8th grades, housed in a building for 7th- through 12th-grade students. SMMS functions much differently than the high school regarding timetables, expectations, rules, curriculum, and unions. The middle school consists of about 300 students, while the high school consists of about 700 students. Similar to other public schools in this area, the organizational structure of SMMS is hierarchical, in which the principal is at the top and has the power to make and overrule many decisions. Under the principal are the two vice principals, teachers, secretaries, custodians, education workers, and librarians. According to the administration, SMMS consists of about 60% Indigenous students. Over the past 15 to 20 years, the representation of Indigenous students has increased significantly. Improving SMMS involves new opportunities related to cultural responsiveness and addressing the impacts of intergenerational trauma caused by traumatic events, such as the residential school system.

The demographic of SMMS students, and the values of SMMS have shaped the leadership lens of this initiative to be guided through an Indigenous perspective. The history of many Indigenous people, including SMMS students and families, includes intergenerational trauma partially caused by the residential school system (Marsh et al., 2015). Unfortunately, many Indigenous students are affected by intergenerational trauma caused by residential schools, which was part of more than 400 years of systematic marginalization (Marsh et al., 2015). An Indigenous perspective is essential and therefore embodied in this initiative, as it is a holistic approach and emphasizes oral traditions, care, respect, culture, language, and community (Munroe et al., 2013). In SMMS, students have access to an Elder and a Four Directions Room. Elders are imperative as they are knowledge keepers of the land and, in a school setting, can connect staff and students to the history, traditions, culture, and language of Indigenous people, as well as community resources. The Four Directions Room is a place where Indigenous students can go to study, eat, and unwind throughout the day. There are two staff who tutor, support, and help students as needed, as well as make meaningful community connections. This program is supported by the FDSB and is modeled in other schools.

Culturally Responsive Framework

A culturally responsive framework is critical to the success of our Indigenous students. Many different terms have been used to explain the idea of further understanding Indigenous culture and used to respect cultures, traditions, values, and belief systems. *Cultural sensitivity, cultural appropriateness, cultural congruence, cultural competency*, and *cultural safety* are some of the terms that have been used (Federation of Saskatchewan Indian Nations, 2014). A more recent term is *cultural responsiveness*. To be culturally responsive in education is to utilize the concept of Two-Eyed Seeing (Information Resources Management Association, 2020), which means "to see from one eye with the strengths of Indigenous knowledge and ways of knowing, and from the other eye with the strengths of Western knowledge and ways of knowing" (Bartlett et al., 2012, p. 335). Elder

Albert Marshal first brought forward the guiding principle of Two-Eyed Seeing in 2004:

> Two-Eyed Seeing adamantly, respectfully, and passionately asks that we bring together our different ways of knowing to motivate people, Aboriginal and non-Aboriginal alike, to use all our understandings so we can leave the world a better place and not compromise the opportunities for our youth (in the sense of Seven Generations) through our own inaction. (Bartlett et al., 2012, p. 335)

Two-Eyed Seeing is fundamental to programming PE for Indigenous students. Cultural responsiveness is described as "respecting where people are from and including their culture in the design and delivery of services or an active process of seeking to accommodate the service to the client's cultural context, values and needs" (Federation of Saskatchewan Indian Nations, 2014, p. 2). Although cultural competence is typically used in the education sector, I will use cultural responsiveness, as the term places the onus on the professionals (i.e., administrators, teachers, and educational assistants) and the organization (i.e., the school and school board) to act in response to the cultural specificity of each student (Armstrong, 2009). A culturally responsive framework is critical and mutually beneficial for the coexistence of both Western and First Nations worldviews. The two systems must come together and be treated as equal to set a foundational stage for reconciliation and respect and, ultimately, eliminate the achievement gap between Indigenous and non-Indigenous students (Federation of Saskatchewan Indian Nations, 2014; Ministry of Indigenous Affairs, 2019). This notion was the understanding of First Nations people when the Treaties were first signed and are present in *The Journey Together: Ontario's Commitment to Reconciliation with Indigenous Peoples* report (Ministry of Indigenous Affairs, 2019).

Finally, the mindset of culturally responsive educators includes a particular set of dispositions and skills that can enable change agents to work creatively and effectively to support all students in diverse settings (Ontario Ministry of Education, 2013). To engage in culturally responsive teaching is to "hold high expectations for learning while recognizing and honouring the strengths that a student's lived experiences and/or home culture bring to the learning environment of the classroom" (Ontario Ministry of Education, p. 6). Villegas and Lucas (2002) encourage teachers to learn about their students and who they are and then to use this information to gain access to the student's learning. Further details are provided throughout this chapter on how a culturally responsive framework has been used to guide change.

Problem of Practice

Many different factors, both internal and external, have directly and indirectly shaped this problem of practice. The problem of practice at SMMS is that too many Indigenous students in SMMS are not meeting the goals of the health and physical education (H&PE) curriculum. Primarily, students are not meeting the following two goals outlined in the H&PE curriculum (Ontario Ministry of Education, 2019, p. 6):

> Students will (1) develop the skills and knowledge that will enable them to enjoy being active and healthy throughout their lives, through opportunities to participate regularly and safely in physical activity and to learn how to develop and improve their own personal fitness; (2) develop the movement competence needed to participate in a range of physical activities, through opportunities to develop movement skills and to apply movement concepts and strategies in games, sports, dance, and various other physical activities

Tools Used in This Improvement Science Project

We began our improvement project as part of an Organizational Improvement Plan (Milko, 2020) by asking why Indigenous students were engaging less than non-Indigenous students in H&PE and why there is a significant gap between non-Indigenous and Indigenous youth in participation levels. A team of teachers engaged in a root-cause analysis and brainstormed possible reasons.

Gathering Information and Data

Next, we gathered information and data. We looked externally first, as we thought there may be information and data we needed to understand and consider before trying to address the problem internally. Some of this key information and data included (1) the *Truth and Reconciliation Commission of Canada: Calls to Action* (Truth and Reconciliation Commission of Canada [TRC], 2015); (2) sedentary levels in Indigenous people versus non-Indigenous people; (3) middle school decline in physical activity and sport, especially with girls; (4) a general decline in youth engagement in physical activity; and (5) nutrition data for Indigenous people.

Then we asked the students. We wanted to understand how they felt about participating in PE to try to uncover any potential issues or barriers. Through interviews, questionnaires, and surveys, we found that students wanted more land-based activities, fewer traditional sports, less pressure to participate, and choice. When students were asked if they liked physical activity, they often said no. When they were asked if they were confident in their abilities to engage in various physical activities, they mostly said no. Students said overall that their engagement in physical activities and PE has decreased from when they were younger, which aligns with research on decreasing physical activity levels from elementary school into middle school and plummeting in high school (ParticipACTION, 2020).

Identify Any Issues That Contributed to the Problems

There are several issues that contribute to an Indigenous student's low level of physical activity in PE. Issues that inhibit physical activity engagement with one student may not be the same for another. Some of these issues include being unmotivated to engage in the programming that was offered, low confidence in the ability to engage in activities successfully, uncomfortable during physical activity when the attention is all on them (common in traditional sports), poor nutrition throughout the day leading up to PE, and fatigued going into PE.

Root Causes

After several discussions between team members and team members and students, along with using external information a data, some root causes were identified. These included intergenerational trauma is impacting our Indigenous students, a lack of culturally responsive pedagogy, and a lack of land-based activities that are traditional to the student's community.

Intergenerational trauma is very prevalent in our community, as only a few kilometers from the school is an old residential school site. Some of our grandparents will not even walk in through the school doors as a result of the trauma they experienced in the residential school system. This trauma is passed down for generations, and the students at SMMS are typically grandchildren to residential school survivors. This is an issue that is important to understand. By developing a culturally responsive program, educators began to understand more about why things are the way they are.

Culturally responsive pedagogy was crucial to the success of this initiative. Culturally responsive educators understand that "all students learn differently and that these differences may be connected to background, language, family structure and social or cultural identity" (Ontario Ministry of Education, 2013, p. 2). Building relationships with family members was one of the most rewarding steps of action that could have been taken. Through interactions with parents and guardians over the phone, at "meet and greets," school barbeques, and extracurriculars, educators developed relationships with family members that opened a conversation about physical activity outside of school hours. It was found that students did many land-based activities at home, including trapping, netting, hiking, and hunting. Some students loved to play baseball, and others, basketball. Interests varied, but it gave teachers insight into what their students like to do and identified students who could help with demonstrations, explanations, and leading activities.

Land-based activities occurred sporadically before we started this improvement project but were not fundamental to the program. Culturally responsive quality PE requires a great deal of planning, as resources need to be gathered and set up, equipment needs to be purchased and organized, and lesson plans need to be prepared. A major advantage of using PE specialists in elementary and middle schools is that they get to put their full focus into planning and facilitating quality PE class, as opposed to creating a PE lesson along with eight other different lessons each day.

The Necessary Solutions

A Quality Daily Physical Education (QDPE) program is a strength of Western knowledge and "ensures that all children who receive it have the opportunity to develop the knowledge, skills, and habits that they need to lead physically active lives now, and just as importantly, into the future" (PHE Canada, 2019, para. 3). Recent research by Dudley (2019) found that when learning goals are the primary focus in PE, students have a much more favorable outcome in motivation to be active, and psychomotor learning, than students who are in PE where fitness is the impetus of the program. PE models where learning goals are the primary focus may include sport education, Teaching Games for Understanding (TGfU), and cooperative learning (Curry & Light, 2013; Hannon & Ratliffe, 2004; Hopper & Kruisselbrink, 2002; Siedentop, 2002).

Learning-Based Models

Learning-based models include three concepts: sport education, TGfU, and cooperative learning. Sport education is when students are put into teams, and sports are run in seasons that are two to three times longer than the typical PE unit. Students plan, practice, and compete together. A schedule of competition is organized at the beginning of the season, which allows players to practice and play within a predictable schedule of fair competition. A culminating event marks the end of a season, during which progress and success are celebrated. After training by the teacher, students begin each class in their groups. Each group is led by a student coach through a warm-up and series of skills planned by the student manager. Small-sided games are often played to increase participation and students compete against other students who are similar in abilities (Siedentop, 2002).

TGfU is a games-based approach whereby students learn an adult game through a modified version in which the rules are modified to the physical, social, and mental development of the students. Students learn to appreciate the game and gain an understanding of why the game has specific rules and how to be tactical within a game. Tactical awareness, decision-making, problem-solving, and skill execution are all learned within the context of the modified game (Curry & Light, 2013; Hopper & Kruisselbrink, 2002).

Cooperative learning is built on four foundational principles: accountability, appreciation and use, feelings of positive interdependence, and heterogeneous groups. Students are organized in small teams and challenge with a goal that they need to accomplish together. There are opportunities to be a performer, an observer, a coach, a manager, and a recorder, depending on the task, in cooperative learning. Students engage in physical activity, build communication skills, learn different perspectives, and build trust among each other through cooperative learning (Hannon & Ratliffe, 2004).

The quality of instruction is a priority when implementing a QDPE program. However, *daily* is the next word in QDPE and a significant part of a successful program. Dudley (2019) found that by increasing curricular time dedicated to PE, students significantly improve in their learning, by over a 0.4 of a standard deviation, across all subjects. This is a significant improvement in student learning, especially considering that the research did not differentiate between high- and low-quality PE programming. For example, we do not know if the programming was learning-based. Nor do we know if the program was taught by a trained physical educator. The QDPE program is discussed more in the next section.

The Two-Eyed Seeing Model

At SMMS, Indigenous students compose 60% of the school population and are significantly more disengaged from PE than non-Indigenous students. The solution to closing the gap was not obvious and not simple. Solutions to physical inactivity in general society are not simple, which is why there are always new exercise devices and methods appearing on the market. The exercise solution is not simple otherwise it would not be a problem in society. Only 25% of 10- to 17-year-olds are meeting the physical activity recommendation within the Canadian 24-Hour Movement Guidelines for children and youth (ParticipACTION, 2020). The rate of non-communicated diseases (NCDs) can be reduced significantly by meeting the Canadian Society for Exercise Physiology (CSEP) physical activity guidelines. At the current rate, 50% of non-Indigenous and 80% of Indigenous youth will develop diabetes or pre-diabetes in their lifetime (Diabetes Canada, 2018). ParticipACTION (2020) also found that only 30% of youth 12- to 17-year-olds met the guidelines; however, this was an average of boys and girls together. In this study, boys were much more active, as 43% met the recommendations whereas only 17% of girls met the recommendations.

In-depth interviews with Indigenous people on Indigenous populations and physical activity show that more emphasis is needed in health initiatives to include traditional physical activities (Wahi et al., 2019). SMMS resides on the traditional lands of the Anishinaabe people and the people of the Metis Nation in the Treaty 3 territory. The Indigenous population at SMMS consists of many Anishinaabe and Metis students. Thus, based on our problem of practice, data gathering, and root-cause analysis, our team decided to change our program based on the population of the students and including the Two-Eyed Seeing approach. Thus, several land-based activities were planned and implemented, such as hiking, snowshoeing, cross-country skiing, building hunting blinds and shelters, snow snake games, building fires, medicine walks, ice fishing, tracking animals, and calling deer and moose.

At the beginning of the school year, a long-term plan was developed that included half of all daily PE classes to be outside. The Grade

8 students would have PE outside for 2 weeks while the Grade 7 students had PE in the gym, and then they would switch. When PE was outside, there was a lot of opportunity for teachers to facilitate land-based programming. At first, students resisted having to go outside, especially when the weather was cold as the winter season began. Many students complained and expressed their discontent for having to go outside in below-freezing temperatures. After approximately 2 to 3 weeks, students began to complain less and shortly after, completely changed their perception. They began asking to go outside. The threshold for taking students outside, as per school board policy, is −25 °C. They began expressing their discontent about having to stay inside. This was a result of using land-based programming, along with experiential programming while outdoors. Students love being outside, but prior to beginning lands-based programming, they had not yet realized that love. Some of the land-based programming included hiking, snowshoeing, cross-country skiing, building hunting blinds and shelters, snow snake games, building fires, medicine walks, ice fishing, tracking animals, and calling deer and moose. Both Indigenous and non-Indigenous students were very interested in land-based learning, and their interest led to increased engagement.

The land-based outdoor activities included strengths from Western knowledge as well. The students participated in a mountain biking program during which they learned how to fix, repair, and ride mountain bikes safely on trails and roads. Any major damage or rebuilds were conducted by the students in the bike academy program. The students in the bike academy accept donations of bike and bike parts from the community, fix the bikes, and then donate them back to children and youth who want a bike but may not be able to afford one. Historically, teachers and students in PE never worked with the bike academy program and typically did not have mountain biking as part of the PE program. Now, PE teachers work with the bike academy, and every student has the opportunity to learn how to bike. Every student is in PE, and only a small group in the bike academy, so this was an important and simple internal connection—important because historically marginalized students do not necessarily have the opportunity to learn how to ride a bicycle at home. Transportation to and from school or extracurriculars may be an issue. Learning how to ride a bicycle provides students with the opportunity to learn an important life skill and to engage in a form of active transportation used across the world. When this connection was first established, it was astonishing to see so many students struggle with riding a bike as many had not had this opportunity before. One of the most amazing parts of being a teacher is to see a student's eyes light up when they feel they can do something with competence and then become more motivated to engage in that activity due to a newfound confidence. This is at the core of physical literacy, and now Indigenous students at SMMS do not enter high school without learning how to ride and fix a mountain bike.

After students learned how to ride a mountain bike safely down the trails and road, they used biking as a way of active transportation to the local pickleball courts and learned how to play pickleball. They also participated in many other outdoor activities, such as cross-country running, orienteering, and played TGfU games on the football field and in the trail system. The students had an enriched PE program that was new to them and exciting. It taught them to enjoy the outdoors and dress appropriately for the weather. The program was led by a PE specialist, who is qualified in teaching PE as well as engaged in annual professional development. PE specialists are an integral part of a QDPE program (PHE Canada, 2019). PE is typically deprioritized in Western education systems as it is viewed as less important than numeracy and literacy skills. New research from Dudley (2019) shows that students in learning-based PE programs are not only more motivated to learn in PE but also more motivated to learn across all subjects. This includes cross-curricular subject matter focused on numeracy and literacy skills.

Plan–Do–Study–Act (PDSA) Cycle

The model for learning is well suited for this type of change, as it is based on a "trial and error" type of approach. This is relevant to increasing physical activity in middle school students, as the research shows that success varies by environment, and what works in one location may not work in another (Lonsdale et al., 2013). The PDSA cycle began with a plan and ended with an action. The PDSA framework, according to Donnelly and Kirk (2015), is beneficial as it "ensures that you do not drift from the initial objectives, that you have actual achievable measurements that are valid and will show improvement if the improvement is realized" (p. 281). Most often, change implementation will require many PDSA cycles to make a successful change (Langley et al., 2009).

The model for improvement begins with three questions: "1) What are we accomplishing? 2) How will we know that a change is an improvement?; and 3) What change can we make that will result in improvement?" (Langley et al., 2009, p. 24). In the context of this OIP, we refers to the distributed leadership team of change agents (i.e., PE teachers, teachers, administrators, education assistance, Elders, and community members). These questions are asked daily throughout the change process. These questions act as a guide and a reminder that change happens over time, and that focus is critical for its success.

Resistance is not necessarily a bad thing. Teachers were supportive of a QDPE program taught by a PE specialist. Even with schedule changes, they knew it was a "students first" approach. When action plans align with belief systems of both the organization and stakeholders involved, it creates reasons for change and creates support for change as opposed to resistance. However, resistance is not necessarily negative. This is one of the most valuable lessons learned. In this case, there was a period during which a QDPE program had to be advocated for and explained so everyone understood the "why." Two-way communication helped with decreasing resistance. However, there is still something about change that is uncomfortable, especially when stakeholders do not understand how the change will impact them. Schedules had to change, but the exact change was unknown until the schedules were created. Having reason and purpose behind the change was fundamental for the change to be a success.

Resistance with students also occurred. Students were not very accepting of having to spend half of their daily PE classes outside, especially in northern Ontario where students are expected to go outside in temperatures as cold as -25 °C. It took approximately 3 weeks of kids going outside in PE before the resistance subsided and students began to accept and be ready to go outside. In fact, the students' tone completely changed as many looked forward to outside PE compared to going to the gym. Students who were upset about going outside at first were now excited to go outside.

Results

The goals of this improvement project have the potential for a much more significant impact beyond the curriculum. The H&PE curriculum is fundamental and evidence-based, and, when prioritized, can positively impact students' health and well-being. Nevertheless, the potential of the curriculum goes beyond the walls of the school. The results of this initiative were eye-opening. Our hopes were high for getting our Indigenous youth more active in PE, and we saw this, but we also found some other indirect results that we were not expecting. First, Indigenous student attendance increased by 12% compared to the previous year. There are many factors besides this initiative that could have caused this, but it makes sense that attendance increased. Students became more confident in themselves to participate, enjoyed participating more, and were more motivated to engage in learning-based PE. This sounds like a pretty good reason to come to school and want to come to school if nothing else. Second, the grades of students did not change significantly. Grades in elementary schools are very subjective and go by most recent and most consistent performance. It is completely up to the teacher to decide what to weigh heavy, light, or not at all. Also, PE specialists are likely to grade much different than generalist teachers in PE do. Third, many students developed a growth mindset and engaged in activities rather than avoid the task and using phrases such as "I can't do this," "I don't want to do this," or "I have never been able to do this anyways." Physical activity appears to breed confidence, and confident children do not talk with a stuck mindset but, rather, a growth mindset. Finally, the disapproval for going outside for PE almost disappeared. Overwhelmingly, most students did not want to go outside for PE in the winter months. However, after 3 weeks of consistently going outside for PE, the students' tone completely changed. Now, instead of expressing discontent for going outside into the cold, they are asking to go.

Lessons Learned for Increasing Equity in Schools

Indigenous students will be more active, happier, build confidence in themselves, and ultimately, lead healthier and more active lifestyles if culturally responsive PE is prioritized in schools. Two by-products of increasing physical literacy in Indigenous students include increasing confidence in themselves, and motivation to engage in physical activity. These are two very important by-products of implementing a Two-Eyed Seeing QDPE program and helping address the TRC's (2015) *Calls to Action* and can lead to closing the gap between Indigenous and non-Indigenous students.

The idea of change can feel insurmountable. Especially in this case, where proposals for a new model required systematic and organizational change that had not existed in the history of the organization. Organizational change is even more difficult when the stakeholder(s) seeking change are not in a position of authority that provides them with the power to implement change. Leaders in these positions are referred to as emerging leaders who, through persuasiveness, can influence leaders with authority to adopt change. In the education system especially, change is typically not a "point A to point B" process, as there are several moving parts that include several different stakeholders who may or may not be impacted by the change.

It is critically important to understand and anticipate that there will be resistance to change. Resistance in one form or another is almost always expected in change, especially organizational change. Resistance, however, is not always a bad thing. Resistance may be the behavior associated with anxiety, or stress, related to the unknown of change. If stakeholders are unsure how they will be affected by change, they may resist change in fear that it might be negative for them. Establishing a vision or purpose and being transparent throughout the entire process helps lower or eliminate resistance.

We also learned to always consider the culture of the students in the school and classroom, using a culturally responsive framework in your school and culturally responsive pedagogy with students. We were reminded to make connections with home often and develop relationships with family members. Students love this and will respect you even more for taking the time to connect with their family.

Finally, change is possible. Do not let doubt or negative thought prevent you from trying to implement change. If you have an idea, bounce it off a few colleagues. If they like it, present it to your team. Establish a committee or group and find a way to establish change. Present the change back to your team and accept constructive feedback while acknowledging that some resistance is okay. Finally, do not give up. Organizational change is not easy but is doable. Be tenacious. Persevere.

Discussion Questions

1. How could you adapt this process to ensure equity in other subjects in your school?
2. What might be some obstacles when trying this improvement strategy in your classroom or school?
3. How ready and equipped do teachers and staff feel to address issues of diversity?
4. What would a culturally responsive PE program look like at your school?
5. Who would be a great advocate or resource for you in this type of culturally responsive improvement work?

References

Armstrong, S. (2009). Culturally responsive family dispute resolution in family relationship centres. *Family Relationships Quarterly*, 2009(13) 3-7. http://handle.uws.edu.au:8081/1959.7/505930

Bartlett, C., Marshall, M., & Marshall, A. (2012). Two-eyed seeing and other lessons learned within a co-learning journey of bringing together indigenous and mainstream knowledges and ways of knowing. *Journal of Environmental Studies and Sciences, 2*(4), 331-340. doi:10.1007/s13412-012-0086-8

Curry, C. & Light, R. (2013). The influence of school context on the implementation of TGfU across a secondary school physical education department. In R. Light, J. Quay, S. Harvey, & A. Mooney (Eds.), *Contemporary developments in games teaching* (pp. 118-132). Routledge. https://www.taylorfrancis.com/chapters/edit/10.4324/9780203797730-16/in%EF%AC%82uence-school-context-implementation-tgfu-across-secondary-school-physical-education-department-christina-curryand-richard-light

Diabetes Canada. (2015). *2015 Report on diabetes: Driving change.* http://www.diabetes.ca/publications-newsletters/advocacy-reports/2015-report-on-diabetes-driving-change

Donnelly, P., & Kirk, P. (2015). Use the PDSA model for effective change management. *Education for Primary Care, 26*(4), 279-281.

Dudley, D. [Change the Game]. (2019, October 8). *Physical literacy as a construct of learning* [Video]. YouTube. https://www.youtube.com/watch?v=KCkOIiUdk9k&app=desktop

Federation of Saskatchewan Indian Nations. (2014). *Cultural responsiveness framework*. Indian Governments of Saskatchewan. https://allnationshope.ca/userdata/files/187/CRF%20-%20Final%20Copy.pdf

Hannon, J., & Ratliffe, T. (2004). Cooperative learning in physical education. *A Journal for Physical and Sport Educators, 17*(5), 29-32. doi:10.1080/08924562.2004.11000362

Hopper, T., & Kruisselbrink, D. (2002, July). Teaching games for understanding: What does it look like and how does it influence student skill learning and game performance? *Avante*, 1-29. http://web.uvic.ca/~thopper/WEB/articles/Advante/TGFUmotorlearn.pdf

Information Resources Management Association. (2020). *Indigenous studies: Breakthroughs in research and practice.* IGI Global.

Langley, G., Moen, R., Nolan, K., Nolan, T., Norman, C., & Provost, L. (2009). *The improvement guide: A practical approach to enhancing organizational performance* (2nd ed.). Jossey-Bass.

Lonsdale, C., Rosenkranz, R. R., Peralta, L. R., Bennie, A., Fahey, P., & Lubans, D. R. (2013). A systematic review and meta-analysis of interventions designed to increase moderate-to-vigorous physical activity in school physical education lessons. *Preventive Medicine, 56*(2), 152–161. doi: 10.1016/j.ypmed.2012.12.004

Marsh, T. N., Coholic, D., Cote-Meek, S. & Najavits, L. M. (2015). Blending aboriginal and western healing methods to treat intergenerational trauma with substance use disorder in aboriginal peoples who live in Northeastern Ontario Canada. *The Canadian Journal of Addiction, 6*(3), 2–12. doi: 10.1186/s12954-015-0046-1

Milko, J. P. (2020). *Improving physical literacy in middle school Indigenous and non-Indigenous students* (The Organizational Improvement Plan at Western University, 154). https://ir.lib.uwo.ca/oip/154

Ministry of Indigenous Affairs. (2019). *The journey together: Ontario's commitment to reconciliation with Indigenous peoples.* https://www.ontario.ca/page/journey-together-ontarios-commitment-reconciliation-indigenous-peoples

Munroe, E. A., Borden, L., Orr, A. M., Toney, D., & Meader, J. (2013). Decolonizing aboriginal education in the 21st century. *McGill Journal of Education, 48*(2), 317–337.

Ontario Ministry of Education. (2013, November). *Culturally responsive pedagogy* (Capacity Building Series, Secretariat Special Edition #35). http://www.edu.gov.on.ca/eng/literacynumeracy/inspire/research/CBS_ResponsivePedagogy.pdf

Ontario Physical and Health Education Association. (n.d.). *Elementary: Sports and activities.* https://safety.ophea.net/safety-plans?module=elementary

ParticipACTION. (2018). *Kids steps sweat = healthier brains.* https://www.participaction.com/en-ca/resources/report-card

ParticipACTION. (2020). *Family influence.* https://www.participaction.com/en-ca/resources/children-and-youth-report-card

PHE Canada. (2019). *Quality daily physical education.* https://phecanada.ca/activate/qdpe

Siedentop, D. (2002). Sport education: A retrospective. *Journal of Teaching in Physical Education, 21*(4), 409–418. doi:10.1123/jtpe.21.4.409

Truth and Reconciliation Commission of Canada. (2015). *Truth and Reconciliation Commission of Canada: Calls to action.* http://trc.ca/assets/pdf/Calls_to_Action_English2.pdf

Villegas, A. M., & Lucas, T. (2002). The culturally responsive teacher. *Educational Leadership, 64*(6), 28–33. https://pdo.ascd.org/lmscourses/PD13OC002/media/Module6_CulturallyResponsiveTeacher.pdf

Wahi, G., Wilson, J., Oster, R., Rain, P., Jack, S. M., Gittelsohn, J., Kandasamy, S., de Souza, R. J., Martin, C. L., Toth, E., & Anand, S. S. (2019). Strategies for promoting healthy nutrition and physical activity among young children: Priorities of two Indigenous communities in Canada. *Current Developments in Nutrition, 4*(1), nzz137. doi:10.1093/cdn/nzz137

Conclusion

CHAPTER FIFTEEN

Moving Forward

CASSANDRA THONSTAD, SUSAN P. CARLILE,
AND DEBORAH S. PETERSON

We cannot wait to change. We have students in our classrooms and schools who need the change to happen *now*. Not next semester. Not next year. Our educational systems were not created with equality or equity in mind. And while improving the entire system is our goal, too, we each have to start small. We have to start in our setting, in each of our classrooms, in each of our schools, improving what is within our sphere of influence and locus of control. As a classroom teacher, we don't have the authority to change the bus schedule, but we can improve what we do once the kids get off the bus. We don't have all the answers but in community with our students, families, and colleagues, we can work on solutions together. Our belief in using improvement science is built on the foundational concepts of Dewey (1990) who "believed that the aim of education is to further our democracy and that a constructivist education—or meaning making by those closest to the learning—will best serve that aim" (Peterson & Carlile, 2019, p. 172). We also want to reiterate our support of Freire's (1993) concepts "that freedom is obtained through contextualized action-oriented and collaborative actions that enhance the humanity of individuals and the community" (p. 172). Bryk et al. (2015) similarly endorse considering the context for change.

Throughout history, schools have furthered political and social ideals, harming the most those with the least social capital. As Isabel Wilkerson noted in *Caste: The Origins of Our Discontent*, the United States has perpetuated a pervasive system of privileging those at the top of the caste system: those who are White, English-speaking, and middle class. As Wilkerson reminds us, those of us with these privileges have a moral duty to speak up and to act when others are treated inequitably. Improvement science gives us the tools and processes to act *today*.

Addressing these societal inequities is a nationwide issue requiring a response from our faith-based organizations, government, education, and community organizations. We each can engage in improvement processes in the areas within our locus of control. Focusing specifically on the efficacy of improvement science, Perry et al. (2020) comment, "Practically, improvement science is what educators and organizational leaders do inherently every day; strive to improve their contexts systemically" (p. 28). The experiences in these chapters amplify the importance of a persistent focus on equity; student, family, and faculty voice; collecting and analyzing disaggregated data; monitoring progress; collaborating with colleagues; and adjusting change ideas based on variability in context.

Persistent Focus on Equity

Educators want to be successful in supporting students. It's in their very nature. With this in mind, we must continue to take a disciplined, systematic approach to the improvements we make to promote equity in our schools. Each of the authors in this book has shared an equity-based, disciplined approach to change describing how teacher leaders address potential obstacles, hurdles, and roadblocks every day in their classrooms. They have solicited the voice of students, families, and teachers to ensure the change they are promoting supports those closest to the issue.

Collecting and Analyzing Disaggregated Data

While grades, test scores, attendance, and referral counts are essential measures to study, they only tell a part of the story. As a classroom teacher reviews their students' test scores, they know who scored highest and who also struggled to get those scores. They remember that one student hadn't eaten lunch that day or how a different student's family was going through a rough divorce. Each test score also has a student's name, face, and story behind it. This is why qualitative data are so important. The personal story of each student, family, and teacher—and a test score—helps us understand what change ideas could lead to improving learning. Through empathy interviews, observational studies, and surveys, we can better see the system as it currently exists. Ultimately, as identified by Thonstad (2019), "in understanding a problem deeply, it is important to recognize that your system is set up to get exactly the results it is getting" (p. 271). Authors Meyer and Bendickson (Chapter 7) and Young (Chapter 5) improved gender equity in literacy when they regularly examined performance data to ensure that their system did not perpetuate inequities. Equity data, empathy interview analyses, and Plan–Do–Study–Act (PDSA) cycles grounded the work of all the authors.

Student, Family, and Faculty Voice

We must partner with our communities and families to determine the best changes idea or ideas to be implemented without taking on too many changes at one time. Peterson and Carlile (2019) agree: "Initiative overload and the current public discourse indicate a propensity to embrace authoritarian solutions that disregard the expertise of our families, student, and teachers and the funds of knowledge they bring to our schools" (p. 169). In Chapter 4, Tredway et al. include exemplary models of student and family voice. In Chapter 2, Anderson's work shows how to include teacher voice.

Monitoring Progress

Monitoring progress is important. Some authors wrote about monitoring improvement weekly; some monitored data monthly; others quarterly. The main idea is not to wait until the end of the year to examine data and plan for a new change idea in the subsequent year. That is too late for the children in our classrooms and schools this year! In Chapter 6, Barnard showed how the improvement idea was modified after *one* PDSA cycle.

Collaborating With Colleagues and the Community

When educational leaders do not take the time to grow their teams and focus on the communities within their contexts, intentional changes may be slow or stagnant, remaining in their initial contexts only, whereby changes happen behind the closed doors of a single teacher's classroom. When working with an improvement science team, we see the importance of understanding who is on your team, ensuring a diverse representation within the group, and being aware of possible biases brought to the table. Teams with only teachers lack the awareness of the impact and effect on classified or administrative team members. As Stimson-Clark wrote about in Chapter 8, including educational assistants in the change process was key. And as Tredway et al. exemplified, without involving students and families and our communities, we do not see the entire picture and what our students bring to school. We need each other, and our work together has to be intentional. As Lencioni (2016) would say, "teamwork is not a virtue, but rather a choice," and this is a choice we must make every day for the sake of our students (p. 207). Anything we can do, we can do better *together*.

Be Prepared to Adopt, Adapt, or Abandon Your Change Idea

In the 6 years we've been teaching improvement science in our principal preparation programs, we have not had one failed improvement effort. This is because we know that if the data show the change idea is not working, our teams must adapt or abandon the change idea. We don't wait for 6 months or a year to analyze the results and determine the next steps. Bryk et al. (2015) remind us "the call to innovation is accompanied by an obligation to document what was done, why it was done, and what was learned" (p. 156). When we intentionally study the implemented change in context, we gain the opportunity to refine practice and honor that there is variability in every classroom and school, and our improvement strategy must reflect that unique context. As we've told the hundreds of teacher and school leaders we've worked with, "school leaders need to understand how variations in context impact a change they want to make to the system. They must lead change efforts quickly and in collaboration with others" (Carlile & Peterson, 2019, p. 197). Leaders also must be ready to support their team in moving through change ideas when the result is not an improvement.

Next Steps: Networked Improvement Communities

Improvement science tells us to start small to implement quickly. When changes are implemented and an improvement occurs, how do we begin to scale that change? Through teamwork and our networked improvement communities (NICs), these changes go from a small-scale to system-wide change. Utilizing NICs cannot be done haphazardly, however. Bryk et al. (2015) argue that "when NIC participants come to know, respect, and trust one another, they are more likely to adopt the innovations of their colleagues and test and refine these innovations in their own contexts" (p. 146). Chapter 3 includes brilliant examples of NICs that dramatically increased literacy results in a short time.

Improving Our Schools Now

In this book, we've shared the experiences of classroom teachers, school leaders, district leaders, students, and families who have worked together to improve their schools. They have shared their journey, their data, their processes, and their outcomes. Although it might be difficult to identify where to start, we encourage you to start small but to start now. You can either find a group of people who also want to improve their practices together with you or start by yourself in your classroom. One of our teacher leaders started by working with students to reduce theft in the classroom. Within 3 months, their thefts were reduced to zero. Another teacher wanted to focus on on-time arrival at class. Within 2 weeks and testing two change ideas, students began arriving on time, thus inspiring the teacher team to focus on creating common, engaging activities for the first 5 minutes of class. These are the people who inspire us and remind us:

We cannot wait to change. We have students in our classrooms and schools who need the change to happen *now*. Holly Altiero inspires us when she says, "By engaging in IS processes, I am empowered and changed. I will continue to lead improvement efforts to ensure every child in our school succeeds, and I will encourage others to do the same" (p. 221). Every child deserves this commitment.

References

Bryk, A. S., Gomez, L. M., Grunow, A., & LeMahieu, P. G. (2015). *Learning to improve: How America's schools can get better at getting better*. Harvard Education Press.

Carlile, S. P., & Peterson, D. S. (2019). Improvement science in equity- based administrative practicum redesign. In R. Crowe, B. N. Hinnant-Crawford, & D. Spaulding (Eds.), *The educational leader's guide to improvement science: Data, design and cases for reflection* (pp. 197–216). Myers Education Press.

Dewey, J. (1990). *The school and society and the child and the curriculum*. The University of Chicago Press. (Original work published 1956).

Freire, P. (1993). *Pedagogy of the oppressed*. The Continuum International Publishing Group.

Lencioni, P. M. (2016). *The ideal team player: How to recognize and cultivate the three essential virtues*. John Wiley & Sons.

Perry, J. A., Zambo, D., & Crow, R. (2020). *The improvement science dissertation in practice: A guide for faculty, committee members, and their students*. Myers Education Press.

Peterson, D. S., & Carlile, S. P. (2019). Preparing school leaders to effectively lead school improvement efforts: Improvement science. In R. Crowe, B. N. Hinnant-Crawford, & D. Spaulding (Eds.), *The educational leader's guide to improvement science: Data, design and cases for reflection* (pp. 167–182). Myers Education Press.

Thonstad, C. (2019). Growth and grading: Overcoming "grades don't matter in middle school." In R. Crowe, B. N. Hinnant-Crawford, & D. Spaulding (Eds.), *The educational leader's guide to improvement science: Data, design and cases for reflection* (pp. 257–273). Myers Education Press.

Wilkerson, I. (2020). *Caste: The origins of our discontent*. Random House.

ABOUT THE AUTHORS

Dr. Deborah S. Peterson served as a school leader for many years prior to her current role as an associate professor at Portland State University. As a practitioner, she was known for increasing equity, community engagement, and student voice while dramatically improving student outcomes. Her teaching and research focus on preparing current and future school leaders to serve as antiracist, culturally responsive leaders for equity. Her work has been published in numerous journals, including *Educational Leadership, Multicultural Matters*, and *School Administrator*, and she has presented at state, national, and international conferences on leadership for equity as well as received numerous grants for her work. Her recent research includes examining the experiences of women leaders in numerous professions. Dr. Peterson resides in Portland, Oregon, where she has led or supported hundreds of school leaders as they implement equity-focused improvements in their schools and classrooms.

Susan P. Carlile has more than 50 years of experience in K–12 education as a teacher, middle and high school principal, director of curriculum and instruction for a large, suburban school district near Portland, Oregon. As a professor of practice and program lead for the Educational Leadership and Policy Program, she has facilitated the leadership development of more than 600 school leaders, received 18 grants for her work, and presented and published in dozens of state, national, and international forums of leadership, including collaborating with change leadership researchers and improvement science experts, including Antony Bryk, Louis Gomez, and Paul LeMahieu. She has a BA in English and Fine Arts from the University of California Berkeley, an MA in Curriculum and Instruction and a leadership certification from the University of Oregon, and graduate work in education at the University of Washington and Harvard University. Most recently, her research has focused on examining the issues facing women in leadership positions and strategies for navigating the workplace to ensure gender, racial, ethnic, linguistic, and socioeconomic equity in education.

Dr. Holly Altiero earned her PhD from Oregon State University in 2018 and her master's degree in education from Lewis and Clark College in 2009. Dr. Altiero holds a prekindergarten through 12th-grade school counseling license and an Initial administrator license from Portland State University. For more than 12 years, Dr. Altiero has worked in elementary, middle, and high school settings in the Portland metro area and has expertise in a variety of school-based programming. Dr. Altiero works primarily as an associate program director for City University of Seattle and has taught at Lewis and Clark College, Portland State University, and Oregon State University. Dr. Altiero is also the founder of Tiered Educational Consulting and has been sought out to teach and train school counselors, teachers, and school leaders on challenging situations and topics such as multicultural considerations in crisis responses, working with homeless youth, suicide prevention and intervention, trauma-informed care in the classroom, secondary classroom trauma, and the impact of technology of child development.

Erin Anderson is an assistant professor of educational leadership and policy studies at the University of Denver. She is the program manager of a state grant that supports the development and facilitation of the professional learning program for leadership teams to integrate liberatory design and improvement science into school improvement work. This design improvement program is co-constructed and delivered in partnership with Denver Public Schools. She is also a member of the Carnegie Foundation for the Advancement of Teaching Improvement Leadership Education and Development Steering Committee. She worked in public middle and high schools in Virginia and New York City, including alternative schools, which initiated her interest in how to make schools more equitable and inclusive spaces for students historically marginalized in the education system and how to improve schools to serve each student's well-being. Her research focuses on planning, leading, and implementing continuous school improvement.

Daniel F. Barnard spent the first 13 years of his career teaching multiage elementary classrooms before he transitioned into English Language Development (ELD) as an ELD specialist and English language instructional coach. Dan builds with blocks, designs marble runs, and reads books with his toddler, and when the weather permits, he hikes and explores around the Pacific Northwest. When the toddler falls asleep, and if the mood is right, he enjoys holding an uninterrupted conversation on one topic for more than four minutes with his wife.

Dr. Linda Bendikson has been working as an independent schooling improvement consultant since 2019. Previous roles include being a principal of a small rural school serving a Māori community; a principal of a large, diverse urban elementary school; a Ministry of Education regional manager; and, most recently, the director of the University of Auckland's Centre for Educational Leadership. Her research focuses on goal theory, schooling improvement, and principal leadership in secondary schools.

Jolia Bossette is a sixth-grade student at Edendale Middle School in San Lorenzo, who loves going outside to swing at the nearby park and listening to music. Jolia was the graduation speaker for her fifth-grade class at Dr. Machado's school, and through her storytelling in the fifth-grade class, her response was a video of her story "My Skin Is Not a Threat."

Shane Brown is a grants and regional educator in the South Coast Education Service District in Coos Bay, Oregon. While his passion will always be social studies, he also teaches math, language arts, and science subjects at a small rural school in the Willamette Valley of Oregon. Shane is a 2015 graduate of Western Oregon University and completed his graduate course work at Portland State University, where he earned his MSEd and principal license in educational leadership and policy in 2020.

288 *Improvement Science*

Kelly Dyer is currently an instructional coach at the University of Texas at Tyler University Academy, which is a K–12 university charter school with a focus in science, technology, engineering, and mathematics (STEM). She is also an adjunct faculty member and Master Teacher for UTeach STEM Teacher preparation program and the Masters in Instructional Coaching in the School of Education. Her research interests include STEM education, dual credit, and blended learning. Dr. Dyer holds a PhD in curriculum and instruction from Texas Tech University.

Keith Grosse has been teaching science and engineering for more than 20 years in the Portland metropolitan area. He uses improvement science in his classroom and when training teachers across the Northwest to develop an innovative, inquiry-based curriculum. He has a master's in curriculum and instruction and recently earned his principal administrator license from Portland State University. He believes academic performance improves and achievement disparities decrease when we nurture a culture where every student feels safe and included, is supported, feels a sense of belonging, and has strong relationships with others.

Corey Jenks is currently a principal resident in Denver Public Schools and is pursuing a master's in educational leadership and policy studies at the University of Denver. As co-founder of Reparative Teaching, Corey has worked in schools to increase equitable access to instruction through the implementation of the tools and resources of this theoretical framework.

Teresa Kennedy is a professor of bilingual STEM education. She focuses on equity, English as a second language, and bilingual education. She is a member of the UTeach STEM teacher preparation faculty and graduate faculty member for the ED in School Improvement in the School of Education. She also serves as the secretary for the UNESCO nongovernmental organization Liaison Committee. Her research interests include bilingual education, early language acquisition, and equity in STEM education. Dr. Kennedy holds a PhD in education from the University of Idaho.

Anne Larkin has served in a variety of leadership roles in two large Colorado school districts over the last 15 years. Her most current role is as a principal and she is pursuing her doctoral degree at the University of Denver. Co-founder of Reparative Teaching, Anne is an activist for equitable access to high-quality education.

Sandy Lochhead is leading efforts to support schools and the district to continuously improve and innovate to solve complex problems and achieve results. Prior to this, she led a team in supporting and developing aspiring, new, and current leaders through various pathways, including a residency, an alternative license program, and a new leader onboarding program. She started her career as a special education teacher, and after completing her master's degree at George Washington University, she served as a general education teacher in Arlington, Virginia. After achieving her National Board Certification, she became interested in supporting others in improving their professional practice in the Office of Professional Learning for Arlington Public Schools. Sandy is currently working on her doctorate at the University of Denver in educational leadership and policy studies. With more than 25 years of experience in education, Sandy is committed to increasing equity in our public schools and eliminating the opportunity gaps.

Moraima Machado is an elementary school principal in San Lorenzo Unified School District and has recently completed her EdD at East Carolina University. Her dissertation is titled *Family Stories Matter: Critical Pedagogy of Storytelling in Fifth-Grade Classrooms*. Born and educated in Caracas, Venezuela, she has worked in education for more than 25 years in different capacities from Spanish bilingual teacher to principalship.

Dr. Frauke Meyer is a senior lecturer in the faculty of education and social work at the University of Auckland. She teaches in the Master of Educational Leadership program. Her research is concerned with school improvement, leadership, and interpersonal leadership practices. The immediate focus of her research is the analysis, assessment, and development of leadership practices that foster school improvement and interpersonal behaviors that promote relational trust.

Matthew Militello is the Wells Fargo Distinguished Professor in Educational Leadership at East Carolina University (ECU). He has held academic positions at the University of Massachusetts and North Carolina State University. Prior to his academic career, Dr. Militello was a middle and high public school teacher and a principal in Michigan. He has more than 60 publications, including six books. Dr. Militello is currently the principal investigator of three large-scale grants and the founding director of ECU's International Educational Doctorate.

Dr. Jarod Milko is a Métis educator in northern Ontario, Canada. He has worked in several capacities in elementary, secondary, and postsecondary education. He is an elementary physical education specialist and Ontario Physical Health and Education Association Ambassador. He has taught physical education from kindergarten to Grade 12 for about a decade and coached a variety of school sports. Dr. Milko is also an instructor for ETFO AQ and a part-time faculty member for the Schulich School of Education in Nipissing University. He graduated with his EdD in educational leadership (K–12) from Western University, where his organizational improvement plan focused on improving physical literacy in middle school Indigenous and non-Indigenous students.

Michael Odell is a professor of STEM education and holds the Sam and Celia Roosth Chair in the College of Education and Psychology. He holds appointments in the School of Education and the College of Engineering. He is the co-founder of the University Academy (UA) Laboratory Schools and serves on the school board. He also provides oversight for the UA curriculum. He is the co-director of the UTeach STEM Teacher Preparation program and the co-director of the EdD in School Improvement Program. His research interests are education policy, sustainable education, problem-based learning, school improvement, and STEM education. Dr. Odell holds a PhD in curriculum and instruction from Indiana University.

Yanira Oliveras-Ortiz is currently the assistant director of the School of Education. She is also the coordinator of the C&I Master's Programs and the co-director of the EdD in School Improvement. Her research interests include instructional leadership, school improvement, and the impact of learning environments on student engagement. Dr. Oliveras-Ortiz serves as the president of the University of Texas Tyler University Academy Charter school board and as the chair of the American Educational Research Association's Supervision's Instructional Leadership SIG. She holds a PhD in curriculum and instruction from Penn State University.

Jaclyn Pedersen currently serves as the director of curriculum, instruction, and assessment for the University of Texas at Tyler University Academy. She led the development of the instructional models currently in place at the laboratory schools. Her prior experience includes teaching secondary mathematics, as well as instructional coaching in the areas of problem-based learning and mathematics. Ms. Pedersen has a master's degree in educational leadership and is currently a doctoral student in the EdD in School Improvement at the University of Texas at Tyler.

Jennifer Rasberry is currently an instructional coach at the University of Texas at Tyler University Academy, which is a K–12 university charter school with a focus on English language arts. She is also an adjunct faculty member in the teacher preparation program focusing on literacy and elementary education. Her research interests include literacy education, blended learning, and school reform. She is currently a student in the University of Texas at Tyler EdD in School Improvement Program.

Jo Ann Simmons is currently the superintendent of the University Academy Laboratory Schools in the College of Education and Psychology University of Texas at Tyler. She is also an adjunct faculty member in the education leadership program and the coordinator of the superintendent program. She is also an adjunct for the EdD in School Improvement. Her research interests include education policy, school reform, and school improvement. Dr. Simmons holds an EdD in educational leadership from Stephen F. Austin State University.

Adrienne Stimson Clark is a licensed special education teacher who works in Hillsboro, Oregon. She has been teaching for the last 10 years, primarily supporting students who experience multiple disabilities, genetic disorders, autism, or cognitive impairments.

Lynda Tredway is the program coordinator for the International EdD at East Carolina University (ECU) and a senior associate at the Institute for Educational Leadership. She collaborates on community learning exchanges and Project 14 with the ECU team. She was founding director of the Principal Leadership Institute at the University of California Berkeley, a secondary teacher in DC schools, and the program coordinator of a teacher residency program, a collaboration of George Washington University and DC schools. In addition to her education work, she is a quilt artist currently working on a project to honor the memory of all persons lynched in the United States.

Cassandra Thonstad has served as a teacher and school administrator for 15 years, in addition to teaching math, math pedagogy, and improvement science at several universities. As a doctoral student at Portland State University and an instructor for improvement science in the College of Education, Cassandra is driven by a passion for improving our PK–12 system, using improvement science with an equity focus and engaging students, teachers, and the community to help learners meet their maximum potential while honoring each student's experience in the classroom.

Laura Vasta is a Denver Public School graduate. She has been very fortunate to spend her career at the school that she went to as a child, Sabin World School. She has been able to wear a variety of hats at Sabin: second-grade teacher, mom of two students (Keegan and Makayla), and assistant principal. She is proudest of the work she led in early literacy; teaching young minds how to read is what gives her hope for the future of our youngest learners. As she transitions into a new role as principal in a new school in Denver Public Schools, she looks forward to replicating this work and ensuring that no child ever walks out of a building not knowing how to read.

Rhiannon Young is a teacher leader in a middle school in the Columbia River Gorge outside Portland, Oregon. She loves to inspire learning in middle school students, and together with her husband, who is a high school teacher, she says that "some days [she] can't believe what a dream job and life [she has]" in rural Oregon. She immediately embraced improvement science as a process for increasing equity in her classroom and school and as a way to involve students in their learning.

Naichen Zhao is a doctoral student in Educational Leadership and Policy Studies in the Morgridge College of Education at the University of Denver. She comes from China and has spent several years teaching English at a university in her home country. She holds a master's degree in translation and interpreting from the University of Nottingham in Britain. Her research interest is bridging the equity gaps for English Language Learners in K–12 education.

INDEX

55 Whys, 3, 198

A

Academy of Success Elementary
 School, 9
action research, 57
activist research, 51, 52, 57, 65
activity traps, 139
advanced mathematics-for-all model,
 187
Advanced Placement (AP), 185, 186
affinity diagram, 196–97
Aguilar, E., 56
aim statement, 16, 17, 110, 113
Allen, J., 54
alternative classroom management
 strategies, 32
Anashinaabi people, 268
Anderson, G.L., 52, 56
Andreoli, P.M., 137, 139
antiracism, 52
Apple, 244, 246, 247, 250–52, 253
Apple Genius, 246
Apple Teachers, 251
Apple Trainers, 251, 253, 254
Armstrong, S., 262
arts-integrated learning, 55
Ashbaker, B., 159–60
authentic learning experiences, 246

B

Bandura, A., 139
Bartlett, C., 261, 262
Bellei, C., 140
Bender, W.N., 32
Bendikson, L., 139
Berliner, D., 185
Berry, R.Q., 167
Biag, M., 116
Bishop, R.S., 86
blended learning (BL), 166–67
Bondy, E., 54
Boone, M.E., 60
Bossette, J., 51, 53, 61, 64, 66–67, 69
Bottge, B.A., 230
Bryk, A.S., xvi, 9, 13, 52, 54, 57, 59, 60,
 61, 63, 139, 164, 175, 282, 283
Building Equity, 80
Bybee, R.W., 166

C

Calkins, L., 78, 85, 86
call-and-response, 56
Calls for Action, 273
Cambridge Grade School, small-group
 instruction improvement at,
 97–98
 AIM statement, 110, 113
 driver diagram, 105–6
 empathy interviews, 99
 equity audits, 101–2
 fishbone diagram, 104–5, 106, 116, 117
 literature review, 99–101
 PSDA cycle 1, 107–9
 PDSA cycle 2, 109–10, 113–14
 PDSA cycle 3, 110–13, 114–16
 problem of practice, 98
 student behavior, 98, 101
 student demographics, 97–98
 student engagement survey, 102–3
 teacher surveys, 103–4
 testing change at, 107–16
 theory of improvement for, 104–7
 tools for improvement, 99–104
 variability and, 106–7
Canadian 24-Hour Movement
 Guidelines, 268
Canadian Society for Exercise
 Physiology (CSEP), 268
Capizzi, A.M., 146
Capper, C., 3, 79, 185, 186, 209, 225, 238
career and technical education (CTE), 224
Carlile, S.P., 89, 211, 279, 281, 283
Carnegie Project for the Education
 Doctorate (CPED), 52
Caste: The Origins of Our Discontent,
 279
change ideas, 18–19, 170
Chopra, R.V., 145
Claro, S., 191
Clifford, D., 9
Cobb, P., 61, 70
Cohen, D.K., 139
collaboration, 140, 279, 282
collective achievement, 254
collective efficacy, 254
Collins, V.K., 212
Colorado Department of Education
 (CDE), 11

295